BIDDING BETTER BRIDGE

BOOKS IN THIS SERIES

BIDDING BETTER BRIDGE

Acol for Americans

by

BEN COHEN

and

RHODA BARROW

Foreword *by Alan Truscott*

South Brunswick
New York: A. S. Barnes and Co.

A. S. Barnes and Co., Inc.
Cranbury, New Jersey 08512

6229
Printed in the United States of America

FOREWORD

The Acol System described with great clarity in this book is first cousin to Standard American bidding methods. Their common grandfather was the Culbertson System of 1933, which included some bidding ideas which rapidly disappeared from circulation in America. The weak no-trump and limited non-forcing jump responses became cornerstones of the Acol System in England, but more than two decades passed before they returned to the American tournament scene.

Today a majority of American experts, influenced by the English example, play a raise of one spade to three spades as non-forcing. A significant and substantial minority play the weak no-trump. A few have adopted the Acol two-bid in preference to Weak Two-bids.

The American enthusiast can graft any or all of these Acol features onto his regular style, and should find an increase in efficiency. He can then take the painless further step of playing Acol in its entirety.

There is one general rule in Acol which clarifies many situations: *Jump bids, unless in a new suit, are not forcing.* For example, suppose the bidding begins:

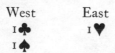

West	East
1♣	1♥
1♠	

What does it mean if East jumps to two no-trump, three clubs, three hearts or three spades?

Ask a group of American experts this question and you would get varied answers. Some would say forcing; some would say non-forcing; some would sub-divide the rebids into two groups; and a few would scratch their heads. In Acol it is easy to remember that all such bids

5

are non-forcing. They take care of many hands worth about 11 points which are awkward to bid in the standard American forcing style.

Bridge enthusiasts are generally eclectic. Reluctant to accept the doctrine of any single authority or system, they pick ideas, which take their fancy or suit their style, from many sources. The result is that practically no two pairs of tournament players play precisely the same systems and conventions. Even the authors of this book concede that Acol has 57 varieties.

Searchers for tidbits (or perhaps tidbids) can find "fourth-suit forcing," an important idea which is applicable in any bidding style; the Swiss convention, which is a substitute for the standard forcing-jump raise; and the rarified Acol four no-trump opening bid. And serious students can broaden their knowledge of the Acol language by attempting the quizzes which end each chapter, and by examining the useful summary at the end of the book.

Alan Truscott

CONTENTS

♠♡♣◇♠♡♣◇♠♡♣◇♠♡♣◇♠♡♣◇♠♡♣◇♠♡♣◇♠♡♣◇

7

INTRODUCTION

♠♡♣◇♠♡♣◇♠♡♣◇♠♡♣◇♠♡♣◇♠♡♣◇♠♡♣◇♠♡♣◇

A surprisingly large number of people are under the impression that Acol is a new system, very much post-war and somewhat untried, so I should like to invite you to take a short trip down Memory Lane.

Acol is, in reality, almost as old as Contract Bridge itself in this country, and was being used by the "experts" as far back as 1934. The late S. J. Simon, of ever-green memory in the world of bridge wrote of it: "Acol is not a system for beginners. It calls for too much common-sense—too many subtle inferences —too many master-bids." This opinion, coming from so eminent an authority and coupled, too, with the phenomenal success achieved by Acol players in match and tournament play had, at the time, the effect of making the general public feel that it was useless to try to learn it.

Throughout the ages, from the Old Testament onwards, there have been prophets. Jules Verne's fantasies and H. G. Wells' peeps into the future are so much common practice, and the science fiction of today we now confidently expect to be the fact of to-morrow. A recent scanning of old files produced a gem— not so much a prophecy as a flat statement of fact. "Acol bidding", says the Bridge Correspondent of the *Yorkshire Post* in November 1938, "whatever its excellence, is never likely to become generally popular." Could any statement have been less accurate! Acol is now by far the most popular and widely used system in this country. It was played by the Commonwealth teams at the World Olympiad in Turin as well as by

13

the highly successful British team, and it gains in popularity every day.

In an account of a Pairs event in June 1938, one newspaper reported with something like amazement the "third-in-hand Acol opening bid of 3 ◇ by West" on:—

♠ x x
♡ K Q x
◇ K J 10 x x x
♣ x x

The report pointed out that the bid, made by an Acol-playing pair*, was the only one which prevented the opposition from finding their "cold" 3 N.T. or 4 ♠ game, as it robbed the opponents of two valuable rounds of bidding. Nowadays, when we prefer to use opening bids of three on hands that contain no defence to a slam, the purist might object. The six-card suit headed by K J 10 but, beyond that, the holding of K Q x in one of the majors, would make the hand unsuitable as a text-book example of an opening three-bid. Even so, the truly Acol-minded will agree that there can be little or nothing "on" East-West after East's pass.

On October 1938 one of the London dailies reported a "spectacular hand where, quite obviously, no pair could have any difficulty in bidding a little slam, but only one pair* reached the lay-down seven, a contract which was reached in only three bids."

♠ 9 5 3
♡ Q 10 5
◇ Q J
♣ A J 10 9 7

♠ 7 2
♡ 8 6 4 3
◇ 10 7 6 3
♣ K 8 2

♠ 4
♡ J 9 7 2
◇ 8 5 4 2
♣ Q 6 5 3

♠ A K Q J 10 8 6
♡ A K
◇ A K 9
♣ 4

The report continues:— "After passes by North and East, South, playing the Acol Two Club system, made a forcing opening bid of 4 N.T., which demands partner to show any aces which are held. Since the bid of 5 ♣ at this

* Mrs Rhoda Barrow and Ben Cohen

14

point would deny the holding of any Ace, North had to respond 6♣ to indicate one Ace. This allowed South to make the spectacular bid of 7♠ which cannot be beaten."

These bids and others like them, so new and remarkable in the thirties, are common practice to us today. The system has, of course, grown and developed, but it is basically the same, and is as sound and dependable as ever it was. Above all, and once again the phrase is ascribed to the late S. J. Simon, Acol is less a system than an attitude of mind. You may call this a catch-phrase if you like—it is a fact. The true Acol player bids his own cards and does not wait for his partner to bid them for him. He keeps to certain basic rules and from there on lets common sense guide him and his partner to the right contract. These basic rules you can learn from this book. The common sense you must supply yourself.

For the purposes of this book it is assumed that the reader is already a bridge player and familiar with the principles of bidding on approach-forcing lines. He may have decided to change to Acol, or be one of the many so-called Acol players for whom the system has somehow become weighted and over-loaded with extraneous conventions and misconceptions. The aim of this book is to present to you the latest, soundest, and finest technique in bidding, and to allay once and for all the confusion as to what is, and what is not, basic Acol; to make clear the principles upon which the system is founded, and to eliminate the endless and often quite needless and pointless elaborations with which so many players have clouded and obscured it. It will also point out to you the choice, where alternatives are available, together with reasons as to preference for one or other.

Acol as a bidding system nowadays is so well known and so very widely used that it seems almost unnecessary to set out again the principles on which it is based. If, however, you play in a variety of different Clubs or at any of the many Bridge Congresses that are held all over the country, it must strike you that though at least 95% of the players use Acol, practically all of them, if separated from their accustomed partners, would be lost.

In the twenty-five years during which Acol has been steadily gaining in popularity both at home and abroad, in rubber bridge at the local club or amongst tournament players, bridge has not stood still. Men like Leo Baron, Samuel M. Stayman, Charles Goren, and a smothering mass of conventions such as Gerber, Texas, Bull Dog and so on, have all contributed to an ever-increasing flood of theory and doctrine with the result that, if you merely say you play "Acol", a strange partner will not know whether you play Blackwood, Norman, or Culbertson Four-Five. He will not know whether you play Herbert (Fishbein), Lower Minor, or Three No Trumps for a take-out over pre-emptive bids. He will not know whether you play "fourth suit forcing". Furthermore, he will not even know whether you play "Acol with weak Two's", a common enough practice, but one at variance with every basic principle of the system. I have even been asked, believe it or not, to play "Acol with Asking Bids" which are, of course, diametrically opposed to the Limit Bids which are the cornerstone of the system.

In fact there are now more than the well known "57 Varieties" of Acol. It is true that the system has no rigid code incapable of flexibility or alteration, and it can—and does—incorporate new conventions or modifications as long as these do not conflict with the basic principles of the system. Within certain limits, variations may reasonably be made to suit individual preferences, but these should not be allowed to stray outside the basic framework of the system which has been tried, tested, and proved by some of the finest players in the world. Those, therefore, who like to think of themselves as Acol players would do well to study their system once again, and to make sure that they know and thoroughly understand this basic framework. In the few instances where alternatives are reasonably available, they should be sure that they are familiar with these too.

Finally, one word to the die-hards, to those who claim that Acol is new-fangled and worthless, or that an opposition bid "poked-in" ruins the sequences. Let these players remember three things. Firstly, that Acol's natural sequences are less liable to damage from interference bidding than any other system. Secondly, so accurate is an Acol player's assessment of his hand that it is far more likely to be the interferer who is damaged, and thirdly that the crimes that are committed in the name of Acol are legion. They prove the bidders, not the system, bad.

B.C. and R.B.
October, 1965.

CHAPTER 1

The Basic Rules

Hand Valuation:

FIRSTLY, though, are you as certain as you think
you are on the important question of hand valuation? Let's go over an excellent guide you can use
until your experience grows.

There are three yardsticks by which the strength
of a hand may be measured, high card point count,
quick tricks and distribution. The point count referred
to throughout the book is the Milton Work's count,
i.e.,

Ace	....	4 points
King	....	3 points
Queen	......	2 points
Jack	......	1 point

In assessing a hand for No Trump bidding, 10's may
be counted as ½ pt., and additional values may be
allowed for good "fillers".

Now with regard to distribution—in assessing your
hand as *opener* or *prospective declarer*, points may be
added for distribution by way of long suits. Add one
point for each card over four in the prospective trump
suit, and one point for each card over four in a side
suit. Thus, applying the Milton Work count to a hand
containing a suit of A K Q x, count 9 points. For a 5-
card suit headed by the same honours count 10 points,
and with a sixth card, count 11 points. Points must not
be added in this way when assessing a hand for No

Trumps, as these bids are judged solely on high card strength.

A different distributional count must be applied when assessing a hand as **responder**. This time, provided you hold primary, or 4-card trump support for your partner's bid, you add points for **shortages in side suits**. For a void add 3 points, for a singleton add two points, and for a doubleton add one point.

♠ K x x x To give one example, in counting
♡ K J x x x this hand as responder to a 1♠ or
◇ x 1♡ opening bid, allow 7 points for
♣ x x x the high cards and 2 points for the
singleton diamond. In response to a
diamond or club opening, however, count 7 points only.

The Quick Trick count is used only on the very big hands. It is, therefore, seldom necessary, but should be known. Only the honour cards in combination are reckoned, and no suit can hold more than two Quick Tricks. No hand, therefore, can hold more than eight. The scale is as follows:—

A K	= 2 Q.T.	K x	= $\frac{1}{2}$ Q.T.
A Q		K J x	= $\frac{1}{2}$ Q.T. and a
A J 10	$\Big\}$ 1$\frac{1}{2}$ Q.T.	Q J 10	$\Big\}$ + value.
K Q J			
A	$\Big\}$ 1 Q.T.	2 + values = $\frac{1}{2}$ Q.T.	
K Q			

Note that a hand with an Ace and King in different suits count 1$\frac{1}{2}$ Q.T., whereas if these two cards are in the same suit it counts 2 Q.T.

All these methods of valuation are somewhat arbitrary and, it must be realised, subject to fluctuation in the light of the bidding. A King, for instance, once a bid in its suit has been made **over** it, can no longer be considered worth its face value of 3 points, whilst a

King held **over** a bid in its suit is worth more than 3 points. Thus a hand may change its original value as the auction proceeds.

A mistake many learners make is to value both long and short suits in the same hand. Remember that, in valuing a hand as opener, only high-card points and length may be counted. When valuing as responder, trump fit is of paramount importance and, with this, short suits outside the trump suit may be valued.

No method of valuation is foolproof. An Ace counted as 4 points may be trumped on the first round and so become worthless. A singleton counted by responder as 2 points may face declarer's singleton Ace. On balance, however, these counts give a pretty sound working guide to the strength of a hand until such time as practice and experience take over.

Now let us go on to the basic rules of the Acol Bidding System.

At the risk of labouring points with which you are already familiar, I should like to set out to begin with the basic principles which should be known, understood, and kept inviolate by all Acol players. If you know them, well and good. If you don't, be sure to learn them now.

1. Acol is an approach-forcing system, that is, many bids call for a reply and some of them insist on one.

2. A vitally important feature is the **light opening bid** which, in conjunction with the system of **limit bids,** is one of its most potent weapons.

3. All No Trump bids, whether original or in response, are rigidly defined in terms of point count.

4. All direct raises of suit bids—the **Acol limit bids**—are rigidly limited in terms of playing strength. They proclaim "This far I can go: now do what you think best as I shall not bid again unless I am forced."

5. Original bids at the one-level are limited by the fact that the hand has not been opened either with a Two Bid or with a Two Club bid.

6. Simple responses are limited by the fact that responder has not made a forcing bid.

7. Except for strategical reasons, particularly in tournament play, the recommended No Trump range is 12-14 points not vulnerable and 15-17 points vulnerable. The range for a Two No Trump opening bid is 20-22 points.

8. Opening bids of Two in any suit other than clubs proclaim hands of strength and quality, too strong for a one-bid and not strong enough for a two-club bid. These opening bids are forcing for one round.

9. The only other forcing opening is the "cipher-bid" of Two Clubs which has no reference to the club holding. It proclaims a minimum of five quick tricks and is unconditionally forcing to game unless opener rebids 2 N.T.

This framework is virtually standardised, at least in Great Britain, and largely in other countries, and the introduction of bidding sequences which violate it bring disaster. Of the situations where there are reasonable alternatives to use, it is not for me to dictate which you should select. All I can do is to present you with the best modern theory, with examples of how it should be applied and, thereafter, leave the rest to you.

One example here should serve to make the point. A well-known international pair held these hands in an

important tournament:—

West	East
♠ A J 7	♠ K 6 5 2
♡ A J 9 6 2	♡ K 8
◇ A 8	◇ K Q J 10 6 5
♣ A Q 6	♣ 2

In one room West opened 2 N.T. and East bid 4♣! No, this is not a mis-print but it gave West a headache, as perhaps it gives you. You see, this pair was playing "Texas", an artificial device for bidding the suit ranking *below* the one really held, so as to make the strong hand which opened in No Trumps into de- clarer in his partner's long suit. West thought that East, therefore, might mean "I want to play in diamonds, but it might be better if the lead came up to you." It was not, however, as simple as that, because the partnership was also playing "Gerber", another convention which uses a 4♣ bid over No Trump openers to ask immediately for the number of Aces held. East and West, although partners for many years, had not then discovered that "Texas" and "Gerber" can conflict. West eventually decided that the 4♣ bid was, as in fact East had intended it, the "Gerber" convention, so he bid 5♣ to announce all four Aces. East now jumped into 7 N.T. which was, unhappily, one down. West's only Queen was not "working", and either the spade or heart lady would have been worth four times the ♣Q.

In the room next door Acol was also being played, and West opened 1♡, not 2NT! This pair was using 2NT to show 21-22 points, not the normal Acol 20-22. East responded with 2◇ and now West, who had deferred his headache as to whether to shade a 2NT opening by one point, had a far worse headache. What bid could he now possibly find to do justice to his hand? A jump to 3NT after a response at the two-level was a gross underbid: a 20-count holding all four Aces is much stronger than a 19-count with only two which would surely justify 3NT. It was impossible to "manufacture" a secondary force in clubs as the diamond support was not all that strong. The hearts were too thin, and in any case not long enough for a jump to 3♡, which might be passed anyway, so what could he do? West found a (forcing!) reverse of 2♠. East bid a simple, correct, and admirable 4♠ and now West really was on the spot. He temporised, not with a Culbertson Four No Trump, but with a 5♣ cue bid. East replied, sensibly enough, with 5◇, reaffirming a good (probably six-card) suit. With the club tenace, the known spade support, the solid diamonds and— note this—the likelihood of getting anything except a heart lead, one would have thought 6NT would have been a sensible bid if 6◇ were rejected on the grounds that the doubleton Ace was not enough support for a rebid suit. But no, West bid 6♠, surely a quite appalling effort.

Both sides said they were playing Acol, and both sides landed themselves in disaster. This was no fault of the system, but fault in the players who failed to apply its basic principles correctly.

In lighter vein, but on the same theme, let me recount to you what must surely be the classic of all successful misunderstandings. At Duplicate Pairs North opened what was intended to be a highly pre-emptive 4♣ and saw no reason to disturb the contract when his partner, South, removed to 4♡. This was eight down, for a mere 400 points undoubled and un-vulnerable, and might have been more down if the bewildered opponents had not defended half the hand before they cottoned on to what had happened. South had thought that North's 4♣ was some new and exotic development of the Acol 4NT opener which asks immediately for Aces, and had replied 4♡ to show that she had one! During the ensuing recriminations someone opened the travelling score sheet, to find that 4♡ vulnerable (620 points) had been made by every other East-West pair in the room!

Let us try to avoid these pitfalls, as well as the dangers of elaborations which, in addition to being confusing, really are not necessary.

We shall in this book, therefore, be dealing with the basic principles which go to make up the Acol system, and which make it essentially different from other approach-forcing systems, as well as with the necessary conventional bids. It will be assumed that the reader is already familiar, for example, with normal opening bids as distinct from the Acol Light Opener, but to clarify possible queries which are not covered in the text, a number of summarised tables have been included at the end of the book.

One other point before we get to work—there is no doubt as to the popularity of the Quiz in this day and age, any more than there can be any doubt of its excellence as a method of learning. For this reason most of the chapters have attached to them a Revision Quiz based on the subject matter of the chapter. If you answer all these correctly, then you can claim to know your Acol. Remember, they are not "catch" questions intended to trip you up, but the sort of hands you are likely to meet in the course of play.

Much thought has been given to the problem of where and how to present these questions. Some readers say that they get bored if they have to turn innumerable pages looking for the answers, and others say that if the answers are not concealed in this way they "cheat" by looking too soon. There is no real compromise between these two extremes and we decided to give the answers immediately following each set of questions. We can only hope that this method will give the greatest satisfaction to the greatest number of readers.

CHAPTER 2

Definitions

BEFORE we get to the real business of bidding, it might be as well to define some of the terms used throughout this book. Their correct interpretation is fundamental to the whole Acol system and many unfortunate contracts would be avoided, and many more good ones reached, if their application were fully understood.

1. **The Light Opening Bid** is one of Acol's most potent weapons. It is made on as little as 9 or 10 high card points, but carries with it the requirement of a safe rebid, either in a second suit, or in a return to the original suit bid at the lowest available level.

You will notice that, though the high-card point count is low, once the additional points have been added for length in the trump suit, an opening hand is seldom, if ever, below a total of 12 points.

2. **The Sign-Off** is the protection offered to the Light Opening Bid. If an opening bid is made on a very light count but good "shape", that is, a six-card or longer suit or two biddable five-card suits, opener can sign off by returning to his own suit at the lowest available level, which says clearly to partner "I have nothing more to say." Responder, having heard a sign-off, should at all times respect it. This is not to say that he must not bid again himself, but if he does, he should do so with the knowledge that his partner is weak and has said so, and will pass at the earliest opportunity, or merely go on repeating his own suit

27

with little or no enthusiasm. An alleged Acol bidding sequence heard recently went as follows:—

West	East	
1 ♠	2 ♡	Now with good Acol bidding such a
2 ♠	2 N.T.	sequence simply cannot happen. West,
3 ♠	3 N.T.	having opened the bidding with 1♠ has,

in spite of his partner's two bids, announced as clearly as if he were permitted to use the words: "I have made an Acol Light Opener. It is based on a long spade suit and I have very little of value beyond this. Let me play this hand in spades. From your bidding thus far I know your strength and I am now the best judge of the final contract—**you have been warned.**" In spite of this, East went on to bid 3 N.T. and, believe it or not, made it. This, however, was not a failure on the part of the system. It was a failure on the part of East, who had grossly underbid his hand with 2 N.T. He failed to remember that, having signed off with his first rebid, *his partner was free to pass the 2 N.T. bid*, and the fact that he did not do so, preferring to try to play in spades, was East's good luck, as it gave him an undeserved chance to bid the game he should have bid earlier.

3. **The Limit Bid,** a corner-stone of the Acol system, is one which immediately announces the full value of responder's hand in reply to his partner's opening bid. It says in plain terms "Thus far I can go and no further. The rest is up to you." A raise of opener's 1♠ to 2♠ denies the values to bid more than 2♠. Similarly, 1♠-3♠ denies the values to bid more constructively or direct to game. Used in conjunction with the Light Opener, these Limit Bids have a very high obstructive value, which will be made clear in the chapter on the subject.

All No Trump bids, whether opening or in response, are Limit Bids, as their values are clearly defined and limited, and deny the values to bid any higher.

4. **A Force** is a bid which demands a response from

partner whatever his holding, and however much he may dislike the idea of having to bid on his hand. At no time must a player who hears his partner force decide to take matters into his own hands and pass. The Acol Opening Two Bid is forcing for one round but some players like to reserve to themselves the right to pass on "a well-balanced Yarborough". They have no such right. Opener may well have game "cold" in his own hand—he has announced by his opening a *minimum* of eight playing tricks in the suit bid, not a maximum. He may well have two long and powerful suits requiring no more than three small cards in one and a shortage in the other from his partner. Here is a hand which was dealt in a duplicate event which illustrates the point:—

West	East
♠ A K Q J 7	♠ 10 4 3
♡ A K 9 8 5 3	♡ 10 7
♢ 6	♢ 10 9 8 5 3 2
♣ 3	♣ 7 6

On this hand West opened 2♡ and one East took matters into his own hands and passed. It does not need much imagination to see what this cost the pair on this round.

Many other forcing situations occur, and these will be dealt with later. The simple point to be learned here is that a force is what it says it is and must be accepted as such by responder.

5. **A Sacrifice Bid** is one made quite deliberately with the knowledge that the contract cannot—or is highly unlikely—to be made. It arises where a partnership is prepared to take a penalty rather than permit the opposition to score a game or slam. It is, for instance, cheaper in terms of points at Duplicate to go down seven tricks doubled and unvulnerable (1,300 points) than to allow the opposition to score a vulnerable small

slam in one of the major suits (1,430 points). The preemptive bids come into this sacrifice category, being weak opening bids or overcalls made at a high level with the deliberate object of obstructing the opponents and possibly shutting them out of the auction.

6. **A Preference Bid** is said to be given by a bidder when he returns to one of his partner's bid suits at the lowest available level. In the sequence 1♠—2◇
2♡—2♠, the
2♠ bid is a mere preference for spades over hearts, and may be no better than a doubleton spade as compared with a singleton heart.

1◇ — 1♡   Here the 2◇ bid, though it raises the
1♠ — 2◇   level of the bidding, is still only a
            weak preference for diamonds, and
a weak preference for spades would be shown by passing.

A jump preference bid returns partner to his first suit at a level one higher than required. In the first
1♠ — 2◇   example above, 3♠ would be a
2♡ — 3♠   jump preference bid showing, not
            mere weak preference, but a very
decided choice. This, in Acol, is *not* forcing though it is, of course, very highly encouraging. The bid would only be made on a hand containing both a marked preference (amounting to good support) for the suit as well as enough outside strength to stand the higher contract.

CHAPTER 3

Light Opening Bids of One and The Sign-Off

♠♡♣◇♠♡♣◇♠♡♣◇♠♡♣◇♠♡♣◇♠♡♣◇♠♡♣◇♠♡♣◇

ACOL players believe firmly in the principle that the safest form of defence is attack, and for this reason the **Acol Light Opening Bid** has been developed. Used in conjunction with the **Sign-Off** and the **Limit Bids**, these **Light Openers** frequently impede the opposition to such an extent that they miss their own best contract and can, too, often pave the way to most profitable "sacrifice" bids.

It must be clearly understood that these light opening bids do not replace normal one-level suit bids. They merely increase the range of the bid at the lower end of the scale whilst the upper limit remains, as before, more or less indeterminate, and limited only by the fact that the hand could not be opened as an Acol Two Bid or an Acol Two Club Bid, both of which cover far stronger hands.

You will be learning about these two types of opening bid in later chapters, so for the moment we shall be dealing only with hands suitable for opening bids of one of a suit. Nor is this the time or the place to go into a detailed description of a normal opening one-bid. Suffice it to remind you that it is made on a point count of about 12 upwards, with a four or five card trump suit. The only criterion is that the hand should contain an honest rebid, either to develop the attack or to provide a safe line of retreat.

Hard and fast rules about opening bids are difficult to make except with particular types of hands. You must learn to accept that the point count of a hand is not the be-all and the end-all as a guide to your bid. You can hold 20 points so distributed that the hand qualifies for an opening Two Club Bid or for a Two No-Trump bid, or which qualifies only for a one bid. The point you must learn here is that opening bids of one of a suit *are* limited, even if no rigid limits can be set. They are limited by the shape, the distribution, or the point count that makes them unsuitable for a stronger opening bid. They can come near to these stronger bids, in which case their strength will be shown later by the appropriate rebid. At the other end of the scale they can come near to being too weak to open at all, which will be shown by a sign-off rebid. When you, in your turn, find yourself responding to an opening bid of one of a suit, therefore, do not forget the negative inference to be drawn from the fact that only a one-bid was made.

ACOL LIGHT OPENING BIDS

Assuming that you are qualified to judge that a hand is suitable for a normal one bid, we can now go on to consider adding the attacking weapon of the **Acol Light Opening Bid**. As already stated, this bid increases the *downward* range of opening one bids, and can be made on a point count of as little as nine provided that the vital safe line of retreat is available. This can be in the form of a six-card suit or two reasonably good five-card suits, both of which offer safe rebids, and on either of these holdings it is a good strategical move to open the attack. A rebid in your own opened suit at the lowest available level must be taken by partner as a *sign-off*, that is, a warning that you have nothing further to add to your original bid. Partner should now be able to judge whether his hand warrants any further action or whether to leave you in your two-level contract. Remember too, that when you open the bidding, say with 1 ♠, the opposition cannot tell whether this is an Acol Light Opener, a normal one bid, or a strong one. Good opponents will not overcall lightly at the two-level, especially when vulnerable, so that by the time the bidding has gone, perhaps N. E. S. W. fourth hand may have very

1 ♠ — 3 ♠ ?,

great difficulty in coming into the auction at so high a level. Here is a hand from actual play which illustrates

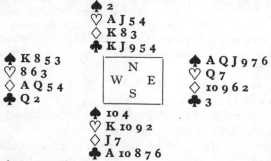

this point to perfection. In this case East opened 1 ♠, a typical Acol Light Opener and South, who was vulnerable, could not consider coming in with his meagre eight points. West made the Acol Limit Bid of 3 ♠ and there the bidding rested as North, still unaware, of course, of the strength or weakness of East's opener, had no possible bid available. East passed, and 3 ♠ exactly was what he made whereas, at other tables where East did not open, North-South found their club fit and, in several instances, bid and made 5♣.

This hand alone proves our point that it pays to open the attack early. So on nine or ten points, if your hand contains a six-card suit, for which you may add 2 points, attack immediately, as the suit provides its own rebid. Incidentally, on East's cards in the hand above, if West had held a 2♥ response, East would just have rebid 2♠, thus signing-off in his six-card suit. If North had intervened he would have taken the opportunity to pass, to show that he had nothing to add and that his rebid would have been a sign-off, and nothing would have been lost.

♠ K 7 5
♥ Q 10 7
♦ A J 9 7 5 3
♣ 5

Having opened 1♦ on this hand, you have a safe rebid of 2♦. Not only that, you have offered your partner a good lead in the event of the opposition trying for a No Trump contract—in fact you may well have ruined their chances of bidding and making a No-Trump game on a "blind" lead from your partner.

It is important to remember that, in Acol, the mere fact of a change of suit rebid by opener is not forcing. It is, therefore, perfectly safe to open the bidding on an equally light hand containing two reasonably good five-cards suits, as a rebid in the second of these suits *is not forcing to partner*, who has the choice of rebidding his own hand, passing the second bid, or merely giving preference to the first bid suit. Thus once again no harm is done by opening and much good may result.

♠ A J 9 5 2
♥ K Q 10 8 6
♦ 9 3
♣ 7

This hand has only ten points, but it contains two good five-card major suits, either of which might easily lead to game. At any rate, an opening bid of 1♠ may well obstruct the opposition, and can cause little or no trouble to partner as long as he knows his basic Acol. To his response of 2♣ or 2◇ you can safely rebid 2♡, confident that he will not become excited by your change of suit and that he can, in fact, pass the bid or merely return you to 2♠ if he is weak himself.

This does not mean that any nine or ten point hand offers a good opening bid, as at all times the requirements for a safe rebid must be met. None of the following examples can be regarded as suitable opening bids as, in spite of their point count, they have neither a six-card nor a suitable second five-card suit:—

♠ A Q 8 6 2	♠ A K 6 2
♡ 9 5 4	♡ Q 5
◇ A 7	◇ Q 6 5 4 2
♣ 9 6 2	♣ 7 6

♠ 9 2	♠ Q 8 3
♡ Q 7 6 4 2	♡ K 7 6 5 2
◇ A K 6 5 2	◇ 8 4
♣ 3	♣ A Q 5

We have now established that the advantages of initiating the attack are tremendous, but before we go on to study how these Light Opening Bids are allied to the Sign-Off and the Limit Bids, let us just look at a few more examples, to make quite sure that the bids are clear to you.

♠ 9 7	Open 1♡ confidently, knowing that
♡ K Q 10 7 5 4	the suit provides its own rebid. 10
◇ K Q 4	points + 2 for the 6-card suit.
♣ 8 2	

♠ Q 9 4	Open 1♣. Although your suit is a
♡ 5	minor and its pre-emptive value, there-
◇ K 10 8	fore, not so great, the same principle
♣ A J 9 8 6 2	holds good. In any case the bid may
	assist you to reach a No Trump
	contract or prevent the opposition from
	doing so. 12 points again.

35

♠ 9 8
♡ A J 9 8 6
◇ K Q 7 5 3
♣ 6

Open 1♡, and over partner's 1♠ or 2♣, rebid 2◇. 10 points + 1 each for the two five-card suits.

♠ A J 9 7 6 4
♡ Q 8 6
◇ K 6 2
♣ 7

As in the first example, your six-card suit provides a safe rebid, and you should open 1♠ without any hesitation. A total of 12 points.

♠ K Q 9 7 5
♡ 8 6
◇ 7
♣ A J 9 7 6

This time open 1♣, anticipating that the bidding will keep low and that you will be able to rebid 1♠. You are not nearly strong enough to open 1♠ and risk having to rebid 3♣ over partner's 2◇ or 2♡. Total, 12 points.

Remember that these Acol Light Opening Bids are in addition to, and not in place of, normal strength opening bids, and are a strong weapon to be added to your armoury provided you use them corrrectly.

THE SIGN-OFF BIDS

The Sign-Off bid, which has been mentioned several times already, is the safeguard which enables the Acol player to make use of the weapon of the Light Opening Bid without undue risk to the partnership. It is made by returning to your own, or your partner's suit, at the lowest available level. Let us examine a few examples. Suppose that you are the dealer and pick up this hand:—

♠ A Q J 8 6 2
♡ K 10 4
◇ 7 5 4
♣ 8

You attack immediately with an opening bid of 1♠. To your partner's response of 2♣, 2◇, or 2♡, you "sign off" with a rebid of 2♠, thereby telling him that you have already shown your full values and that any further developments are up to him.

It may be that his hand is such that he refuses to be silenced, in which case you just continue signing-off, or pass at any appropriate moment.

1♠ — 2◇   On the hand just described, you sign-off
2♠ — 3♣   immediately with a bid of 2♠, and to
?   partner's rebid of 3♣ you sign-off
           again with a weak preference bid of 3◇.

By this time partner should have realised that you have nothing more than an Acol Light Opener, and it is on his own head if he wishes to go on. It would be highly unimaginative to make your second sign-off by bidding 3♠, as you have a singleton of one of your partner's suits and three cards in the other.

1♠ — 2♡   Your second rebid this time is a
2♠ — 3♣   weak preference to 3♡, which you
?   must remember *is still a sign-off*. You
           announced your Light Opener with

your 2♠ rebid in spite of which for reasons which at the moment only he can know, partner still wishes to make a further try. Your 3♡ bid is only a return to his first suit at the lowest available level, giving nothing more than a preference for hearts over clubs, and will not be read by him as encouragement.

1♠ — 2♡   Here your next, and most forceful
2♠ — 3♡   sign-off is to pass. Partner knows
?   that you signed off on the first round
           and he has not forced so you must

just take it from him that he prefers to play in hearts, and don't be tempted to find a raise you haven't got.

1♠ — 2◇   Your knowledge that your partner
2♠ — 2 N.T. has a diamond suit plus (from his
?   second bid) a minimum of 11 points,
           does not make you revise your

opinion that you had a weak opener and once again you sign off, this time in 3♠. If partner does not see the red light and pass now, he is no Acol player.

It goes without saying that if partner *is* an Acol player and fully awake to the fundamentals of basic Acol, he will have recognised your first rebid for what it is and will only have pressed on if his own hand merits it. In other words, nothing will be lost, because partner is bidding on *with the knowledge of your weakness.* From this it follows that, hearing your announcement of weakness, partner is at liberty to pass as soon as he likes.

1♠ — 2♡
2♠ — ?

2♠ is more than likely to be the end of the auction if the opposition does not come to life (and we have already seen how difficult this may be for them). You must therefore, at all costs try to avoid using a sign-off bid if you have better than an Acol Light Opener.

♠ A Q 10 7 4
♡ 5 2
◇ A K 5
♣ K Q 4

On such a hand as this, no sign-off of 2♠ must pass your lips. If partner responds in clubs or diamonds you can raise his suit. If he bids 2♡, then 3 N.T. from you would be no more than the truth.

It follows further that you must become Acol-minded about the revaluation of your hand in the light of partner's bids. Take our first example, on which we did nothing but sign off to anything partner bid, and change it by only one card:—

♠ A Q J 8 6 2
♡ K 10 4 2
◇ 7 5
♣ 8

This is still virtually the same 1♠ Light Opener, and calls for nothing but a sign-off if partner responds in clubs or diamonds. Indeed, if he bids both these suits, it rapidly becomes one of those rare hands on which you begin to wish you *hadn't* opened. If this should occur, remember that there is an element of risk in practically every bid, and that for the one occasion on which you come to grief there will be fifty on which you gain. But to go back to this hand—if partner responds 2♡ to your 1♠, the value of your hand, although nothing can improve the high card count, rises immediately. You cannot afford, with short clubs and diamonds and such a good heart fit, to risk being passed out in 2♠. Your hand, in the light of partner's bid, is no longer excessively weak and you now can—no, *must*—raise to 3♡. This is not a contradiction of all that has been said about signing off, because you no longer wish to sign off.

A word about intervening bids before we leave the sign-off. If the opponent on your left overcalls you, this may affect your partner's bid. South's bid at the
(N. E. S.)
two level (1♠ 2◇ 2♡) will be substantially the same as it would have been without the intervention and you can make your appropriate sign-off undisturbed. If South is forced to bid at the three-level though,
(N. E. S.)
(1♠ 2♡ 3◇) he should be relied on to hold either support for your spades or compensating values, so you can afford to offer your sign-off at the 3♠ level. An intervening bid over your partner, that is, on your right, gives your partner another chance to bid and so releases you from the obligation to "keep the bidding open". You can, therefore use such a bid as an opportunity to pass, which is equivalent to telling your partner that, without the intervention, your rebid would have been a sign-off, and any "free" rebid over such intervention will be taken to indicate additional strength.

REVISION QUIZ ON CHAPTER 3

(1) What opening bid would you make on the following hands?

- (a) ♠ K J 9 6 4 2: ♡ A 6 5: ◇ 7: ♣ K 9 4:
- (b) ♠ K 5 3: ♡ Q 10 9 8 7 2: ◇ A 4: ♣ 8 3:
- (c) ♠ Q 4: ♡ K 10 9 6 3: ◇ A 5 4 3: ♣ J 3:
- (d) ♠ 5: ♡ 6 4: ◇ A K Q 10 6 3 2: ♣ K 4 3:
- (e) ♠ K 5: ♡ K J 9 6 3: ◇ K Q 8 4 2: ♣ 3:

(2) Assume that you opened 1♠ and partner responded with 2♡. What is your rebid on these hands?

- (a) ♠ K J 10 8 4 3: ♡ A 4: ◇ K 9 3: ♣ 6 3:
- (b) ♠ A K Q 10 7 6 5: ♡ Q 9 7 5: ◇ K: ♣ 9:
- (c) ♠ K Q 10 9 6: ♡ Q 4: ◇ K Q 10 8 3: ♣ A:
- (d) ♠ A Q 9 6 4: ♡ J 4: ◇ K 4: ♣ A Q 9 6:
- (e) ♠ A K J 9 4 2: ♡ —: ◇ Q J 9 3: ♣ A 4 3:

(3) What opening bid would you make on the following hands, and what would you rebid if partner responded with 2♣?

- (a) ♠ K 10 8 4 2: ♡ A Q 9 6 5: ◇ Q 5: ♣ 4:
- (b) ♠ 8 6: ♡ 5: ◇ A K 10 9 7 3: ♣ Q J 9 8:
- (c) ♠ 5 3: ♡ A K Q 5 4: ◇ 8 4 3: ♣ 10 6 2:
- (d) ♠ A K Q 6 3 2: ♡ 8 6: ◇ 7 4: ♣ Q 3 2:
- (e) ♠ K 4: ♡ 9 6: ◇ A Q J 8 5 3 2: ♣ 8 3:

ANSWERS TO REVISION QUIZ ON CHAPTER 3

(1) (a) 1♠   Your six-card suit provides a safe sign-off rebid.

(b) 1♡   Here again, you can safely rebid your six-card heart suit.

(c) Pass   You have nothing you can honestly rebid on this hand, so you must not open the bidding.

(d) 1◇   You can bid, rebid, and continue to rebid, in diamonds.

(e) 1♡   Here both your five-card suits are reasonably good so you open with one of the higher-ranking of two adjacent suits, that is, hearts, and later bid your diamonds.

(2) (a) 2♠   You made an Acol Light Opener, and can only rebid in your six-card suit.

(b) 4♡   You had nearly a 2♠ opening bid here. Partner will not take your jump to game in his suit as a shut-out if his hand is strong for his bid.

(c) 3◇   This was a full-strength, not a light, opener, and your diamonds are good enough to show at the three-level, especially as ♡ Q 4 is by no means a misfit with partner's hearts.

(d) 3♣   Partner will know your spades are longer than your clubs or, with two equally long black suits, you would have opened 1♣.

(e) 2♠   Although you have 15 points, you are not strong enough to bid anything else, especially with a complete misfit in partner's hearts.

(3) (a) You would open 1♠ and, over 2♣, rebid 2♡. As the change of suit is not forcing, partner may pass or just return you to spades.

(b) You would open 1♢ and raise 2♣ to 3♣. You really don't want to sign off here and anyway, clubs are a wonderful fit.

(c) Perhaps not quite a fair one—as you would not open in the first place you won't have to rebid!

(d) You would open 1♠ and rebid 2♠. You have nothing else to say.

(e) Here again, you would open 1♢ and rebid 2♢, and continue repeating diamonds till partner gets the message.

CHAPTER 4

The Limit Bids

♠♡♣◇♠♡♣◇♠♡♣◇♠♣◇♠♡♣◇♠♣♡♣◇♠♡♣◇

HAVING got clear in our minds the important basic principle of the Acol Light Opening Bids guarded by the Sign-Off Bids, let us now turn to the bids which are the corner-stone of the Acol system, the **Limit Bids**. These can be made in suits or in No Trumps, but their essential purpose remains unchanged, to bid the hand to the full extent of its value telling partner at once, "Thus far I can go and no farther: I shall not bid again unless forced." Within these terms of reference both members of the partnership lose no time in assessing their combined strength or weakness, as the case may be.

So far we have discussed only the opener's way out of danger, by way of a sign-off bid, if his partner responds with a simple approach-forcing change of suit. Now let us take the same opening hand that we

♠ A Q J 8 6 2
♡ K 10 4
◇ 7 5 3
♣ 8

used in Chapter 3 and consider it in the light of responder's possible Limit Bid in reply. Remember now that you will be looking at the situation from the other point of view. Having opened with an Acol Light Opener, you have heard your partner make a Limit Bid and you are now concerned not with signing off, but with deciding on the final contract, *which your partner has said he leaves to your judgment.*

Having opened 1♠ you hear 2♠ from your partner. "I have a weak hand", you interpret this to mean, "but it includes adequate support for your spades". Here are two examples which are typical of responder's possible holding for his bid:—

♠ 9 5 4 3	and	♠ 9 7 5 4 3
♡ 9 8 3 2		♡ 7
◇ K 4		◇ 9 6 2
♣ K 6 2		♣ K 10 5 4

What should you bid now? Obviously there is just one perfect bid and that is a pass. Two weak hands together won't make a game and the only excuse for further signs of life from either partner is obstruction of the opposition if they start to bid. Look at either of these two hands as possible dummies opposite our opening hand, and you will see how accurately the bidding has been judged.

1♠ — 3♠ this time. Here you understand that responder's support for spades is good again, and that he has some honour strength or shortages outside. Not enough, mark you, to make a forcing bid, *or he would have*. This is one of the great virtues of the Limit Bids— they strike the higher limit as well as the lower. This time responder will have something like the hand quoted for West on p. 33,

♠ K 8 5 3	or perhaps	♠ 10 8 5 4 3
♡ 8 6 3		♡ 6
◇ A Q 5 4		◇ A Q 5 4
♣ Q 2		♣ Q 6 3

What should you bid this time? You, knowing the lightness of your opener, will pass without even a sigh. If partner knows his basic Acol, you will need to find every card, plus the opposition, playing to assist you if you are to make a game.

1♠ — 4♠. In the original version of Acol this direct jump to game was a strong Limit Bid, not to be taken as a shut-out if opener were strong for his bid. In practice, however, it was found that many slams were missed in this way as opener, possibly short of first-round controls, feared to investigate further.

Modern technique has developed a new way of dealing with these hands by way of the 4♣ — 4◇ convention, which is fully explained in Ch. 16 so, meanwhile, let us deal with the direct raise to game as it is used today.

The bid is purely pre-emptive and is only a Limit Bid in the sense that, though there may be a play for game on distribution, the thing of paramount importance is to block the opponents' bidding to the full, as with an opening pre-emptive bid. The indications are exceptionally good trump support, a poor high-card count, but strength by way of voids or singletons.

♠ J 8 6 4 3 2 This 5-point hand, which increases
♡ 7   to 9 points by counting two for
◇ 5   each singleton, is an admirable
♣ K J 10 7 6   example of a direct raise of 1♠ to
               4♠.

♠ 8   In the minors, as the raise to game
♡ 7 4   would be at a higher level, slightly
◇ Q 10 8 5 4   more high-card strength is required.
♣ K Q J 8 6   say about 8 points. Here, if partner
               opens 1◇, the major suit shortages
increase the count to 11 points, and a direct raise to 5◇ may cause havoc in the opposition ranks.

There are one or two points which should be stressed here before we go on to consider the No Trump responses which are also Limit Bids.

Immediately responder makes a Limit Bid, several things have been achieved. Firstly, the "captaincy", or control of the bidding, has been firmly planted on the opener. Responder has got his whole hand off his chest in one bid, and from then on will only bid again if his partner forces him to do so.

Secondly, the opener knows within reasonably close limits the combined strength of the two hands, and must accept that the responsibility is his from then on. There are, and there always will be, close decisions to be made. A very lucky "fit" and fortunate distribution may result in the making of a game which has not been bid and, alternatively, a game which has been bid may come to grief on adverse distribution. Far more often, however, if players learn to use their basic Acol accurately, the right contract will be reached, the right games bid, and the right hands left in part-scores.

Last, and by no means least, the Limit Bid will have cast a high pre-emptive barrier across the auction which, whilst not taking the opener and his partner beyond their depth, obstructs the opposition to the full.

It is difficult to set very exact limits on these bids, as so many factors must be taken into consideration. An Ace-Queen, for instance, over an intervening bid in that suit, must be worth more than its face-value of six points, but as a rough guide, the following counts may be used:—

> 5—9 points   ......raise one to two.
> 10—12 „   ....raise one to three.
> 13 and over.......bid in a new suit (See Ch. 16).

Remember that these counts include distributional points as explained earlier, and that they pre-suppose primary or 4-card trump support, without which suit Limit Bids should be avoided.

When in doubt, it is better with these Limit Bids to err on the high side. That is to say, when you are not quite certain whether your hand warrants a raise to two or to three of your partner's suit—when, in fact, you wish you might bid 2½♠ to his 1♠, bid 3♠, not 2♠. It won't happen very often because generally some feature of the hand will tip the scales in favour of one bid or the other, but when in real doubt, make the higher bid. The logic of this is that the higher bid retains to the highest degree the pre-emptive value of the Limit Bid. The less you and your partner have between you the more there is for the opposition so, in case partner's opener were very weak, you do not want to err on the side of making it easy for the opposition. Particularly when making a Limit Bid over an intervening bid, which in itself warns partner of a concentration of strength on his left, call up to your highest possible limit to obstruct fourth hand. Remember that it will pay you to go one down, even doubled and vulnerable, to prevent the opposition's unvulnerable game, and that you can afford two down doubled and vulnerable in exchange for their vulnerable game.

Generally speaking, if your hand qualifies for a Limit Bid response, it is better to make it immediately than to look for another bid, as so many players do. This applies very particularly if you have already passed, that is to say, if partner has opened the auction third or fourth in hand. A change of suit from responder *after an original pass* is not forcing, even for one round. Suppose you held:—

♠ 9 5　　　Not having passed, you might be
♡ J 9 8 6　　tempted to respond 2♢ to partner's
♢ K Q 9 6 2　1♡, but the direct limit bid of 3♡
♣ K 3　　　is far better technique.

Once having passed you *must* respond 3♡, as you cannot afford to risk a change-of-suit bid which is no longer forcing, and in which you may be left when you are more than happy to play in hearts.

One final word before we go on to the next item on our programme. One of the many reasons why the Acol system is so very successful is that its Limit Bids give so little information away to the opposition.

1♠—2♠	1♠—3♠	1♠—4♠	1♠—2NT	and so
4♠	4♠		3NT	

on—these brief sequences, in preference to a complicated series of bids going all around the mulberry bush before arriving at the same contract, tell the opposition virtually nothing except in a general way that spades and a variety of other high cards are held. No possible weakness or spot where attack is least likely to be appreciated has been shown up, and this may well make the difference between making the contract or being one down, or may assist towards getting those vital overtricks that every Duplicate player prizes so highly.

We have spoken of these Limit Bids so far as though they applied exclusively to the major suits, but this is not the case and they can be used equally well with the minors. Bear in mind, though, that five of a minor is a lot of tricks to have to make, and partner is very likely to leave a raise from one to three diamonds, for example, when he would not pass a raise from one to three of a major. So offer another suit if you can, as this may well help towards a No Trump contract. But if your best and only reasonable bid is a direct Limit Bid in partner's minor suit, then don't hesitate to make it, and perhaps partner may himself be able to make a try for No Trumps. As you will learn in a later chapter, opener may have found himself forced into making a "prepared" bid in either of the minor suits. If this is the case, and you give a direct raise in the suit, he will rebid in the appropriate number of No Trumps—and anyway, he'll have a minimum of three of the suit. If he opened with a natural suit bid, your Limit raise may be all he wants to know for a game contract.

There is no such thing as a direct limit bid of a raise from one to four in the minors except as a purely pre-emptive measure on weakness rather than strength. The jump to the four level cuts out the 3NT possibility.

♠ 9 5   If partner opens 1 ♡ raise to 2 ♡. If
♡ Q 10 8 6   he opens 1 ◇, bid 1 ♡, which may
◇ Q 10 8 6   enable him to go into No Trumps.
♣ K 7 4   If you've already passed originally,
                 raise 1 ◇ to 2 ◇, as you might be
left in 1 ♡ with this good diamond fit available.

LIMIT BID RESPONSES IN NO-TRUMPS

For the moment we will keep to our same opening hand. Let's quote it again for convenience of reference:—

♠ A Q J 8 6 2   As before you open 1♠ and partner
♡ K 10 4   responds 1 N.T. We all know this one—
◇ 7 5 3   a horrible hand without much spade
♣ 8   support or there would have been a
                 1♠ - 2♠ bid on it. It will be as weak as
5 - 9 points, and virtually responder's only excuse for bidding is to keep the auction open in case you are very strong or can rebid in a second suit which will provide a better fit than spades. Few people think of this as one of the Limit Bids but it is, because it immediately casts the gloom of responder's exceedingly limited strength across the table.

It is, perhaps, worth mentioning here that a frequent mistake made is to respond in two of a suit instead of with 1NT on a hand such as this:—

♠ 9 3
♡ Q 7 2
◇ Q J 9 6 4
♣ J 7 2

Many players would make a 2◇ response to 1♠ on this hand, whereas it only barely qualifies for 1 N.T. If partner's second suit happens to be diamonds, you are quite certain to find your 2◇ bid raised, whereupon you may well land in disaster, whereas if you announce your weakness with 1 N.T. and partner offers a 2◇ rebid you can pass with a clear conscience knowing that, having heard your limit bid on the first round, partner will not expect you to keep the bidding open again except, perhaps, to give him preference to his first suit if you do indeed prefer it. Had partner made the opening bid of 1◇, you would have made the equally dismal Limit response of 2◇ denying, as we have already learned, the values to say anything better.

It should also be pointed out that the reason why you must bid 1NT instead of 2◇ is that you would be raising the level of the bidding when you are not strong enough to do so. As responder to an opening bid, and provided always that your hand does not contain an immediate Limit Bid in the suit opened, you may always respond with a bid at the one-level even on a very meagre suit (as poor as J 10 x x) subject to your having sufficient values for a 1 N.T. response. In other words, a change-of-suit response at the one-level does not promise any better holding than the 5 - 9 points required for a 1 N.T. bid, whereas to respond at the two-level (1♠ - 2◇) shows a minimum of 8 points with a 5-card suit, or perhaps 7 points with a 6-card suit.

We'll return now, though, to our original position, a 1♠ opener to which partner has responded 1 N.T. On our old favourite there is only one logical thing to do in the light of the information received, and that is to return smartly to 2♠. This is no longer a sign-off, but a decision as to the final contract in the light of partner's Limit Bid. There are, however, a variety of other courses of action available to the opening bidder, depending on his specific hand. Take the following examples:—

(a)   ♠ A K J 8 5   On a hand like this, pass the
       ♡ Q 10 4   1 N.T. There really cannot be a
       ◇ K 7   game on with a *maximum* com-
       ♣ J 10 8   bined count of 23 points, and 1
                   N.T. may well be easier to make
than 2♠. Remember, responder's 1 N.T. was a Limit Bid, and there is no forced response to Limit Bids.

(b)   ♠ 9 8   This hand was given as an
       ♡ A J 9 8 6   example of a Light Opener on
       ◇ K Q 7 5 3   p. 36, the hand containing two
       ♣ 6   biddable suits. Here, having
                   opened 1♡, bid 2◇ over partner's
1 N.T. He will pass if diamonds suit him better than hearts, or give you prefence to your first suit.

(c)   ♠ A K 10 7 6   Here again, over 1 N.T. in
       ♡ Q 6 5   response to your opening 1♠,
       ◇ A J 10 6   show your second suit with a bid
       ♣ 9   of 2◇. You have a decided
                   allergy for a No Trump contract
and partner, as well as being weak, had not enough spades to give you a direct limit raise in the suit. He may well have a reasonably good fit for diamonds, which he was unable to bid himself at the two level. If not, he'll give you preference to 2♣, but the worst that can happen to you cannot be very serious.

(d) On a very strong hand—one, perhaps, only just short of an opening two bid, where you feel that there must be a game on if partner can produce even as weak a "free" bid as 1 N.T., you can make a jump-switch, forcing him to bid again. He may only give you preference to your first suit, or raise your second suit if you have struck a fit, or merely relapse into 3 N.T. if he cares for none of it. Whatever he does, you won't become unduly excited, as you already know from his first response how very limited his hand is.

For a jump-switch rebid your hand might be something like this:—

♠ A K J 5 4   It doesn't quite qualify for an opening
♡ A Q 10 6 3   Two Bid (see Chapter 13), it is most
◇ K 5   unsuitable for a No Trump contract,
♣ 8   and requires very little of a fit with
              partner to produce game.

(e) On a more or less balanced opening hand of 17-18 points you can try out with a raise to 2 N.T. *This in itself is another Limit Bid*, denying the strength to bid game direct, but responder will read it for what it is, passing if his 1 N.T. were a minimum and going on to 3 N.T. if it were a maximum.

♠ A Q J 6   This hand is typical of this class and,
♡ K 8 7   if partner has 8 or 9 points instead of the
◇ J 10 8   possible 5, 6 or 7, has every chance of
♣ A Q 4   producing game in No Trumps.

(f) On a 19-point hand, the same as the one above, except for the addition of the Queen of either of the red suits for example, you should bid the game direct yourself, as even if partner has the bare minimum of 5 points you will have 24 between you which, especially if you find a reasonable fit, has every chance of playing for game.

A similar series of bids at one higher level can follow responder's 2 N.T. Limit Bid. In this case responder announces a balanced hand of 11-12 points, and opener should not find it very hard to judge his best course of action. As before, he will have the choice of passing 2 N.T., rebidding three or four of his original suit, showing a second suit, or bidding 3 N.T. On our original hand he would return to 3 ♠, which responder can be trusted not to disturb. Such a sequence as 1 ♠ — 2 N.T. simply cannot occur if players 3 ♠ — 3 N.T. or 4 ♠ know their basic Acol. Either the 2 N.T. Limit Bid was wrong in the first place, or responder wants his head examined if he cannot learn to take no for an answer.

The hand given in (d) on the previous page illustrates a rather special point here. In this case opener's rebid over 2 N.T. must be 4 ♡ not 3 ♡ because responder, having made a Limit Bid, *is at liberty to pass anything but a force*. He will not interpret a 4 ♡ bid as a force, as both hands are limited by their previous bids, and his only action will be to give preference to the first bid suit if he prefers it. The sequence 1 ♠ - 2 N.T. - 4 ◇, though, must not be passed. As game has not yet been bid it remains a game force, as well as a request to partner to give preference either to 4 ♠ or 5 ◇, opener holding a good hand unsuitable for a No Trump contract.

A direct raise from one of a suit to 3 N.T. shows a balanced hand of 13-15 points and is, of course, a strong Limit Bid. It is not a shut-out and partner can go on for a slam try or pass, or merely remove to four of his own suit as he sees fit.

This direct 3 N.T. is an unpleasant bid to have to make as it rather blocks exploration for a possibly better contract and it should, therefore, be avoided if a reasonable alternative bid can be found. Just occasionally this is not possible, but particularly when the hand appears to give promise of a slam contract, a forcing-to-game suit jump-switch should be preferred. This may safely be made in a short suit in a denomination lower than the opener's suit when adequate support for partner's suit is held, as the final contract can always be returned by responder to that denomination. For a full explanation of this position you should turn to the chapter on forcing responses.

SECOND ROUND RESPONDER'S JUMP BIDS

A number of second-round jump bids by responder come into the Limit Bid category and are, therefore, NOT forcing, although they are clearly highly invitational, inviting a game contract, though not demanding it. In this sequence, there are five jump bids available to responder. 3♡ would obviously be forcing, as would 2♡ (see p. 266, Fourth Suit Forcing), but the other four, 3♣, 3◇, 3♠ and 2 N.T., are Limit Bids.

South	North
1♣	1◇
1♠	?

Obviously, since responder is making this second try, they *invite* further action from opener and, in practice, they show something like 11 points in a hopeful hand. A couple of examples should suffice.

♠ A J 9 3
♡ 7 6
◇ K 10 9 6 4
♣ Q 8

Opener bids 1♣ and you respond 1◇. Opposite opener's rebid of 1♠, a spade game seems probable, though not certain. Rebid 3♠, inviting opener to bid the fourth if he has values to spare, or to pass if minimum,

♠ J 3
♡ J 9
◇ A K Q 9 6 5
♣ J 10 4

but holding a hand like this, responder's rebid is 3◇. This shows the quality of the suit, and opener is at liberty to pass, rebid clubs or spades at the minimum level or, if holding a good stop in hearts, convert to 3 N.T.

REVISION QUIZ ON CHAPTER 4

1. Assume that your partner has opened the bidding with
1♠. What is your response on the following hands?

(a) ♠ Q 7 6 3; ♡ J 3: ◇ 10 9 7 4 2: ♣ K 3:
(b) ♠ K J 9 3: ♡ K 4 3: ◇ 6 5: ♣ K 9 4 2:
(c) ♠ 10 9 8 5 4: ♡ 3 2: ◇ K Q 10 7 6: ♣ 4:
(d) ♠ K J 9 4: ♡ 5: ◇ Q J 9 6 5 4 3: ♣ 4:
(e) ♠ K Q 10: ♡ K Q J 9 6 4: ◇ 6 3: ♣ 5 4:

2. Assume that your partner has opened the bidding with
1♡. What is your response on the following hands?

(a) ♠ Q J 9: ♡ Q 4: ◇ J 9 7 3: ♣ 10 9 8 6:
(b) ♠ J 10 9 6: ♡ K 4: ◇ Q J 5 4: ♣ K J 3:
(c) ♠ Q J 7: ♡ J: ◇ Q 10 6 3 2: ♣ 7 4 3 2:
(d) ♠ Q 5 4 2: ♡ J 10: ◇ Q 5 4 3: ♣ Q 7 5:
(e) ♠ A Q 9: ♡ J 10 3: ◇ Q J 6 3: ♣ Q J 9:

3. Assume that you opened the bidding with 1♡. What is
your rebid if partner responds with 1 N.T.?

(a) ♣ K 7 5: ♡ Q 10 9 7 4 2: ◇ K 3: ♣ A 4:
(b) ♠ K 4: ♡ A K Q 9 6 5: ◇ A 4 2: ♣ 7 4:

What is your rebid if partner responds 2 N.T.?

(c) ♠ J 4: ♡ A K J 9 6 3 2: ◇ A 4: ♣ 10 9:
(d) ♠ Q J 4: ♡ A K Q 6 2: ◇ Q J 4: ♣ J 10:
(e) ♠ J 6: ♡ A K Q 9 7: ◇ J 10 7: ♣ J 6 4:

What is your rebid if partner responds 3 N.T.?

(f) ♠ Q 4: ♡ K J 10 9 7 5 3: ◇ A 4: ♣ Q 5:
(g) ♠ Q 9 3: ♡ A K Q 5 4: ◇ 9 6 2: ♣ K 4:
(h) ♠ 9: ♡ A K J 9 6: ◇ A J 9 4 2: ♣ K Q:

ANSWERS TO REVISION QUIZ
ON CHAPTER 4

1. (a) 2♠ A simple Limit Bid in spades, by far the best and most expressive on this hand.

    (b) 3♠ This is the stronger Limit Bid, of course, and tells your partner you are too strong to bid 2♠ and not strong enough to bid more.

    (c) 4♠ A purely pre-emptive bid based on trump support and "shape".

    (d) 3♠ If opener has a fit with you in diamonds, this will merely be an asset towards a spade contract.

    (e) 2♡ There's nothing odd about this one—a perfectly straight-forward take-out into your own good suit.

(2) (a) 1 N.T. On 6 points you must keep the bidding open and you have no other bid.

    (b) 2 N.T. A Limit Bid showing just what you have— a balanced hand with 11-12 points.

    (c) 1 N.T. Your hand is unsuitable for No Trumps but you are not strong enough to show a suit at the two-level. All you can hope for is that partner can show a second suit.

    (d) 1♠ Some players would bid 1 N.T., but 1♠ is better style and more constructive *unless* you've previously passed, when the 1 N.T. response is wiser.

    (e) 3 N.T. You have 13 balanced points and no other constructive bid, so bid your limit at once.

3. (a) 2♡ All you can do is rebid your six-card suit. You are now responsible for selecting the final contract.

(b) 3♡   You are too strong for a mere 2♡ bid. Tell your partner that your hearts are long and strong and that you had better than a Light Opener. He will pass if he is minimum.

(c) 4♡   With a known minimum of 11 points with partner you want to be in game. You prefer hearts to No Trumps and the final contract is up to you.

(d) 3 N.T.   You have something in every suit and your hearts should be most helpful.

(e) Pass   Pass in sleep, as they say. Partner's balanced 11 points plus your 12 are unlikely to produce game and you have no reason to think 3♡ would be a better contract than 2 N.T.

(f) 4♡   Obviously a better bet from your point of view. Responder, having bid No Trumps, certainly won't have worse than a doubleton in your suit.

(g) Pass.   3 N.T. should be as good a contract as any other.

(h) 4♢   Apart from being allergic to No Trumps, you have two good suits, either of which could produce slam, let alone game, if you find the right fit. Partner must bid again, even if only to return you to 4♡.

CHAPTER 5

One No Trump Opening Bids and Responses

♠♡♣◇♠♡♣◇♠♡♣◇♠♡♣◇♠♡♣◇♠♡♣◇♠♡♣◇

THE No Trump bids and responses in Acol are as vital a part of the basic system as the Light Opening Bids and Limit Bids, and are being explained after these only because some item must be discussed first. They are, as has already been said, all Limit Bids, as they are made on clearly defined and limited point counts. Only in the realms of suit responses to opening No Trump bids do we get away from the Limit Bid response and turn to bids where judgment and "Acol-mindedness" take over.

Standard basic Acol advocates that an opening bid of 1 N.T. should be made on a balanced hand of 12-14 points unvulnerable and 15-17 points vulnerable. Here, however, we come to the first of the "reasonable alternatives" mentioned in the Introduction. You will meet people who say they play "Acol with variable No Trumps" and you will not know, without further questioning, what point counts they have in mind. You will meet people who say they play "weak throughout" and again, there are different interpretations of this. You will meet others who want to play the "three-quarter No Trump", which means weak except when vulnerable against unvulnerable opponents, and in addition to this complication, the point counts again may differ. There is still another variety where you may be required to play "weak throughout except as fourth hand opener", and so on. These variations cannot be classed as reasonable alternatives and my advice to you is to refuse to have anything to do with them—they are all too easily forgotten in the heat of battle, and may well cause disaster. You will be well advised, therefore, to equip yourself with the full mechanics of the variable No Trump bidding, the only reasonable alternative to which is "weak throughout", and as the mechanics of the first include the second, you will have nothing further to learn.

There is a lot to say for either "variable" or "weak throughout", and perhaps the ultimate choice should be left to individual temperament. At Match Pointed Pairs particularly though, the advantages of using the weak No Trump throughout are tremendous. For one thing, the frequency with which suitable hands occur gives its use very wide scope, and 1 N.T. is the most pre-emptive of the opening one bids. It is difficult to overcall on a modest hand, and it is difficult to deal with in the "balancing" position. Furthermore, left in, it can be most difficult to defend, and many is the declarer who has sneaked away with his 90 points for 1 N.T. bid and made when the opposition have two, or even three, of a suit "on". Even the loss of 100 points for one down vulnerable scores well at Match Points against the opposition's 110 for 2♡ or 2♠. On the other hand, 1 N.T. on 12 points vulnerable, doubled and left in, can well cause the most almighty "bottom", being a tempting target for opponents with superior strength. Personally, this is a risk which I am fully prepared to take as I am of the opinion that, for the once you will get into trouble, you will gain a dozen times and, to my mind, this is a very fair exchange. If you don't like the nervous strain of what *may* happen, then stick to "variable", but remember that then you will very likely be opening one of a minor suit which can easily be overcalled by your opponents. True, you won't risk your "bottom", but you will miss many a "top".

From now on, then, we shall not speak of vulnerable or unvulnerable No Trump bids, but of weak or strong. Weak is 12-14 points, and strong is 15-17 points. Whatever the agreed strength, a No Trump opening bid should be made on a balanced hand of 4-3-3-3 pattern or perhaps on 4-4-3-2. There are also a number of strategic positions when it may be made on a hand of 5-3-3-2 pattern when the five-card suit is a good minor, but such strategy is not a basic part of the Acol system and this is no place to discuss it. Remember, then, your basic point counts—evenly balanced hands of 12-14 points for "weak" and 15-17 points for "strong".

RESPONSES IN NO TRUMPS

Before we go on to the specific features which make the Acol No Trump bidding so important, make sure you know the simple basic No Trump responses. They are based on the assumption that, given a reasonable proportion of the good breaks, 25 points between the two hands will produce game. The counts are calculated on the basis of balanced hands, the objective, of course, being to reach a contract of 3 N.T. with a combined count of 25 points. Good "intermediates" such as 9's and 10's, must be given full weight when assessing a hand either for an opening bid or for a response, and 10's, in fact, should be counted as $\frac{1}{2}$ point.

Opener bids:	Responder:
1 N.T. weak (12—14 points)	Raises to 2 N.T. on 11—12 points
	Raises to 3 N.T. on 12+ or 13 points
1 N.T. strong (15—17 points)	Raises to 2 N.T. on 8—9 points
	Raises to 3 N.T. on 9+ points.

A very simple method of remembering responder's counts is for responder to add his points to opener's known minimum. If this gives a total of 23 or 24 points, he should raise to 2 N.T. and opener, holding better than a minimum, will bid the third. If the total comes to 25 points, responder should raise direct to 3 N.T. not, of course, forgetting to allow additional values for good intermediates or a long suit. A few examples should serve to make this clear:—

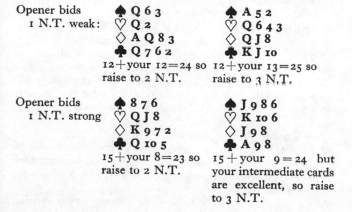

Opener bids 1 N.T. weak:

♠ Q 6 3
♡ Q 2
◇ A Q 8 3
♣ Q 7 6 2
12+ your 12=24 so raise to 2 N.T.

♠ A 5 2
♡ Q 6 4 3
◇ Q J 8
♣ K J 10
12+ your 13=25 so raise to 3 N.T.

Opener bids 1 N.T. strong

♠ 8 7 6
♡ Q J 8
◇ K 9 7 2
♣ Q 10 5
15+ your 8=23 so raise to 2 N.T.

♠ J 9 8 6
♡ K 10 6
◇ J 9 8
♣ A 9 8
15 + your 9 = 24 but your intermediate cards are excellent, so raise to 3 N.T.

From this you will realise that, though you may occasionally get into a contract of 3 N.T. on only 24 points, you are seldom likely to be out of it on 25 points, and a lucky distribution or finesse has often brought the contract home on fewer points than these.

WEAK TAKE-OUT RESPONSES

A take-out of 1 N.T. into two of a suit by responder is a weak bid, and should be made on an unbalanced hand with a long suit—at least five—more likely to be of use as trumps than in a No Trump contract. Opener's hand is already limited strictly by the known point count of his opening bid and he must never, *never*, **never** rebid 2 N.T. Just very occasionally, with a maximum No Trump and a good fit for the suit bid, he may raise to three of the suit, but no more.

This weak take-out applies to the spade, heart, and diamond suits. Clubs are a very special case on their own and will be dealt with in detail in the next chapter. Meanwhile, we had better look at a few examples of this weak take-out.

♠ 10 8 7 5 4 2
♡ 7
◇ 7 5
♣ Q 7 5 2

Whether partner's No Trump is weak or strong, bid 2♠ on this hand. It is worthless unless you are allowed to use your spades as trumps.

The known strength of the opener may well affect responder's bid. For instance, opposite a weak No Trump,

♠ J 7 6
♡ 8
◇ A K 9 8 6
♣ J 8 6 2

this hand offers little or no chance of making game, and 1 N.T. should be taken out into 2◇. But opposite a strong No Trump the minimum combined count is 24 points which

plus your five-card suit, offers great hopes: raise a strong No Trump to 2 N.T.

♠ 8 4
♡ Q 10
◇ K J 9 7 4
♣ 8 7 6 4

Whatever the strength of the opening No Trump, you should respond 2◇ on this hand, which you have some hope of making, whereas the outcome of a No Trump contract must be highly dubious.

A bid of 2♣ over 1 N.T. has a specialised conventional meaning which we shall deal with later but this, of course, means that you cannot make the normal weak take-out into 2♣. If, therefore, your hand is such that you would like to make this bid, you bid 2♣ over 1 N.T., and repeat clubs—3♣—over partner's response. This will tell him that you would have liked to have made the weak take-out in the first place. In these circumstances a very weak hand with only a five-card club suit is probably best left in 1 N.T., so that the 2♣ bid followed by the 3♣ repeat should virtually only be made on a six-card suit and complete garbage.

These weak take-out bids are an essential part of basic Acol. They do not, as some of the die-hards still claim, rob you of good suit contracts because the whole machinery to find the right suit contract, either in part-score or in game, is fully and simply developed. Responder is in the happy position of knowing the strength of his partner's bid within very exact limits and can act accordingly.

SUIT JUMP TAKE-OUT RESPONSES

We have already considered responder's action on balanced hands containing a reasonable point count, and on unbalanced hands with a low point count. Now we can go on to unbalanced hands with a much better count or "shape", where a take-out into three of a suit—and this includes clubs this time—is the order of the day. This jump take-out is a strength-showing bid, forcing to game at least, either in the suit or in No Trumps.

♠ A 7
♡ Q J 9 8 4 2
◇ 10 9
♣ J 10 9

Opposite a weak No Trump this hand would offer a weak take-out into 2♡, but opposite a strong No Trump you should bid 3♡. On such a distribution you want to be in game, and would obviously prefer a heart contract to No Trumps. Opener will respond 3 N.T. or 4♡, according to his hand.

♠ A 9 8
♡ 9 8 5
◇ K J 10 6 4 3
♣ 7

Bid 2◇ opposite a weak No Trump and 3◇ opposite a strong No Trump. You have a long minor suit plus an entry, so you must force, and partner has the option of bidding 3 N.T. or going on to 5◇. Had your diamonds and clubs been reversed you would have bid 2♣ over a weak 1 N.T. and repeated 3♣ over opener's response. Opposite a strong No Trump you would bid 3♣ immediately.

A distinction must be drawn between the jump take-out in the majors and in the minors. In the case of the majors you would prefer a game contract at the four-level but with the minors, five is a lot to make, and opener is likely to take the bid as an invitation to bid 3 N.T. if he can. You must, therefore, be prepared to stand a 3 N.T. contract, or to go on to a game contract in your minor suit if you make a jump bid in one of them.

♠ K Q 10
♡ A Q 6
◇ K J 10 8 7
♣ 5 3

On this hand you would assuredly bid 3◇ whatever partner's opening strength. If weak, and he rebids 3 N.T., that should be a happy contract, and should he prefer a raise to 4◇ there could be little wrong with a cue bid of 4♡ to test the possibilities of a slam. If he's opened a strong No Trump, you're interested in the possibilities of a slam from the moment you look at your hand.

One more example, this time of another aspect of this No Trump bidding:—

♠ 9 8
♡ 8 7
◇ A K J 10 7 4
♣ 9 6 5

Opposite partner's weak No Trump you bid 2◇ without question, but opposite a strong No Trump you should raise to 3 N.T. immediately. Here, with only your long diamonds, it is better to raise in No Trumps than to force in the suit. Your minor suit should be good for a *minimum* of five tricks, and six if partner has the ◇Q in which case, with any luck, he'll be able to run off nine tricks before the opposition has time to get awkward.

Other jump take-out bids which we should touch on in this section are the immediate calls of four in either major or minor suits, and the jump to five of a minor.

A jump take-out to four of a major shows an exceed-

♠ A J 10 9 8 7 4
♡ 6
◇ 9
♣ J 7 6 4

ingly unbalanced hand containing a long major suit and precious little else. The bid announces promptly that the hand is worthless except with this suit as trumps, and asks to be left undisturbed to play in the major suit game.

An immediate raise to four diamonds is pre-emptive, and would be made on a hand which is virtually a "blizzard" in the majors though containing a long suit of diamonds—say seven or eight to the K Q. A jump to 4♣ cannot be made in this position, as the bid is conventional. It will be explained in the next chapter.

A somewhat stronger hand, either in clubs or diamonds, should be bid directly to game in the suit.

♠ 9
♡ A 6
◇ 8 6
♣ K Q 9 8 6 5 3 2

It is unlikely that this direct jump to game will mean a missed slam, as partner's No Trump opener will have to take care of a minimum of five losers. On the other hand, on such a collection as this, 5♣ may well be a make against a blind opposition lead, apart from which the bid is so highly pre-emptive that it would be brave opponents who would dare to seek a major suit contract over it.

REVISION QUIZ ON CHAPTER 5

1. Playing weak No Trump throughout, what do you open on the following hands?

    (a) ♠ K 9 4: ♡ Q 10 2: ◇ A J 9 4: ♣ Q J 6:

    (b) ♠ K J 10: ♡ Q 10 9 8: ◇ K J: ♣ A J 4 3:

    (c) ♠ Q 4 3: ♡ Q J 4: ◇ Q 7 4: ♣ A K 6 3:

    (d) ♠ A Q 4: ♡ 8 7 4 2: ◇ K Q 10: ♣ A Q 10:

    (e) ♠ Q 10 4: ♡ Q 9 3 : ◇ A K 9 5 2: ♣ Q 4:

    (f) ♠ A Q: ♡ A Q: ◇ 10 9 8 7 4: ♣ J 10 9 8:

    (g) ♠ A K 7: ♡ 9 5 4 3: ◇ A K 6: ♣ J 4 2:

    (h) ♠ A Q 6 2: ♡ K 9 3: ◇ 7 4 3: ♣ K 10 6:

    (i) ♠ A K 5: ♡ 10 7 3 2: ◇ A 6 2: ♣ A Q 5:

    (j) ♠ 7 6 3 2: ♡ A Q 6: ◇ K 6 5: ♣ A Q 5:

Now what do you open on them if you are vulnerable and playing "variable"?

2. If partner has opened 1 N.T. (12—14 points) what do you respond on the following hands?

    (a) ♠ Q 7 6 5 3 2: ♡ 7: ◇ 8 4 2: ♣ K 7 3:

    (b) ♠ Q 7 6: ♡ K J 9: ◇ A 3: ♣ Q J 9 8 5:

    (c) ♠ Q 9 2: ♡ K 7 3: ◇ K 5 4: ♣ A 6 3 2:

    (d) ♠ Q 10 9: ♡ K 10 9: ◇ K 9 4: ♣ A 10 3 2:

    (e) ♠ A Q 6: ♡ K Q 10: ◇ 7 4: ♣ K J 10 8 7:

    (f) ♠ 7: ♡ A Q 10 9 6 4 3: ◇ 8 7 5 3: ♣ 4:

    (g) ♠ 7: ♡ 6 2: ◇ K Q 9 6 5 4 3 2: ♣ 8 4:

    (h) ♠ 7: ♡ A 7: ◇ K Q 9 6 5 4 3 2: ♣ 9 4:

    (i) ♠ Q 9: ♡ J 3: ◇ K J 8 4 2: ♣ 7 6 4 3:

    (j) ♠ K Q 10 9 8 3: ♡ 7: ◇ A Q 4: ♣ K J 9:

ANSWERS TO REVISION QUIZ ON CHAPTER 5

1. (a) 1 N.T. A balanced 13-point hand is ideal for the bid.

   (b) 1♣ It is better to open 1♣ than 1♡, as 1♣ gives the better chance of finding a fit with your partner.

   (c) 1 N.T. Bid the whole hand at once—1 N.T. is far more pre-emptive than your alternative of 1♣.

   (d) 1♡ With 17 good points you cannot bid 1 N.T. and you can afford to show the heart suit.

   (e) 1 N.T. 13 points and a good 5-card minor. This is a good strategic bid on such a hand.

   (f) 1 N.T. If you fall into the trap of opening 1◇, what can you possibly rebid?

   (g) 1◇ This is a moment for a "prepared" 1◇, hoping that your partner will bid hearts, but only if he bids 2♣ will you have to make an overbid of 2 N.T.

   (h) 1 N.T. If you feel tempted to open 1♠, ask yourself how you propose to rebid this hand.

   (i) 1♡ Almost the same hand as in (d) above, and just to see if you remembered.

   (j) 1♣ Too strong for 1 N.T., not strong enough for 1♠—(see Chapter 7).

Now bidding these hands again using the 15—17 point No Trump when you are vulnerable:—

   (a) 1◇ Open your 4-card suit in preference to 1♣.

   (b) 1 N.T. A perfect strong 1 N.T. opener.

   (c) 1♣ This time you can't make use of the pre-emptive value of a 1 N.T. bid as you are not strong enough.

   (d) 1 N.T. Still within the limits for a strong No Trump which you bid in preference to the weak heart suit.

(e) 1◇   A bit difficult, because your only rebid is going to be 2◇ but you must open something.

(f) 1◇   Other than passing on this 13-point hand, you must break some rule to find a bid, and this seems the least of a number of evils.

(g) 1 N.T.   No trouble this time.

(h) 1♣   You dare not open 1♠ as you have no possible rebid, so you open 1♣ *and rebid in No Trumps*. (See Chapter 7).

(i) 1 N.T.   Automatic—17 points, well balanced.

(j) 1 N.T.   Again automatic—a well balanced 15 points.

2. (a) 2♠   A simple weak take-out into your long suit.

(b) 3 N.T.   You have the full necessary count plus a most valuable five-card suit.

(c) 2 N.T.   Opener's minimum of 12+your 12=24. Leave the decision to him.

(d) 3 N.T.   The same arithmetic, but your "intermediates" are so strong that you can bid 3 N.T. direct.

(e) 3♣   You are far too strong to make a weak take-out and partner must now bid 3 N.T. or raise your clubs.

(f) 4♡   A direct bid to game in the majors means a long suit and practically nothing else.

(g) 4◇   This is highly pre-emptive, and is only bid on a hand with nothing whatever in the major suits.

(h) 5◇   Stronger by just that Ace, but still worth a game bid in diamonds rather than a try at No Trumps.

(i) 2◇   Back to a simple weak take-out on a hand where you have some hope of making provided you are allowed to use your suit as trumps.

(j) 3♠   A straight-forward jump take-out into a good suit in which you would prefer to play. Partner will keep open by raising or bidding 3 N.T.

CHAPTER 6

One No Trump and The Club Suit

♠♡♣◇♠♡♣◇♠♡♣◇♠♡♣◇♠♡♣◇♠♡♣◇♠♡♣◇

WE have now covered all the responses to 1 N.T. except those in the club suit and both 2♣ and 4♣ over 1 N.T. are, as already pointed out, conventional bids, requiring special explanation.

2♣ over 1 N.T. calls on partner to show his four-card major suit if he has one and thus, by finding a "fit", to prevent a No Trump hand from being torn to pieces—a most humiliating situation which can occur when responder happens to have no stop in opener's own weakest suit.

This bid was first invented by Ewart Kempson and then further developed by J. C. H. Marx. It went to America where Samuel M. Stayman elaborated it and publicised it as a part of his system. Since then Richard Skinner had published even bigger, better and brighter elaborations, none of which are of interest to Acol players. Indeed, the Acol system does not use the Stayman Convention at all, although this 2♣ over 1 N.T. has become almost universally known by that name. A name is not, in any case, necessary. Once a player has announced that he is using Acol it should be implicit that he uses a 2♣ bid over 1 N.T. as a means of fit-finding. This is one of Acol's basic principles.

The bid is not a contradiction of the simple take-out into two of a suit which we have already gone into. The 2♣ take-out is a bid to be used when responder would, virtually, like to discuss with partner the eventual contract whereas, with the simple take-out he is telling, not discussing.

There is no limiting qualification imposed on a responder who wants to use this take-out bid, and it may, in fact, be made on anything from a Yarborough to a rock-crusher. There are, however, two important positions where it must not be used:

(a) On balanced responding hands which are themselves suitable for No Trump contracts.
(b) Where a clear-cut take-out into a suit, either forcing or otherwise, is indicated.

It is quite as important to learn when *not* to use this bid as when to use it. Stating the limitations another way, then, you may bid 2♣ over 1 N.T. when, though interested in a possible major suit contract,

(a) You have no straight-forward weak take-out
OR
(b) You have no straight-forward forcing bid available.

It is important here to stress that the 2♣ bidder has, at this stage, taken over control of the bidding, which must now be allowed to develop along the lines he indicates.

Opener's choice of a rebid after hearing his partner bid 2♣ is simple:

(a) If he holds one four-card major suit, he bids it at the two-level.
(b) If he has two four-card major suits he bids the spades first and can later, if expedient, show the hearts. This is merely a matter of following the Acol principle of bidding the higher ranking of two adjacent and equal suits first.

(c) Having no four-card major suit, he rebids 2◇ *irrespective of either his diamond holding or his point count.* This is of paramount importance, as it leaves responder free to make what will now be a weak take-out bid at the two-level.

Responder's next bid is equally simple. The initiative belongs to him and:

(a) If opener's rebid suits his hand he can pass or raise, according to his strength.
(b) If the bid does not suit, he can bid or jump bid his own best suit or revert to No Trumps.
(c) On very rare occasions he may make a forcing bid of 3◇ over 2◇.

As usual, the best way of making these positions quite clear will be by way of a number of examples. Assume in all these that partner has opened with a weak, that is 12-14 point, No Trump.

♠ A 7 6 4 3
♡ J 9 6 3
◇ J 10 7
♣ 4

This hand is quite obviously far better equipped for a major suit contract than for No Trumps. Over 1 N.T., therefore, bid 2♣. Pass partner's response of 2♡ or 2♠, but over his 2◇ response make a weak take-out of 2♠.

♠ A 7 5 4
♡ J 9 7 6 3
◇ J 10 7
♣ 4

Just the same story, except that your own best of two evils is hearts. Pass partner's 2♡ or 2♠ bid, but bid 2♡ over 2◇.

♠ 9 8 6 4
♡ 9 7 4 2
◇ 8 6 4 3
♣ 4

This quite horrible selection could hardly be more unpleasant for a No Trump contract. Respond 2♣ and pass any rebid from partner, even 2◇. With a known maximum holding of six cards between the two major suits, opener is practically certain to have either three or four diamonds.

Besides this, your 2♣ bid may well discourage a fourth hand protective double.

♠ J 9 8 7 5 4
♡ J 8 4 2
◇ 6 3
♣ 6

Bid 2♣ over 1 N.T. and pass either 2♡ or 2♠. Over 2◇, bid 2♠.

♠ 9 8 7 5 4
♡ 8 7 6 4
◇ 7 5
♣ 6 2

As in the example above, bid 2♣ over 1 N.T., pass 2♡ or 2♠ and bid 2♠ over 2◇.

♠ K Q 9 7 4
♡ A J 9 4
◇ 6 3 2
♣ 4

Bid 2♣ over 1 N.T. Raise either 2♡ or 2♠ to the three-level, but bid 2♠ over 2◇. Had partner's No Trump opener been strong you would raise either major suit to game or bid 3 N.T. over 2◇.

♠ J 4
♡ J 7
◇ 10 8 4
♣ Q 9 7 5 4 2

Bid 2♣ and repeat 3♣ over any response from partner. The hand is useless except with clubs as trumps, and this is your only way of signing-off in clubs.

♠ K Q 5 4
♡ 6
◇ K 7 5 3
♣ Q J 10 4

Using "weak throughout" bid 2♣ and pass 2♠ *or* 2◇. Bid 2 N.T. over 2♡ as the count is good enough for you to feel like inviting partner to "have a go" if he is maximum, especially once you know that he has a stopper of at least four cards in hearts. Over a strong No Trump opener you would want to be in game, either 3 N.T. or 4♠.

♠ J 7 6
♡ 8
◇ A K 9 8 6
♣ J 8 6 2

This is the hand we considered on p. 62 before going into these 2♣ bids. Many players would feel reluctant to raise direct to 3 N.T. with the singleton heart, even opposite to a strong No Trump. If you feel like that, consider what happens if you bid 2♣ and partner responds 2♡—you can now bid 3 N.T. knowing he has a four-card stopper. But if he bids 2♠ over 2♣, what can you do next? You are not interested in a spade contract, are you? This, therefore, is one of the occasions for *not* using the 2♣ bid but for making the direct raise in No Trumps.

♠ K J 9 7 5 4   Bid 2♣ over 1 N.T. and raise either
♡ Q J 10 3   major to game. If partner responds
◊ 8   2◊, however, make a jump bid to
♣ A 3   3♠. This is one of the rare occasions
                    where you want to be in game anyway,
but take the opportunity of finding out on the way up if you have a fit with partner in either of the major suits.

♠ A Q 6 5   Bid 2♣ over 1 N.T. If using weak
♡ A J 8 5   No Trump, over 2◊ bid 2 N.T. or
◊ 9 7 5   raise either major to three. Opposite
♣ 8 3   a strong No Trump, bid 3 N.T. over
                    partner's 2◊, or raise either major
suit to game.

With regard to (c), responder's rebid of 3◊ mentioned as being forcing, the occasion for the use of this bid will only arise very rarely but, like all other conventions, when it does it can be very useful. Having opened 1 N.T. and responded 2◊ to his partner's fit-finding bid of 2♣, responder's subsequent rebid of 3◊ is forcing, calling on opener to show the *best* of his two major suits. These suits are already known to be less than 4-card ones by virtue of the 2◊ denial bid, and opener must now give preference to length over honour strength in his reply to 3◊. That is to say, with three hearts and two spades, he must bid 3♡, or with three spades and two hearts, he must bid 3♠. Holding equal length in both, he bids the one containing the better honours.

This convention may be used to cover the occasional hand where responder's hand is of game-going strength but two-suited in the majors. Having failed to find opener with a 4-card fit for either, responder still prefers to look for a suit contract and, the opening bid having been 1 N.T., he is assured of being able to find at least a three-card fit for one or other of his suits.

♠ A Q J 8 7
♡ K Q 10 9 8
◇ 6
♣ 3 2

1 N.T.—2♣
2◇—3◇
?

Here the point count justifies a game contract, even opposite to a weak No Trump opening bid, but clearly either 4♡ or 4♠ will be more attractive than 3 N.T. The bidding could then go: Over 3◇ opener will show his best major suit which responder will raise to four.

This 3◇ bid also, of course, works as a transfer bid, leaving the opening No Trump hand concealed, and also with the lead coming up to, not through, it.

Remember that the key-note of this 2♣ bid is its fit-finding efficiency. Here is a hand from actual play in a duplicate pairs event where a surprising number of responders failed to realise their potential strength:

♠ 9 7
♡ A 10 9 7 6
◇ A J 8 6
♣ J 10

10 points—not enough to raise opener's weak No Trump, so several responders made the weak take-out bid of 2♡ which was, of course, left undisturbed by opener. Another who held this hand considered long and deeply and finally produced a raise to 2 N.T. which again opener passed. He had 13 points but only K x in spades. The truly Acol-minded, though, realised that here was a hand which would be upgraded out of all proportion to its point-count if a fit were found, and made the bid of 2♣. To partner's rebid of 2◇ or 2♠ you would revert to 2 N.T. and no one in their senses could accuse you of making an over-bid. To a response of 2♡, though, how the picture changes! A direct raise to 4♡ becomes a "must", and those who took this view were amply rewarded, as the hand played for 4♡ + 1.

Just one peep from the other side of the picture.

♠ K Q 7 6
♡ K J 6 5
◇ A 10 7
♣ J 10

As opener, it would be somewhat misleading to bid 1 ♠ on this hand with the idea of rebidding 2 ♡, so you get out of your trouble by bidding 1 N.T. (if, as I hope, you are playing "weak throughout"). Now your partner bids 2 ♣ and you bid, of course, the higher ranking of your two four-card major suits, that is, spades. To this partner produces a rebid of 2 N.T. Now you know a number of things: partner was interested in your major suit holdings and his interest faded when he heard you had spades—in fact he must have hearts. His hand is better than a weak take-out or he would have bid 2 ♡ or passed 1 N.T. in the first place, so you can read him for about 11 points with a four-card heart suit and weakness in spades. So try him out now with a bid of 3 ♡. Your hand is a maximum for your bid but you're not too happy about the club suit yourself and partner, knowing that you have eight cards between the two major suits, can make his choice between 3 N.T. and 4 ♡.

One word of warning here, on the importance of learning when not to use this convention—and this applies equally to the use you will learn later of 3 ♣ over 2 N.T. Used injudiciously, it can give much gratuitous information to the opposition, who will not be slow to take advantage of the count offered by the knowledge that declarer has less than four cards in any particular suit. 1 N.T.—2 ♣—2 ♡, you will realise, denies four cards in spades, and similarly 2 ♣ followed by 2 ◇ denies four cards in either of the majors. This is negative information it is true, but it may be invaluable to your opponents. Unless responder is sure, therefore, that there will be great benefits if a suit fit is found, he should prefer any direct raise in No Trumps that his strength indicates.

Before going on, this seems an appropriate moment to make clear two other points which often seem to cause confusion. If the opening 1 N.T. bid is doubled by the next hand, responder's 2♣ bid is now a natural weak take-out and not conventional. It is also possible that responder may pass an opening 1 N.T. because his only weak take-out would have been into 2♣ and he does not wish to have to repeat these at the 3♣ level. If fourth hand then doubles and it is passed round, the opening bidder's partner may now make his 2♣ take out, which will be natural and not conventional.

N.	E.	S.	W.	
1NT	—	—	x	On this sequence, South will only be making a weak take-out of the double, feeling that the hand will play better in 2♣ than in 1 N.T. doubled.
—	—	2♣		

Secondly if, as in this case, North's opening 1 N.T. is immediately overcalled with an intervening 2♣, a

N.	E.	S.	W.	
1NT	2♣	x		double by South takes the place of the 2♣ he cannot now bid himself, becoming a fit-finding bid

and not a business double. This is the only exception, and any other intervening suit bid doubled by South in this position is strictly for business.

THE GERBER CONVENTION

The bid of 4♣ over 1 N.T. has a very special significance, and one which fills a long-felt want. True to the Acol principle of incorporating bids and conventions which do not conflict with its basic principles, the Gerber Convention is now added to your weapons. It is an immediate announcement of interest in a slam and, at the same time, a request to show the number of Aces held. Opener responds 4◇ with no Aces, 4♡ with one, 4♠ with two, 4 N.T. with three, and 5♣ with all four. As it is almost inconceivable that the 4♣ bid was made on an Aceless hand, this leaves the subsequent bid of 5♣ free as a request to show Kings on the same "step" principle. Any other bid than 5♣ in this position is a sign-off and should be left undisturbed by the original opening 1 N.T. bidder.

1NT—4♣ (Gerber)   The 4♡ bid shows one Ace which
4♡—4NT   is, presumably, insufficient for partner's hopes, and he signs off in 4 N.T.

1NT—4♣   This time, apparently, one Ace is good
4♡ —5♣   enough, so now the enquiry is about
6♣ — ?   Kings. The 6♣ bid shows all four and partner is now free to choose the final contract. Note that these responses would be impossible if "weak throughout" is being used, as they account for 16 points (one Ace and four Kings, and opener could only hold one more Jack to be within the limits of even a 15-17 point No Trump.

♠ A   A bid of 5◇ over 1 N.T. would be
♡ 9   madness on a hand like this, and a
◇ K Q J 9 7 6 5 2   jump take-out into 3◇ is liable to
♣ A 7 6   leave you in a qaundary for a suitable rebid over partner's almost inevitable 3 N.T. An immediate 4 N.T. bid is "out" as this would be taken as quantitative and might well be left by opener. A bid of 4♣, however, will elicit the invaluable information that partner has either one or both the missing Aces, and 5♣ will then account for the Kings.

It must be remembered that the 4♣ bidder has taken control of the bidding and, no suit having as yet been agreed, his discretion as to the final contract must be accepted. If opener admits to two Aces and one King on this last example, there will be thirteen tricks on top in No Trumps.

REVISION QUIZ ON CHAPTER 6

1. What do you bid over partner's opening 1 N.T. (12—14 points)?

    (a) ♠ A J 9 2: ♡ K J 10 3: ◇ 10 9 8 6 3: ♣ —:

    (b) ♠ A J 9 6 2: ♡ 4 3: ◇ K 10 4 3: ♣ 6 2:

    (c) ♠ 8: ♡ K 10 9 4: ◇ K Q 8 6 4 2: ♣ Q 4:

    (d) ♠ K 9 6 5 4: ♡ Q 9 6 2: ◇ 4: ♣ J 9 8:

    (e) ♠ K Q 9 5: ♡ K Q 9 5: ◇ 7 4: ♣ A 10 3:

2. Over partner's weak 1 N.T. opening bid you respond 2♣ and partner bids 2♡. What is your next bid?

    (a) ♠ 7: ♡ Q 10 8 4: ◇ A K 6: ♣ K 10 7 3 2:

    (b) ♠ K Q 6 3 2: ♡ 6: ◇ Q 7 4: ♣ K 10 7 3:

    (c) ♠ Q 10 9 4: ♡ A 4: ◇ K J 9: ♣ A 9 8 2:

    (d) ♠ K 10 9 6: ♡ Q 10 9 6: ◇ A 8 6 4: ♣ 4:

    (e) ♠ K Q J 9 5: ♡ K Q 7 4: ◇ Q 4: ♣ Q 4:

3. What do you bid over partner's opening 1 N.T., weak, and how do you plan to continue the bidding?

    (a) ♠ K Q 10 9 7 4: ♡ A Q 7 2: ◇ 6 3: ♣ 3:

    (b) ♠ Q 7 5 4: ♡ K 6 3 2: ◇ A J 4 2: ♣ 2:

    (c) ♠ Q 3 2: ♡ K 8 4 3: ◇ A 6 3: ♣ K J 6:

    (d) ♠ Q 4 2: ♡ 7 6 3: ◇ 8 2: ♣ K J 7 6 2:

    (e) ♠ A 7: ♡ K Q J 6: ◇ A K Q 10 7 6: ♣ 7:

ANSWERS TO REVISION QUIZ ON CHAPTER 6

1. (a) 2♣ Then pass anything partner says, including 2◇.

   (b) 2♠ A simple weak take-out bid.

   (c) 2♣ Pass 2♡ or 2◇ and bid (rather reluctantly) 2 N.T. over 2♠.

   (d) 2♣ Pass 2♠ or 2♡ or bid 2♠ over 2◇.

   (e) 2♣ Over 2◇ raise to 3 N.T. Raise either major to four.

2. (a) 4♡ A perfect fit and enough strength to raise to game.

   (b) 2♠ This now becomes a weak take-out. If partner had bid 2♠ you would have passed.

   (c) 3 N.T. As you have not found the spade fit you hoped for, raise direct to game.

   (d) 3♡ You have found the fit you hoped for, but are not quite strong enough to go direct to game yourself.

   (e) 4♡ Don't make the mistake of showing your spades with the known 4-4 fit in hearts.

3. (a) 2♣ first, and if partner shows either major, you plan to raise direct to game in it. If he bids 2◇ you will bid 3♣.

   (b) 2♣ and you plan to pass 2◇ and raise either major to three.

   (c) 3 N.T. direct. Evenly balanced—enough points.

   (d) No bid. You can't make a weak take-out into 2♣ as you don't want to rebid 3♣.

   (e) 4♣ The "Gerber" request to partner to show Aces. If he admits to holding two you plan to bid 7◇ direct. You could enquire about Kings with a 5♣ bid on the way, just in case his N.T. were made up with Queens and Jacks, of course.

Acol and The "Prepared" Minor Suit Bids

♠♡♣◇♠♡♣◇♠♡♣◇♠♡♣◇♠♡♣◇♠♡♣◇♠♡♣◇

THE Acol attitude towards the "prepared" bids in the minor suits merits a chapter to itself, and it is fair to say that 1♣ is one of the most abused opening bids of the lot.

From the opening bidder's point of view, when either of the minor suits is held, an opening bid in one of them differs in no way from an opening bid in the majors, but far too many players nowadays have adopted the use of a "prepared" minor suit bid, especially a "prepared" 1♣, using it almost at random when they can think of nothing else to do. This is a habit very deeply to be deplored. Acol does not advocate the over-use of the principle of preparedness which can, when carried as it so often is, to unnecessary lengths, result in bidding your partner's cards for him. This, as we have already learned, is the very antithesis of basic Acol where every bid is aimed at bidding your own cards simply and fully.

Correctly used, the "prepared" 1♣ or 1◇ occur in Acol in only two situations. The first of these is if you are using the 15-17 point vulnerable No Trump and you pick up a balanced hand of 12-14 points which is too strong to pass and not strong enough to open 1 N.T. Nor is it strong enough to risk opening a four-card major, as the hand would then have no sound rebid at the two-level. So you resort, though reluctantly, to 1♣ or 1◇, but as you must never, *never*, **never** make a "prepared" minor suit bid with less than three cards in the suit, and one of them a high honour, you select either clubs or diamonds, which ever fits the occasion best. Not vulnerable, of course, on this sort of hand, or playing "weak throughout", you can open 1 N.T., and with 15 or more points you can usually open one of your four-card suit and rebid in No Trumps.

The second situation when a "prepared" minor suit bid may be necessary is when you are not vulnerable, or when you are playing "weak throughout", which means that your No Trump bid is never stronger than 12-14 points. Then, just occasionally, you may pick up a 15-point hand, or perhaps even a 16-point one, on which your four-card suit is really not biddable—is, in fact, virtually of interest only as support if partner bids that suit. Then, once again, you may be forced into opening 1♣ or 1◇. Take, as an example, the following hand:—

♠ 8 6 4 2   Here the hand generally is not good
♡ A Q 7   enough to announce a biddable suit of
◇ K Q 3   spades and you may open 1♣, but if
♣ K J 5   you strengthen it by the inclusion of the
            ♠Q in place of the ♠8 you can well
afford to open 1♠. If you leave the spades at ♠ 8 6 4 2 and make the clubs ♣ K Q J, then your outside values compensate for the weakness of the spades and you can again open one of that suit. Or make it like this:—

♠ 8 6 4 2   Now you can open 1♠ regardless. If
♡ A K 8   partner responds in No Trumps, raise
◇ K Q 3   him. If he insists on a spade contract,
♣ K Q 7   then he'll have at least four spades in
            support and your chances of making
will be good anyway.

Allowing for the use of a prepared bid even in these

situations is a violation of the natural quality of Acol bidding, as you are opening with a bid in a suit in which you do not wish to be taken seriously. It is, however, an evil which must be endured, but there is one important stipulation which has not yet been mentioned, and this must be attached *before the bid is used in any circumstances.* If you open the auction with a "prepared" minor suit bid, your rebid, if you have not got primary support for your partner's suit response, **must be in No Trumps.** This is not only to try to avoid misleading your partner more than has already been necessary, but to protect you from getting preference from your partner in a suit which you don't, in fact, prefer, a most ignominious position in which to find yourself. Apart from these considerations, it is essential that you should take the earliest possible opportunity of announcing that you were forced to make an unnatural opening bid.

If you open a prepared 1♣ on a hand such as this:

♠ A Q 7 3   and partner responds 1♡, rebid 1 N.T.,
♡ Q 8 3   not 1♠. The hand is, of course, an
◇ K 7 3   excellent weak One No Trump opener.
♣ Q 10 3   Playing "variable" and being vulnerable, some of you may feel the urge to open 1♠, but if you do, what possible honest rebid have you got? So open 1♣ and rebid 1 N.T. over 1◇ or 1♡. If partner bids spades, of course, raise him.

So the rule is that, having felt forced to open with a "prepared" minor, rebid in No Trumps unless you can support partner when he has elected to respond in your four-card suit. If both minors qualify by virtue of being three-card suits headed by a high honour, open 1♣ in preference to 1◇.

From all this it will be apparent that an opening bid of one of a minor can almost always be taken by responder as a natural bid to which he can respond naturally. He has, however, whatever point count is being used for No Trump bidding, the choice of all three suits for a one-level response over 1♣ and of both majors for a one-level response over 1◇. It follows, therefore, that a response of One No Trump over either of these bids can afford to attach to itself some further significance. The significance that the Acol system attaches is that a No Trump response to a 1♣ opening bid promises a balanced hand and a point count of 8 - 10, not the 5 - 9 you would expect over a major suit, and that over 1◇ it promises 7 - 9 points.

Conversely you will realise that if partner responds 1 N.T. to your 1♣ bid, you can rely on him for a minimum of 8 points, and similarly for a minimum of 7 points over an opening 1◇, and your immediate No Trump raises can be de-valued accordingly. Over 1♣ - 1 N.T., a 17 or 18 point hand becomes worth a direct raise to 3 N.T., as the minimum combined count will be 25 points (See Chapter 5).

To summarise, therefore,

(a) Never use a "prepared" minor if you have a more natural bid available,
and

(b) Never use a "prepared" minor with less than three cards, one of them a high honour, in the suit.

♠ 8 7 6 5
♡ J 6 4 3
◇ A K 8
♣ A K

On such a hand as this, a 1♣ bid being "out" as there are only two cards in the suit, I should prefer to open 1◇ to either 1♡ or 1♠, and to support either major if bid by responder. Over the opening 1◇, responder can make a one-level bid in either hearts or spades on a minimum hand with 5 points, and will prefer this to 1 N.T. A major suit fit, therefore, will not be missed by the use of a 1 ◇ opening bid on this hand.

♠ J 7 4 2   This is another hand which should be
♡ A Q 6   opened with 1 ◇ when the 12-14 point
◇ A K J   No Trump is being used. There is no
♣ 8 4 3   honour, let alone a high one, in the club
suit, and it will serve you right if you open 1♣ and partner raises you to 2♣ on six or seven points and four to the nine of clubs. Having opened 1 ◇, if partner responds 1 ♡ you can rebid 1 N.T., if he responds 1♠ you can raise to 2♠, and if he bids 2♣ you can bid 2 N.T.

Finally, at the risk of labouring the point, never resort to a "prepared" bid in either suit if you can find a satisfactory opening bid which allows for an honest rebid in a natural sequence.

REVISION QUIZ ON CHAPTER 7

1. If you are using the variable No Trump (12-14 points not vulnerable, and 15-17 points vulnerable), what do you open if not vulnerable on the following hands?

(a) ♠ 9 8 5 3: ♡ A Q 4: ◇ K Q 5: ♣ K J 3:
(b) ♠ 7 6 3 2: ♡ K Q 9: ◇ A Q 10: ♣ A Q J:
(c) ♠ Q 10 8 6: ♡ J 10 6 :◇ A Q 3: ♣ A K 4:
(d) ♠ K Q 6: ♡ 8 6 4 3: ◇ K J 10: ♣ A J 4:
(e) ♠ J 9 6 3: ♡ J 10 6 4: ◇ A Q: ♣ A K 4:
(f) ♠ K 8 6 3: ♡ K 9 8 4: ◇ A Q 7: ♣ 9 5:

And what if you are vulnerable on these?

(g) ♠ 9 5 3 2: ♡ A Q 6: ◇ K Q 7: ♣ K 10 8:
(h) ♠ K J 4: ♡ 8 6 4 3: ◇ A J 9: ♣ K Q 10:
(i) ♠ A K Q: ♡ K 8 6: ◇ A 6 4 2: ♣ A 9 6:
(j) ♠ K Q 6: ♡ J 9 8 7: ◇ A Q 4: ♣ A Q 5:
(k) ♠ J 8 4 2: ♡ J 9 6 4: ◇ A Q: ♣ A Q 4:
(l) ♠ J 8 4 2: ♡ J 9 6 4: ◇ A Q 4: ♣ A Q:

Now reverse the vulnerability. What do you bid, vulnerable, on hands (a) to (f) above?

What do you bid unvulnerable on hands (g) to (l) above?

ANSWERS TO REVISION QUIZ ON
CHAPTER 7

1. (a) 1♣   One point too strong for an unvulnerable No Trump and the spades really are not biddable.

(b) 1♠   The spades may be equally unbiddable, but the rest of the hand is so strong that you can afford to make this opening.

(c) 1♠   This is a biddable suit within the meaning of the Act.

(d) 1 N.T.   No comment except that this is an automatic bid.

(e) 1♣   Too strong for 1 N.T. and 1♣ is safer than one of either of the majors, which will be excellent in support of partner—or as an undisclosed menace to the opposition.

(f) 1 N.T.   You really cannot give such a false picture of your hand as to bid one of your majors, especially as this would give you no sensible rebid.

(g) 1♣   Not strong enough for a vulnerable No Trump and apart from the weakness of the spade suit, you would have no available rebid.

(h) 1♣   Again, not strong enough for a No Trump but this time it is your heart suit that is too weak and which offers no rebid.

(i) 1♢   In spite of its 20 points this is an unpleasant type of hand, the concentration of points in the spades making it top-heavy. You don't really want to be in game unless partner can make a "free" response, and you're far too strong for 1 N.T. whatever the score.

(j) 1♡   Too strong for a 15-17 point No Trump, and the hearts are perfectly biddable, especially when your honest rebid will be in No Trumps.

(k) 1♣   You will be happy to support either major

87

if bid by partner, and if he bids 1◇ you will
bid 1 N.T.

(l) 1◇   Only two clubs in the hand, so don't use a
"prepared" club, but a "prepared" 1◇, and
rebid in No Trumps or support either major.

Now reversing the vulnerability, let's see what difference
this makes to the opening bids. On (a) to (f) vulnerable,
and using the 15-17 point No Trump:—

(a) 1 N.T. 15 points—just right.

(b) 1♠   Too good for 1 N.T., so bid the spades and
rebid in No Trumps.

(c) 1 N.T. If partner bids 2♣ asking for a major suit
take-out you will bid 2♠.

(d) 1♣   Not strong enough for 1 N.T., and the
hearts are really only interesting as support
on a hand of this medium strength.

(e) 1 N.T. With 15 points you can get the whole hand
off your chest with one bid again, as well as
having a good response to partner's possible
2♣.

(f) 1◇   This is your only alternative to a pass, as the
hand cannot be bid in No Trumps and has
no rebid if you open with a major.

On (g) to (l), unvulnerable, using 12-14 points for a No
Trump:—

(g) 1 N.T. 14 points—a maximum for the bid, but still
the best bid on the hand.

(h) 1 N.T. As above, with no further comment.

(i) 1◇   The first hand that calls for the same bid,
whether vulnerable or not, and for the same
reasons.

(j) 1♡   Again, the same bid, and for the same
reasons.

(k) 1 N.T. A 4-4-3-2 distribution such as this comes
within the scope of a No Trump, and the
point-count is right.

(l) 1 N.T. No need on these hands to make a "prepared" bid of any sort. One of the virtues
of using "weak throughout" is the frequency
with which you can use the bid, dispensing,
again and again, with the unnatural bids,

CHAPTER 8

Opener's Rebids

IN earlier chapters we have discussed certain rebids by the opener, but only in so far as these concern an interpretation of Limit Bids and signing off. Now it is necessary to go a step further and to define a little more clearly the type of **Limit Bid,** as one might call it, mentioned in paragraphs (d) and (e) of Chapter 4.

In the bad old days when any change of suit was forcing, West was under a firm obligation to bid over East's 2♡, and his 2 N.T. in this situation meant that, whilst recognising that he must keep the bidding open, he had nothing else to show. In Acol, this is very far from being the case, and West is under no obligation whatsoever to bid over East's 2♡. He made a sign-off as his rebid, so, not having been forced, he has the free choice of passing, giving a weak preference to 2♠, or retreating to 3♢. The fact that he does not take advantage of any of these sign-off bids must mean something positive. This particular sequence would only occur if West's opener were of the type which, even though containing a point count higher than is required for a Light Opener, can only be rebid as 2♢.

West	East
1♢	1♠
2♢	2♡
2 N.T.	

♠ 8 7 2
♡ Q 8
◇ A K 10 8 7
♣ K Q 4

Here, for example, in spite of its 14 points, the hand has no other first rebid than 2◇. Note though, that nothing will have been lost if responder is not strong enough to find a second bid and, as a corollary to this, that the fact of hearing opener make a sign-off must not deter responder from bidding again if he has the values in his own hand.

Responder having produced a second bid, opener now has the opportunity of saying that, in spite of his rebid, he has more than a sign-off. With only Q x in hearts he could hardly bid No Trumps as his first rebid but now, given this chance, he bids 2 N.T. which is *not* a sign-off but an announcement of additional strength. As he does not support hearts or spades, this must be in clubs. Obviously the hand is limited, as opener does not bid game direct, and now it is up to responder to decide on the final contract. He may pass 2 N.T., raise to 3 N.T., or rebid in either of his own suits.

Another sequence heard recently was the following:

1♠—2♡
2 N.T.—3 N.T.

This final contract proved disastrous, whereupon declarer fumed at his partner—"My 2 N.T. bid *told* you I had nothing more to show, so why did you put me to three?" He, I need hardly say, was no Acol player because, far from saying he had no more to show, he had announced a hand of 15—17 points!

The simple table given on the next page, which you should know by heart, will make these rebids clear, but remember that the point counts given are calculated on quite a conservative basis and that they also assume balanced hands. If you have useful suit lengths or good intermediate cards, that is nines and tens, the requirements can be shaded. No alibis, please, for your failure to bid to game "because I was one short of the point count, partner", when your hand is stuffed with tens and nines or your own suit is solid and you've got a stop in another.

If partner has responded to your opening bid with:—	Your rebid of:—
1. A bid of any other suit at the one level, (i.e., 1♡—1♠)	1 N.T. shows 14 to 16 points. 2 N.T. shows 16+ to 18 points. 3 N.T. shows a minimum of 19 points.
2. A bid of another suit at the two-level, (i.e., 1♡—2◇)	2 N.T. shows 15 to 17 points. 3 N.T. shows a minimum of 18 points.
3. A bid of 1 N.T.	2 N.T. shows 17 or 18 points. 3 N.T. shows 19 points.

All these rebids by opener are Limit Bids and responder need not bid again though he will, of course, do so if his original response were better than minimum. In the cases of Nos: 1 and 2 in the table, responder's strength is, as yet, virtually unknown. For a take-out into a different suit at the one level, he may be as weak as 5 points, and at the two-level as weak as 8 points, while the upper limit of his hand is indeterminate, and limited only by the fact that it was not good enough (or unsuitable) for an immediate force. In the case of No: 3, opener already knows that his partner's hand is limited to between 5-9 points but his own strength may be such that, if the response is maximum or near maximum, when for instance, he himself has 17-18 points, he wants to be in game. Responder will not bid again unless this condition is fulfilled. On 19 points, opener takes matters into his own hands and bids the game direct, as even responder's bare minimum of 5 points will give the hands a combined count of 24 points.

Don't lose sight of the fact that, as opener, you

might wish to make a No-Trump rebid if your partner makes an immediate raise, a suit Limit Bid, as his response. For instance, if you open 1 ♠ on:

♠ A Q 10 6   If partner's response is a raise to 2 ♠
♡ Q J 9   you would not feel inclined to pass
◇ K J 10   without being sure that responder is
♣ K 10 7   minimum so you rebid 2 N.T. This
shows just what you have, an evenly balanced hand of 17 points. The bid, as before, is not forcing but is encouraging and responder can pass if his hand is weak and balanced or return you to 3 ♠ if too unbalanced to tolerate a No-Trump contract. Alternatively, if maximum for his bid, he can raise to either 3 N.T. or 4 ♠.

Before leaving this section of rebids, I should like to refer you back to page 84 of Chapter 7 where, in discussing the minor suit bids and responder's take-out into 1 N.T., I pointed out that 1 N.T. over 1 ♣ carried a point count of 8-10, and over 1 ◇, 7-9 points. Do not forget, therefore, that in the case of No: 3 in the table, opener's rebid requirements can be scaled down if responder's 1 N.T. bid is being made over 1 ♣ or 1 ◇.

One or two other types of opener's rebid should be mentioned here, the first of which is a jump rebid in his own suit after responder's simple change of suit.

1 ♡—1 ♠   This rebid would be indicated on a hand
3 ♡   such as:

♠ 10 9   The hand is not strong enough
♡ A Q J 10 8 2 for an original Two Bid, contains
◇ K J 3   no rebid other than a repeat of
♣ A 6   the heart suit, and is far too
strong for what would be a sign-off of 2 ♡. The bid should be used to announce a hand of seven playing tricks at the suit named, with a six-card trump suit. This bid is not forcing, being in

itself a Limit Bid, but it goes without saying that responder will not pass if he can help it. Particularly if made in the minor suits, responder, with a reasonable hand, is quite likely to have a try for 3 N.T., which may be a very good chance. With the hand on the previous page, for instance, if responder rebids 3 N.T. there is no need to panic. He has bid spades, your weakest suit, and you have stops in both the minors. In any case partner won't have made his 3 N.T. bid with nothing but a bare minimum in the first place.

A simple raise by opener of responder's suit speaks for

♠ A Q 9 8 7
♡ K Q 9
◇ J 7
♣ Q J 4

itself. On such a hand you would obviously bid 1♠ and raise a response of 2♡ to 3♡. Again, this is not a forcing bid and responder may pass if he sees fit.

This vital basic Acol principle of bidding your own cards and not your partner's cannot be stressed too often. If you have the values to bid game direct, do so, and don't wait for your partner to do it because he very likely won't.

1♡—1♠
3♠

In this sequence opener's rebid of 3♠ is once again, not forcing, and it denies the necessary strength to bid game direct. This hand would be an excellent example of this double raise of partner's 1♠ over your opening 1♡. If you get the impression that

♠ K 10 8 2
♡ A Q 8 7 6
◇ Q 4
♣ K 6

you should bid a direct 4♠ on it, remember that, by his response at the one-level, partner has promised you no more than 5—9 points with a four-card spade suit,

so leave the rest to him. If that is all he has, he will pass, but with a reasonable hand he will take the hint, and bid game.

1 ♡ — 1 ♠   This sequence is quite a different
3 ◇   story, and here opener's jump
            rebid in a new suit is uncon-
ditionally forcing. It is a bid which should be made
when, with any sort of "free" bid from partner opener
sees a game as certain and a slam as possible.

♠ K 3   This would be a very typical example
♡ A Q 10 8 4   of a hand suitable for this jump rebid.
◇ K Q J 9   It will be at least a strong hand, and
♣ A 5   probably two, or semi-two suited.

♠ A 4   Here is an example from actual
♡ K Q 10 7 6   tournament play. My partner, South,
◇ A J 9 8 7   opened 1♣ to which I responded 1♡,
♣ 6   and my partner* then rebid 3◇.

After this rebid it didn't take much
imagination on my part to bid the
Grand Slam in diamonds, as if South
is two, or even semi-two suited, as
well as strong enough to make a
♠ K 7 6   forcing rebid, there can be little
♡ A   missing. Note, by the way, that the
◇ K Q 10 6   North hand was not worth an im-
♣ A Q J 9 7   mediate responding force on account
                of the club misfit.

One final word before we go on to the next item on
our programme. Bid to the full limit of your hand
when, as opener, you have to make a rebid. Never make
a sign-off bid if you can possibly avoid it when your
hand is stronger than a Light Opener, and don't make
a simple change-of-suit rebid *which in Acol responder
may pass*, when you are strong enough to force.

*Mrs. Rhoda Barrow.

REVISION QUIZ ON CHAPTER 8

1. Having opened the bidding with 1♥, your partner responds 1♠. What is your rebid on the following hands?

   (a) ♠ Q 10: ♥ A K 9 4 3: ◇ K 9 6: ♣ Q J 4:

   (b) ♠ Q 4: ♥ A K Q 5 4: ◇ K 9 5: ♣ K J 4:

   (c) ♠ J 4: ♥ A K Q 9 8: ◇ Q J 9: ♣ A Q 4:

   (d) ♠ 10 5: ♥ A K J 10 7 4: ◇ A 5: ♣ K 9 2:

   (e) ♠ Q 3: ♥ A Q J 9 4 3: ◇ 10 5 9: ♣ K 3:

   (f) ♠ Q 9: ♥ A Q J 10 8 5 4: ◇ A 4 2: ♣ 5:

2. Having again opened the bidding with 1♥, partner responds 2◇. What is your rebid on the following hands?

   (a) ♠ 9 3: ♥ K J 9 6 4 2: ◇ K 4: ♣ A J 6:

   (b) ♠ K 10 3: ♥ A K 10 5 4: ◇ Q 3: ♣ A 4 2:

   (c) ♠ A J 5: ♥ K Q 10 9 6: ◇ Q J: ♣ K Q 10:

   (d) ♠ 8: ♥ K Q J 10 7 6 4: ◇ Q J 3: ♣ A J:

   (e) ♠ 10 6: ♥ A K J 4 2: ◇ J 9 4 2: ♣ A J:

   (f) ♠ K Q 9 4: ♥ A J 10 9 6: ◇ A 4: ♣ K 3:

ANSWERS TO REVISION QUIZ ON CHAPTER 8

1. (a) 1 N.T. You don't want to sign off in 2♡ and you have something in every suit as well as the right point count.

   (b) 2 N.T. Again, your point count justifies this bid in preference to any other.

   (c) 3 N.T. You take it into your own hands and bid game direct. Even with an absolute minimum from partner you have 24 points between you.

   (d) 3♡ Too strong for a sign-off, not strong enough for a game bid, and unsuitable for a No Trump bid. Announce your long strong trump suit in this way.

   (e) 2♡ Just our old friend, the sign-off after a typical Acol Light Opener.

   (f) 4♡ This time you can hardly do less than have a try for game, and from your point of view it must be in hearts.

2. (a) 2♡ The simple sign-off once more—there is no other bid.

   (b) 2 N.T. No need to sign off here with 16 points.

   (c) 3 N.T. Partner should have at least 8 points to bid at the two-level, so you should have 26 between you and you have a stop in every suit.

   (d) 3♡ Exactly the same story as in (d) in No: 1 above.

   (e) 3◇ A simple raise of partner's suit, showing him a fit. Not forcing.

   (f) 3♠ On this strong hand you make a jump take-out in a new suit, forcing, and partner must keep it open either by supporting one of your suits, rebidding his diamonds, or relapsing into No Trumps.

CHAPTER 9

Showing Shape

♠♡♣◇♠♡♣◇♠♡♣◇♠♡♣◇♠♡♣◇♠♡♣◇♠♡♣◇♠♡♣◇

THERE are various other bidding situations which, in connection with opening bids and rebids, require mention, especially in a book covering the whole of the basic system of Acol. One of these is the important question of how to show your partner your shape—and Ladies, I do *not* mean your vital statistics. I mean the pattern of the distribution of your hand, as it is most important for your partner to be able to judge which of your suits, if you are bidding more than one, you really ought to play in.

If you, as opener, have two suits you want to show, you should remember that the most natural order of bidding is:

1. The longer suit before the shorter, i.e., a six-card suit before a five-card suit.
2. The higher ranking suit before the lower, i.e., spades before hearts.
3. The stronger suit before the weaker, i.e., A K Q x x before Q J x x x.

These rules, I should like to make it clear, are not hard and fast. They are inevitably overlapping and somewhat conflicting, and there will be many occasions on which you will have to judge for yourself which should take precedence. You may also need to pave the way for a satisfactory rebid, and this brings us to one emphatic exception to Rule 2 above which is that when the two equal lengthed suits you wish to show are spades and clubs, you should bid the clubs first.

Remember always two vital Acol principles:—

1. Make the most natural bid available to you in the circumstances existing at the time

and

2. In bidding two suits, you are asking partner to give you preference for one or the other, and you must be careful to give him the information as to which you do actually prefer.

Hands with two suits of equal length—both biddable —normally come quite simply within the rules for natural bidding, with the one exception of clubs and spades. Two-suited hands, where the suits are of different length, however, require rather special treatment, particularly in the rebidding, if you are to be sure of giving partner the right information. He equally, of course, should be able to interpret your bids and apply the results to his own actions.

An important point to understand, and one which, once understood, should clarify the difficulties many players seem to experience with two-suiters is this— if you open the bidding with one suit and then rebid twice in another suit, this implies a holding of at least five cards in the second suit *or it would not be rebiddable*. Under Rule 1 on the previous page you have learned that you should bid first your longer suit. If, therefore, your first bid suit is longer than your second suit which, because it has been rebid, must be of at least five cards in length, then your first bid suit must be even longer, or at least six card in length.

This is something which inexperienced players often find most confusing, but if you think about it, it is quite logical.

In this sequence 1♡ has been opened
and responder makes what is doubtless a normal call of 2◇. Now opener
rebids 2♠. This is a "reverse"—
a bid out of the natural order, and by virtue of the fact that
the showing of two suits asks partner to give preference for
one or the other, implies enough strength to be given preference to the next higher level of 3♡. When responder merely
repeats his diamonds, opener rebids 3♠, not 3♡ which
would ask for a simple preference. Therefore, quite clearly,
as the spades have been rebid, they are a five-card suit. In
spite of the rule about bidding the higher-ranking of two
equally long suits first, opener has bid the lower ranking and
his only reason for doing this should be that it is the longer
of the two suits, which must mean at least a six-card heart
suit. The hand pattern may, of course, be 7—6, or something
less fantastic such as 7-5-1 or 6-5-2, but the first bid suit
will be the longer.

Your general rule, therefore, with two good biddable
suits of equal length, is to bid the longer suit first
and then to bid *and rebid* the shorter. Our example
sequence would be used on a hand such as this:—

 This is not quite strong enough for an
opening two bid in either suit, but
with partner bidding at all is powerful
enough to bid in this way.

Change the hand by reducing the heart suit to five,
and you would open 1♠ in the normal way. Make it
six spades and five hearts, and you would open 1♠
and then bid and rebid the hearts. Take another
pattern:—

♠ A K J 8   Here you would open 1♡ and, being
♡ K Q J 9 7 strong enough, would rebid 2♠ over
◇ 7   partner's 2◇ or 2♣, but your *second*
♣ K 10 4   rebid would be in hearts again.

There is an exception to this, and that is when one
of the suits is six cards long and the other only four.

In this case you should bid and repeat your long suit before showing the shorter. Even exceptions have their own exceptions, though, and that is if the four-card suit is heavily headed by honours. Take this hand:—

♠ 7
♡ A J 9 7 5 3
◇ A K J 10
♣ A 5

Here you have almost a 2♡ opener, but not quite. Bid 1♡ and if partner responds 1♠, rebid 3◇, which is the only way you can do justice to the hand. If, however, partner now takes 3◇ into 3 N.T., you show your 6-4-2-1 pattern by taking out into 4♡.

4-4-4-1 HAND PATTERNS

The opening bids on hands of a 4-4-4-1 pattern pose a problem of their own although Acol, as usual, provides a simple and logical way of dealing with them.

For many years the rule was very simple—on hands with three biddable suits, open the suit below the singleton. This meant that with a singleton spade you bid 1♡, with a singleton heart you bid 1◇, with a singleton diamond you bid 1♣ and, considering the suits as forming a circle, with a singleton club you bid 1♠. This rule did not prove entirely satisfactory, and Acol has refined it as follows:

> With hands of 4-4-4-1 pattern containing three biddable suits, open the suit below the singleton **except when the singleton is in clubs, when open 1♡.**

Opener's Hand: *Responder's Hands:*

Opener's Hand		(a)	(b)	(c)
♠ A J 5 4		♠ 8 3	♠ 8 3	♠ 8 3
♡ K Q 8 3		♡ J 10 7 6	♡ J 5	♡ A 5 4 2
◇ A Q 9 5		◇ K 4	◇ K 10 6 3	◇ K 4 3
♣ 2		♣ K Q 9 7 5	♣ K 9 7 5 4	♣ A 5 4 2

Consider the first hand given opposite to the three possible variations for responder's hand. If opener bids 1♠, holding hand (a) responder will bid 2♣. Now if opener rebids 2♢ responder can do no more except, possibly, "correct" to 2♠, and opener cannot possibly bid his hearts at the three-level, so the perfect fit will have been missed. If responder holds hand (b) he will doubtless bid 1 N.T. over an opening 1♠ and now—what? Opener's rebid is just a guess and if he picks his hearts in preference to his diamonds, once again the perfect fit will have been missed. On hand (c) responder will almost certainly elect to bid 2 N.T. over 1♠, and for the third time opener will be on a guess, though the heart fit stares the partnership in the face if it can be found.

All this difficulty can be avoided if, when the singleton is clubs, the opening bid is 1♡. If responder has a reasonable spade suit he will bid it himself. If he responds 2♣, therefore, you can rebid 2♢, confident that you are not missing a spade fit, and that the best fitting of the two red suits will be agreed for the final contract. If partner responds 1♠ or 2♢ to 1♡, you have effectively eliminated all problems as to your rebid, and over any No Trump response you can also offer diamonds, knowing that the spade fit has not materialised. The risk of missing a heart contract, of course, does not arise, as you have bid the suit yourself.

There is one other point to be made about these 4-4-4-1 hand patterns, and that is that sometimes one of the three suits is very weak or, in other words, of value only as support if partner bids it. Such hands you should treat as two-suiters to be bid according to the natural rules.

♠ 8
♡ 9 7 5 4
◇ A K 5 4
♣ A Q 8 3

When deciding what to bid on this 13 point hand, disregard the hearts, as they do not constitute a biddable suit at this point. Open 1◇, which leaves you a perfectly normal rebid of 2♣, and only if partner responds in hearts, become excited about your holding in this suit, even if you increase the point-count by making the ♠8 into the ♠A. Now you must still bid 1◇, because the hand is not suitable for a rebid in No Trumps.

REVISION QUIZ ON CHAPTER 9

1. What would you open on the following hands, and why?

  (a) ♠ K 10 9 4: ♡ 7: ◇ A Q J 9: ♣ K Q J 3:

  (b) ♠ A J 8 6: ♡ K Q 10 5: ◇ 4: ♣ Q 10 9 3:

  (c) ♠ A J 8 6: ♡ K Q 10 5: ◇ Q 10 9 3: ♣ 4:

  (d) ♠ A K 10 6: ♡ 8 6 4 2: ◇ A Q 9 3: ♣ A:

  (e) ♠ K Q 10 6: ♡ A Q 9 6: ◇ 9 7 6 5: ♣ A:

2. Assuming no opposition interference and a simple suit take-out by responder, how would you plan the bidding of these hands, as opener?

  (a) ♠ 9: ♡ A K 10 9 3: ◇ A J 10 9 6 4: ♣ 6:

  (b) ♠ 4 3: ♡ —: ◇ A J 10 9 6 4: ♣ K Q 10 9 5:

  (c) ♠ 6 2: ♡ A J 9 6 4 3: ◇ A K Q 10: ♣ A:

  (d) ♠ A J 10 9 4 2: ♡ K 9 3 2: ◇ K 5: ♣ J:

  (e) ♠ K Q 10 9 6: ♡ 6 3: ◇ A: ♣ A J 5 4 3:

  (f) ♠ K Q 9 6 4 3: ♡ —: ◇ 4: ♣ K Q 10 9 6 3:

  (g) ♠ A K Q 5 4: ♡ K 10 9 7 4 3 2: ◇ —: ♣ A:

  (h) ♠ Q J 9 4: ♡ A K 10 9 5: ◇ 6 3: ♣ K J:

ANSWERS TO REVISION QUIZ ON CH. 9

1. (a) 1◇   A normal "suit below the singleton" with three biddable suits.

   (b) 1♣   This is another of the same—the suit below the singleton.

   (c) 1♡   This is the exception—three biddable suits and the singleton in clubs.

   (d) 1◇   This may facilitate a 1♡ response on a 4-card suit and you are strong enough to bid 2♠ over a 2♣ response.

   (e) 1♠   This hand must be regarded as a two-suiter in spades and hearts. Bid the higher ranking first and follow with hearts unless you are able to support a diamond bid from partner.

2. (a) Open 1◇, which is the longer of the two suits, and then bid and *repeat*, hearts. This will tell partner that your longer suit is diamonds and that as your hearts are rebiddable (at least five) your diamonds must be at least six.

   (b) Open 1◇ and show clubs on the next round. On the third round (if any) rebid the clubs.

   (c) Open 1♡ and show the diamonds on the next round with a jump force, i.e., 1♡—1♠—3◇. If partner retreats into 3 N.T., show your "shape" by taking out into 4♡.

   (d) Open 1♠ and repeat 2♠ on the next round—a simple sign-off bid, unless partner bids hearts, which raise to 3♡.

   (e) Open 1♣ and rebid 1♠. This is the exception to the rule of bidding the higher ranking of two equal suits.

   (f) Open 1♣ again. The same rule holds good even if they are both now six-card suits.

   (g) Open 1♡, the longer suit, and make a jump switch in spades on the next round. Repeat spades to show they are rebiddable (five) and that hearts, therefore, are longer.

   (h) Open 1♡. Support if partner bids spades, otherwise rebid 2 N.T. over 2♣ or 2◇—only a slight overbid.

CHAPTER 10

Trial Bids and Cue Bids

IT is, perhaps, somewhat unusual to discuss these two types of opener's rebid in the same chapter. The truth of the matter is that, as Iain Macleod said in his fine book *Bridge Is An Easy Game*, all Cue Bids are Trial Bids, but not all Trial Bids are Cue Bids. Both bids are, however, exploratory, and this link brings them together. Trial bids are normally used when seeking a game contract which appears to depend on 'fit'. They ask for information but do not give it. Cue Bids are also Trial Bids in that they seek information about the best final contract, generally when there is a possible final slam in question, but Cue Bids also *give* information, as they confirm first round control of the suit so bid. Both, needless to say, are unconditionally forcing for one round.

TRIAL BIDS

Let us take the Trial Bids first. Under the old methods, if you had a good opening bid to which your partner responded with a simple raise to two of your suit, and if you felt that you were not quite worth a game bid on your own, you would have bid a tentative three of your suit the idea, of course, being to test the strength of your partner's raise. If maximum he would bid game—if minimum he would pass. This method, being completely hit-and-miss, failed to take into account the all-important question of 'fit'. Two

105

huge hands opposite each other can come well and truly to grief if they don't fit, whereas it is not even unknown for the most cheeky of 'sacrifice' bids to make because their slender resources fitted like peas in a pod.

Just very occasionally you may pick up a hand on which partner raises your opening one-bid to two and your only concern is to discover whether the raise has been given on a minimum or maximum. In such rare cases a "test" raise to three would be in order, asking partner to go on to game if better than he need be for his previous bid ($1\heartsuit$—$2\heartsuit$—$3\heartsuit$?) but far more often than not the $3\heartsuit$ bid would be wasted vocal effort. The Acol Trial Bids have been specifically developed to replace guesswork bids with ones asking a definite question to which partner can reply, sometimes negatively, sometimes positively, and sometimes by 'passing the buck'. His hand is already known to be almost painfully weak, a simple raise of an opening one-bid being, as we have seen, about the most depressing that responder can offer. Opener himself was not strong enough to start with anything better than a one-bid, so what possible useful information can now be given at the three level which cannot be sought by means of a Trial Bid at a lower level? Furthermore it is foreign to the whole conception of Acol bidding to introduce complicated and unnecessary bids which add conventional meanings to simple situations, and to tamper with the basic structure of the Limit Bids is unthinkable.

Trial Bids were so christened by Iain Macleod, who also helped to develop them, and they are now an integral part of the Acol system. To carry the use of these bids to the full extent propounded in his chapter on the subject is, perhaps, not everybody's choice. In any case such precise shades of meaning require a close partnership understanding which is beyond the scope of this book. Here you are learning how to use basic Acol with any presentable Acol-playing partner without coming to grief. We will confine ourselves, therefore, to the main basic use of these bids, which is to discover whether that vitally essential 'fit' is present in doubtful game hands. The bids are exploratory purely and simply, and give no information other than the somewhat negative inference that the bidder would like some form of assistance in the suit in which the Trial Bid is made.

The classic situation for the use of a Trial Bid is after responder has raised opener's one-bid to two in the same suit. This applies especially in the case of the major suits, the minors being treated somewhat differently.

Let us assume that the bidding has gone 1♠—2♠. Opener, holding better than an Acol Light Opening Bid and, in fact, seeing a good chance of making game if the two hands fit, now rebids three of the side-suit *in whivh he wants some help*, say 3◇. This says to responder: "I know from your simple raise that you have a pretty poor hand. I myself, though, am better than minimum, and if your raise is better than minimum I should like to be in a game contract. If, however, you are minimum, and if you have no help for me in diamonds, then you had better sign off in 3♠." The core of the question posed by the 3◇ Trial Bid is the diamond situation. "Partner", it says, "I want to be in game if your 2♠ bid is good, but we needn't go on to 4♠ if it isn't. On the other hand, if there appears to be any doubt about it, diamonds seem to be my danger-spot, and if you can offer me any help there, that ought to be the deciding factor." As for what can be considered 'help', a void or singleton with four-card trump support would be invaluable, and even a doubleton must be considered adequate; honours too, of course, but the Ace, King or Queen covered. Jacks and tens are seldom of much assistance. In other words, on the sequence we are considering, on a bare minimum 2♠ raise responder merely converts the 3◇ Trial Bid to 3♠. On a maximum 2♠ raise he bids 4♠ direct, irrespective of his other holdings, or he can let his holding in the diamond suit tip the scales. He has one other alternative, and that is to 'pass the buck' if he can find another bid at the same level which tells something about his hand.

This method of exploratory Trials Bids, telling responder where help is most needed, avoids the necessity for the partnership to go to game 'blind' on ill-fitting hands and is, in fact, precise instead of general. Consider the case of a responder who has raised his partner's 1♠ to 2♠ on any of the following hands:—

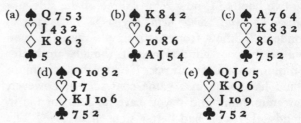

(a) ♠ Q 7 5 3   (b) ♠ K 8 4 2   (c) ♠ A 7 6 4
    ♡ J 4 3 2   ♡ 6 4   ♡ K 8 3 2
    ◇ K 8 6 3   ◇ 10 8 6   ◇ 8 6
    ♣ 5   ♣ A J 5 4   ♣ 7 5 2

   (d) ♠ Q 10 8 2   (e) ♠ Q J 6 5
     ♡ J 7   ♡ K Q 6
     ◇ K J 10 6   ◇ J 10 9
     ♣ 7 5 2   ♣ 7 5 2

If opener now rebids 3♠, what does responder do? Undoubtedly closes his eyes and guesses. But if partner makes a Trial Bid of 3♣, how very different the situation is! On hand (a) responder goes happily and directly to 4♠. His trump support is adequate, and if the club suit is going to be the deciding factor, he can take care of all but the first round by ruffing. On hand (b) he equally bids 4♠ without hesitation. The ♣A is just what the doctor ordered and although the hand is not much better than its 2♠ raise, it does contain what partner is worrying about. On hand (c) he signs off in 3♠. He has not got any plus-values to his original raise, and if club assistance is required, then his holding can be nothing but liability. On hand (d) a different situation arises. Here he still has the adequate trump support but he has no help whatsoever to offer in clubs—still that wretched liability, in fact. But, whilst unable to offer help with clubs, he has an undisclosed asset in his diamonds, which he was not strong enough to show by bidding the suit. It costs him nothing now to respond to 3♣ with 3◇, clearly indicating a hold on that suit whilst denying ability to help with clubs. This, of course, is passing the buck at a level where it costs nothing. Had opener made his Trial Bid in diamonds, responder could not have passed the buck except in 3♡, as to bid 4♣ would raise the level of the bidding and force a 4♠ contract in any event. Hand (e) holds a direct raise to 4♠ in spite of the lack of assistance in clubs. It was a maximum for the raise to 2♠ in the first place.

To make the situation even clearer, compare a typical 1♠ opening with a couple of the many possible 2♠ responses:—

♠ K Q 10 7 6 2   Responder:♠ A 8 5 4 or (2) ♠ A 8 5 4
♡ K 7 2   (1) ♡ Q J 6 3   ♡ J 6 3
◇ 8   ◇ J 6 3   ◇ Q J 6 3
♣ A 10 9   ♣ 7 2   ♣ 7 2

4♠ is almost certain to be made if responder holds hand No: 1 and almost equally certain to go down if he holds hand No: 2. Note that responder's point count and "shape" are exactly the same on both hands, and if opener rebid 3♠ he would be absolutely at sea as to whether to raise to 4♠ or not. Using Trial Bids, opener selects hearts as his most likely danger-spot, and makes the Trial Bid of 3♡. On hand No: 2, responder signs off in 3♠. Hand No: 1 has the required assistance in hearts making the combined hands worth a game contract.

This hand No: 1, however, brings in one other aspect of a Trial Bid made in *a second major suit*. Opener, in addition to the major suit opened, may also hold a second four-card major suit, and if a 4-4 fit can be found the original long suit can most probably be used for discards. If opener makes a Trial Bid in the second major, responder should raise that suit on a good four-card fit such as the one in hand No: 1. He himself cannot know whether opener has a second suit or is making a simple Trial Bid, but as he intends to give a game-raise to the Trial Bid in any case, he may as well offer the information that, should this be a second suit, he has four-card support for it. On the hand such as the one given for opener above, where the 3♡ bid is a Trial Bid only, no harm is done, and opener converts to 4♠. Simple, isn't it? And all done, not by kindness or guesswork, but by a little intelligent exploration.

In the minor suits this use of Trial Bids at the two-level is infrequent. 5♣ or 5◇ is a very high contract to hope to reach in the face of responder's simple raise from one to two. It could just conceivably occur, of course, but a far more likely resting place will be a part-score or a No-Trump contract. Assuming, then, that you have a hand such as:—

♠ A 6 5
♡ 8
◇ A 10 9
♣ K Q 10 9 5 4

Partner has raised your opening (non-vulnerable and, therefore, genuine club bid) from 1♣ to 2♣, it won't take much more than the ♣A to make that suit good for six tricks, and a stop in hearts will give you a very good chance to run off nine tricks in No Trumps. So "try" with 2◇. *Responder should learn, when replying to Trial Bids at the two-level in the minors, to show any reasonable stop he may hold rather than to worry about the suit in which the Trial Bid is made.* As opener is unlikely to be heading towards a 5♣ or 5◇ contract, he must be hoping for a No Trump contract, and wither a 2♡ or 2♠ response may be just what he wants to hear. The bid does nothing to block a 3♣ contract, which opener must be prepared to stand, and it cannot mislead opener, as obviously 1♡ or 1♠ would have been a happier response than 2♣ if it had been available.

On a very unbalanced hand such as:

♠ 8 4
♡ J 8 7 6
◇ K 7
♣ A 8 6 3 2

responder can make a jump bid in clubs, which again cannot be misleading. The 2♣ raise is already so limiting on the hand that a jump can only mean long trump support, a shortage somewhere, unsuitability for a No-Trump contract, and willingness to go on in the knowledge that opener is better than minimum.

Before we leave Trial Bids, there is one other point which I should like to make very clear. If opener is strong enough to bid game direct after getting a simple raise he should do so, without making a Trial Bid. It is always possible that responder's simple raise does not contain the help needed and a denial by way of a sign-off, when opener has specifically asked if help is available in any particular suit, may well tip off the opposition that this is their best line of attack. From this it should be plain that you should not make a Trial Bid unless you think you are strong enough to stand a contract at the three-level even if partner signs off and your announced weak suit is attacked first.

CUE BIDS

The range of raises from one to three is where Trial Bids and Cue Bids merge into one another, or rather, the exploratory Trial Bids give way to the Informatory Trial, or Cue Bids. With a weak response such as a single raise, giving information to responder is not likely to be vitally important, but if he is strong enough to have given a double raise or any other strong response, he may well be the one capable of judging whether to go on to a slam or not.

A Cue Bid is never made until the trump suit has been agreed, either directly or by inference. 1 ♠—3 ♠ paves the way for a Cue Bid, as there can be no doubt as to what trumps are going to be. Similarly 1 ♠ followed by a 2 ◊ overcall from the opposition and 3 ◊ from responder settles spades as trumps, also being a Cue Bid in its own right. Opener, knowing that spades are agreed, may now make a direct Cue Bid in reply.

♠ A Q 10 9 7 6	N.	E.	S.	W.
♡ A 10 9	1 ♠	2 ◊	3 ◊	No
◊ 9 7 6	3 ♡			
♣ K				

North It costs North nothing in this position to show the heart control. South can then decide whether to take the contract simply to 4 ♠ or higher.

A Cue Bid shows first round control of the suit so bid, and suggests interest in a higher contract than the

one immediately available if partner holds the right
controls. In this sequence the 4♣ is a Cue Bid. It

<table>
<tr><td>1♠—3♠</td><td>shows either the Ace or a void in clubs</td></tr>
<tr><td>4♣— ?</td><td>and willingness to hear about partner's
controls instead of settling, without further</td></tr>
</table>

investigation, on a game contract of 4♠. Thus partner,
holding an Ace or void in either hearts or diamonds,
can show this at the four-level without jeopardising the
game contract if it is not the control opener needs.
Having nothing further to show, he can sign off in 4♠.

♠ A K J 6 4   Take this hand, an obvious 1♠
♡ K Q 3   opener, to which partner responds
◇ 8 7   with 3♠. Partner may have a wide
♣ A Q 5   variety of holdings to justify his bid
             but none of these, other than control
of diamonds, will help towards a slam. Opener, then, makes
a Cue Bid of 4♣ over 3♠, and responder in turn can now
make a Cue Bid. Let us take several of his possible response
hands :—

(a) ♠ Q 9 8 3   (b) ♠ Q 9 8 3   (c) ♠ Q 9 8 3 2
    ♡ A J 9   ♡ 6 2   ♡ J 10 5 4
    ◇ 6 3   ◇ A J 9   ◇ K J 9 2
    ♣ K J 6 3   ♣ K J 6 3   ♣ —

It is an accepted rule that the lowest ranking control
must be shown first on a Cue Bid. On hand (a), therefore, when responder bids 4♡ over opener's 4♣ Cue
Bid, he is denying the possession of the ◇A, so opener
can sign off in 4♠ telling responder that, alas, the
information he had hoped to hear was not forthcoming.
On hand (b), when opener hears a 4◇ response to 4♣,
he will bid an immediate 6♠. Remember that there
is no likelihood of this being an underbid, as responder
has already limited the strength of his hand by his
raise to 3♠. On hand (c) responder himself signs off
in 4♠. He knows that his own first-round control,

H   113

the void in clubs, is only a duplication of his partner's. Change opener's hand a little:—

♠ A K J 6 4
♡ A Q 5
◇ K Q 3
♣ 8 7

Now, if opener wishes to make a Cue Bid, it must be 4♡ so that any reply he gets, other than 4♠, must be at the five-level. Responder, with the barest minimum for his bid, must not force this position, and it is his duty to sign off, even if he could show a control, when he has nothing extra to what he has already bid.

♠ Q 9 8 3 2
♡ A 8
◇ A 9 8
♣ 9 8 6

On such a hand as this you would respond 3♠ to 1♠. If opener now makes a Cue Bid of 4♣ you should show the ◇A in response. This, being the lower ranking of the two Aces held, does not deny the holding of the ♡A, whereas showing the ♡A would deny the holding of the ◇A.

Thus a Cue Bid is one both giving information about, and asking for information on, first round controls after the trump suit has been agreed. It is usually best to make such a bid at the lowest available level and responder should follow these general rules:

(a) Holding the bare minimum for his bid he should sign off in the agreed trump suit.

(b) With better than a bare minimum he should reply with a Cue Bid in a new suit, or take any other action that his hand warrants.

(c) If doubtful, but provided that the bid does not raise the level of the contract, he should make a new Cue Bid if he has one in his hand.

As mentioned earlier, the trump suit may be settled by inference by responder's immediate overcall of an opponent's intervening bid, as in this sequence:—

W.	N.	E.	S.
—	1♡	1♠	2♠

Here South's is a powerful bid, forcing to game and suggesting slam possibilities in hearts. It is also a Cue Bid because it agrees trumps as hearts whilst, at

the same time, confirming first round control of spades.
South, in our sequence, would be happy to make the bid on
such a holding as:—

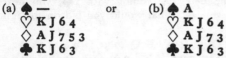

(a) ♠ —   or   (b) ♠ A
   ♡ K J 6 4   ♡ K J 6 4
   ◇ A J 7 5 3   ◇ A J 7 3
   ♣ K J 6 3   ♣ K J 6 3

Note the economy of bidding space. There is no
need to force in another suit or make risky jump bids
in hearts which, being a Limit Bid, is not forcing and
may be passed. Both the trump suit and the control
in spades are announced immediately.

In connection with the sequence above, though, it
should be pointed out that South has made a Cue Bid
showing spade control so he need not subsequently
show this control again. On either of the responder's
hands given we might get the bidding:—

W.	N.	E.	S.
—	1♡	1♠	2♠
—	3♣	—	?

North is Cue-Bidding his ♣A,
knowing that South agrees hearts
as trumps and has first round
control of spades. South, therefore, can next show his ◇A by bidding 3◇.

REVISION QUIZ ON CHAPTER 10

1. Having opened the bidding with 1♠, you hear your partner raise to 2♠. What would you bid on the following hands?

    (a) ♠ A Q 9 7 4: ♡ K Q 10 5: ◇ 9 8 2: ♣ A:
    (b) ♠ A Q 9 7 4: ♡ K J 9 6: ◇ A 4: ♣ A 3:
    (c) ♠ K J 9 4 3 2: ♡ A 9 6: ◇ Q 7 2: ♣ 6:
    (d) ♠ A Q 10 7 4 3: ♡ K J: ◇ Q 10 9: ♣ A 5:
    (e) ♠ Q J 9 7 4 3: ♡ A: ◇ A K J: ♣ 7 5 2:
    (f) ♠ K Q 10 9 7 5: ♡ 9 8 4 3: ◇ K 4: ♣ A:

2. Having opened the bidding with 1◇, you hear your partner raise to 2◇. What would you bid on the following hands?

    (a) ♠ Q 10 4: ♡ A 5: ◇ K Q 10 8 4: ♣ A Q 6:
    (b) ♠ Q 4: ♡ K 3: ◇ A K J 9 4 3: ♣ A 10 4:
    (c) ♠ J 5: ♡ A Q: ◇ K J 10 8 6 4: ♣ K Q 10:
    (d) ♠ A Q 6: ♡ Q 10 4: ◇ K Q 10 8 4: ♣ A 5:
    (e) ♠ K J 9: ♡ 6 3: ◇ A K Q 7 4 3: ♣ K J:
    (f) ♠ K J 10: ♡ A Q 9: ◇ K Q 10 8 4: ♣ 7 5:

3. Your partner having opened the bidding with 1♠, you raised to 2♠ on the following hands, and partner then made the bid shown. What would you bid next?

    (a) 1♠—2♠ ♠ Q 9 8 7: ♡ J 9 7 6: ◇ 8: ♣ Q 9 6 5:
    3◇— ?
    (d) Ditto ♠ Q 9 8 7: ♡ K J 9 8: ◇ 8 7 6: ♣ 9 8:
    (c) 1♠—2♠ ♠ Q 9 8 7: ♡ K J 9 8: ◇ 8: ♣ 9 8 7 6:
    3♡— ?
    (d) Ditto ♠ Q 9 8 7: ♡ 9 6 5: ◇ K J 9: ♣ 9 8 7:

4. To your 1♠ opening bid, partner responded 3♠. What do you bid next on the following hands?

    (a) ♠ A Q 10 7 4 3: ♡ A Q 6 3: ◇ K Q 6: ♣ —:
    (b) ♠ K Q 10 9 4: ♡ 9 5: ◇ A Q 10: ♣ A K 4:
    (c) ♠ A Q 9 5 4: ♡ 10 9 7 6: ◇ A 6: ♣ A 7:
    (d) ♠ A J 9 7 4 3: ♡ 6 5 2: ◇ 4: ♣ K J 5:

ANSWERS TO REVISION QUIZ
ON CHAPTER 10

1. (a) 3◇   A Trial Bid saying that your main weakness appears to be in diamonds and asking if the 2♠ raise contained any help in it.

   (b) 4♠   A direct game bid with no need for a Trial Bid on the way.

   (c) No.   If partner can only raise to 2♠ you do not want to be in a game contract.

   (d) 3◇   A Trial Bid, again in the suit in which you would like some assistance.

   (e) 3♣   If partner's single raise contains both top spade honours he won't have any club help but you will still have a good play for game if he raises direct to 4♠ on his trump holding.

   (f) 3♡   Heart assistance, either in honours or a short suit, would be vital to a game contract.

2. (a) 3♣   If partner has the ◇A and responds by showing a spade stop, you have a good chance for 3 N.T.

   (b) 3♣   If partner can show a spade stop, and with the lead coming up to you, you again have a good chance of 3 N.T., failing which, 4◇ should be pretty safe.

   (c) 2♡   Here again you are interested in a spade stop.

   (d) 2♠   This tells partner that you are strong and suggests that he might try 2 N.T. if he has any "plus" to his 2◇ raise, or show whatever stop he has on the way up.

   (e) 2♠   You are pretty certain of six diamond tricks, but must hear about a heart stop before you try No Trumps.

   (f) 2♡   If partner offers you a spade stop you know clubs will be wide open and will revert to 3◇.

3. (a) 3♠ You have the barest minimum for your bid in spite of the diamond singleton, so sign off.

   (b) 3♡ You cannot help in diamonds, but it costs nothing to "pass the buck" with 3♡ in this case.

   (c) 4♡ You have "help" in hearts, whether partner has a second suit or not. This, plus your singleton and spade support, makes a game contract most attractive.

   (d) 3♠ No help anywhere, and you can't show the diamond stop without raising the level, so sign off.

4. (a) 4♣ A Cue Bid, showing first round control by virtue of the void. If partner can show the ◇A it will be lovely, but the ♣A will be duplication of values.

   (b) 4♣ You must know whether partner can control the hearts before getting yourself above the game level.

   (c) 4♠ You don't even *want* to investigate slams here. Settle for the game contract direct.

   (d) No. An Acol Light Opener answered by a Limit Bid which is not forcing so on your very minimum hand you accept the opportunity to pass.

CHAPTER 11

The Acol Opening Two Club
Bid and Responses

♠♡♣♢♠♡♣♢♠♡♣♢♠♡♣♢♠♡♣♢♠♡♣♢♠♡♣♢

I should have liked to have gone on next to the bidding of the bigger No Trump hands, where the point count comes beyond the limits set in Chapter 5. To understand these fully, however, it is necessary first to have a clear understanding of the Acol opening Two Club bids and responses. We shall, therefore, deal with these next, though in this chapter we shall be confining ourselves to the opening Two Club bids which do *not* come within the category of evenly balanced hands suitable for No Trump openings.

The Acol Opening Two Club is a cipher bid. It bears no relation at all to the actual club holding and is an announcement of strength only. Unhappily for most of us, Two Club opening bids come all too rarely though when they do, the 2 ♢ negative response comes with almost gramophone-like regularity. However, the Two Club openers *do* come, as well as positive responses, and if we don't want to miss the opportunities that the fates offer, we must learn how to take advantage of these powerful hands.

Except in the cases when the Two Club opener rebids in No Trumps, which we shall be dealing with separately in Chapter 12, the bid carries with it three conditions:

1. It is unconditionally forcing to game.
2. It guarantees a minimum of five quick tricks.

3. It guarantees sufficient playing strength to predict that a game contract can be fulfilled with little or no assistance from partner.

Remember that all three of these conditions must be fulfilled before a hand qualifies for a Two Club opening bid. Five arid quick tricks with no "shape" or playing strength would be unlikely to qualify for better than an opening bid of one of a suit.

♠ A 6 5
♡ A 7 5
◇ A K 8 6
♣ A 4 3

On a hand such as this, for example, it would be madness to force your partner to bid on unconditionally until a game contract were reached. Open the bidding with a simple 1◇ and await developments.

Having got this point clear, let us look at a few examples of hands which do qualify as Two Club opening bids, but remember that we are not at present touching on the well balanced hands with a high point count of the No Trump type.

♠ A K Q 10 8
♡ A K 6
◇ K Q
♣ A 9 4

This hand contains six quick tricks and is so strong from a playing point of view that it qualifies unreservedly for a 2♣ opening bid. Rebid 2♠ over partner's probable 2◇.

♠ K Q 10 9
♡ A K J 7 3
◇ 8 6
♣ A 7

Five quick tricks in this one, and a most powerful game-going hand. Open 2♣ and rebid 2♡ over 2◇.

♠ K 6
♡ —
◇ A K J 9
♣ A K Q 9 7 6 3

This hand contains only 4½ quick tricks, but its predominating suit is clubs. Although a slight overbid, it is impossible to show its strength in any other way than by opening 2♣. Rebid 3♣ to anything responder may say, and he will know that you may be a trifle under the normal requirements for your opening bid.

OPENER'S JUMP REBID

2♣—2◇   The 3♡ jump rebid in this situation asks
3♡   partner to cue-bid any Ace he may
         hold—in other words, to cue-bid his
Ace, if any, in reply. Obviously if he held two, or an
Ace and a King, he would not have bid 2◇ in the first
place, so he can only have one Ace, if that.

In the original version this jump rebid, in addition
to asking responder if he had an Ace in spite of his
negative 2◇, promised a solid and self-supporting
trump suit. It was subsequently realised, however,
that this was not a situation in which responder needed
this information, opener being the one in charge and
the one capable of judging the best final contract when
he knew whether or not his partner had an Ace. The
negative response, denying an Ace, is 3 N.T. Look

♠ A K Q   at this hand. It has no long solid
♡ K Q J   suit, yet if responder has one Ace
◇ K Q J 10   the final contract should be 6
♣ A K Q   N.T. After opening 2♣ and
               getting 2◇ from responder, jump
to 3♠. If responder cue-bids either red Ace, go
straight to 6 N.T. If he signs off in 3 N.T. showing
no Ace, simply pass.

♠ A   This is an obvious 2♣ opening bid.
♡ A K Q J 9 8 3 You might, of course, get a positive
◇ K Q   response, but you are far more likely
♣ K Q 10   to get the negative 2◇ which means
               that there cannot be less than one
Ace missing. You make the jump rebid of 3♡, to which
partner will respond 3 N.T. with no Ace, or 4♣ or 4◇ if he
holds the ace in either of these suits. A 3 N.T. response you
would convert to 4♡, but with one Ace in partner's hand
you can bid 6♡ direct.

♠ K Q J 10 6 5   Here, if partner holds either Ace,
♡ A K 7   opener wants to play in 6♠, but
◇ 6   missing both, he may as well play
♣ A K Q   quietly in 4♠. So he bids 3♠ to his
partner's 2◇ response to his original
2♣. He could obviously get the information by way of one
of the slam conventions, but an unnecessary five-contract
when no slam is available only offers that much more chance
to the opposition to find some awkward ruffing position to
produce a setting trick.

RESPONDING TO AN ACOL TWO CLUB BID

An opening Two Club bid is unconditionally forcing
for one round, and unconditionally forcing to game
unless opener rebids in No Trumps. We shall be
dealing with this latter situation in Chapter 12, but
at the moment we are concerned with responder's
course of action when he hears his partner open Two
Clubs. His "negative" reply, which must be made
even on a complete Yarborough, is 2◇. It denies the
holding of anything as good as either:—

1. An Ace and a King.
2. A biddable suit (see below) and 1½ quick tricks.
3. Any nine point hand.

It is appropriate at the moment to discuss what is
meant by a "biddable" suit, and in modern terms a
four-card major suit is always biddable provided it
can be shown without raising the level of the bidding.
That is to say, 1♠ may be shown over an opening 1♡
on a holding such as ♠ Q 10 x x and an outside Ace
or King, whereas this same holding transposed to
hearts could not be shown over a 1♠ opening, and
responder would have to bid 1 N.T. So, at the forcing
level of a 2♣ opening bid, it is both correct and

permissible, and provided the requirements for a positive response are held, to show a four-card major suit in preference to 2 N.T.

In practice it is unwise to do this unless the four-card suit is reasonably good, that is to say, headed by at least one high honour and backed by better than "little x's", and I personally should regard K 10 x x as the very minimum to make the suit "biddable". If it is necessary to raise the level of the bidding, as it is in order to give a positive response in either of the minor suits, then a five-card suit must be regarded as the minimum necessary.

Provided the opening bidder is aware that the positive response of 2♡ or 2♠ may be made on such a four-card suit, no trouble should arise, as subsequent rounds of bidding should give ample time to determine whether or not the suit is re-biddable, i.e. five or more cards long.

West	East
♠ A K 5 3	♠ 10 9
♡ A Q J 6	♡ K 10 7 5
◇ K 10	◇ A 5 3
♣ A Q 10	♣ 9 7 6 4

Here is an example of a hand on which West's opening bid must, clearly, be 2♣, though it is not the type of hand on which it is intended to force to game in a suit. It is a typical 2♣ opener with a rebid of 2 N.T. showing 23—24 points (see Chapter 12). East, however, has the requirements for a positive response, that is, an Ace and a King, though he has not got what the older methods demanded, a five or six card suit. If he gives the positive response of 2 N.T., though, from this point onwards it is virtually impossible to catch up with the bidding. If West *does* decide to show a suit over 2 N.T., it will be spades, and the hand will end up being played in 3 N.T. or blindly bid to 6 N.T. which will go down, whereas 6♡ depends only on finding the adverse club honours split.

With the necessary values for a positive response but lacking a biddable suit under these terms of reference, responder should bid 2 N.T.

If, however, responder has had to produce a negative bid of 2◇, *he must subsequently continue to keep the bidding open until a game contract has been reached unless opener rebids in No Trumps.* Responder's second negative, if he is forced to make one, is 2 N.T., but he may, if he is lucky, be able to raise the suit bid by opener, or even bid one of his own. He may even— blissful day!—be able to make a positive response in the first place, which he should do on the lines already explained. An immediate response of 2 N.T. would show the holding of either an Ace and a King, or any nine points, without a biddable suit. A bid of 2♡ or 2♠ would show at least a four-card major headed by as good as K 10 together with the other "positive" requirements. A positive response when the club suit is well held would, of course, be 3♣, and similarly a positive response in diamonds must be 3◇ as 2◇ would be the negative.

CONVENTIONAL RESPONDER'S REBIDS

There are two specialised conventional bids in the "response" class which you should learn before we go on to examples, and both these are available for use after responder has made the original negative bid of 2◇. The first of these is an immediate double raise in whatever suit opener rebids, as in the sequence shown

2♣—2◇   here. This bid proclaims a hand with
2♠—4♠   good trump support, some honour strength, *and no Ace or void.* It is not a shut-out bid, and opener is free to make a slam try if

he sees fit, though the 4♠ bid is specifically limited. Responder is known to hold less honour strength than the very modest requirements for a positive response to 2♣, no Ace, and no void. The only thing he has is trump support and some scattered points. This hand would be a typical example. If opener, after your 2◇

♠ Q 8 6 4   negative to his original Two Club
♡ Q 7 3 2   bid, rebids 2♡ or 2♠, raise to
◇ K 9 8 6   four of that suit. If he rebids 3◇,
♣ 7   raise to 5◇.

2♣—2◇   Similarly, responder's rebid of 3 N.T.
2♠—3 N.T.   shows an evenly balanced hand with
                     about 7—8 points and *no Ace or*
♠ 8 3   *void*. It also, by implication, denies
♡ Q 6 5 4   "adequate trump support" for
◇ K 9 8   opener's suit. On this typical example,
♣ Q 9 8 3   rebid 3 N.T. over opener's 2♠ or
                     4♡ over his 2♡ rebid.

Remember that as responder has denied an Ace again, a bid of 4 N.T. from opener would now be the Acol Direct King convention, by-passing the request for Aces and asking for Kings. (See p. 252).

RESPONDER'S JUMP REBID

The second of these specialised conventional responses—again after a 2◇ negative, is when responder, at his next turn, makes a jump bid in a new suit. By this he shows *a solid suit without the Ace*, which information may be invaluable to partner. On this

♠ 7 4   hand responder, having none of
♡ K Q J 10 8 4   the requirements for a positive
◇ J 8 7   response, must bid 2◇ first but,
♣ 9 6   when opener rebids, perhaps with
                 2♠, he makes a jump rebid of

4♡. Opener can now read him for at least a six-card solid suit missing the Ace, which makes "adequate trump support" very much easier to judge. Note that if the suit were solid and headed by the Ace, responder would have held a positive reply in the first place.

Now let us look at a selection of examples, to see whether you have got these bids and responses clear.

♠ 8
♡ 9 6 5 2
◇ 8 7 3 2
♣ 9 7 6 5

Respond 2◇ to 2♣. If opener next bids 2♠, give a further negative of 2 N.T. If he bids one of the other three suits raise it, even if reluctantly. You couldn't dislike your hand more, but you are under an unconditional obligation to keep the bidding open to game.

♠ Q 7
♡ J 7 2
◇ 10 9 8 6
♣ 10 9 8 6

Respond 2◇ to 2♣ and to 2♠ again give a further negative of 2 N.T. With your reasonably good intermediates, probably your best bet is to go on repeating No Trumps.

♠ K 9 7
♡ 9 6 5 2
◇ K 10 7
♣ Q J 9

This hand contains a positive response of 9 points with no biddable suit so, instead of the eternal 2◇, you are now able to bid 2 N.T.

♠ 9 6
♡ K 10 8 7 6
◇ A 9 8
♣ 6 4 2

This hand contains a simple positive response of 2♡ to 2♣, by virtue of an Ace and a King and a biddable heart suit.

♠ Q 9 7 2
♡ 8
◇ K 8 3 2
♣ Q 6 5 4

You must make a negative response of 2◇ on the first round but if partner rebids 2♠ you would raise direct to 4♠. 3♣ or 3◇ you would also raise to four, and to 2♡ you would bid 2 N.T.

♠ 9 8
♡ 9 8 7 6
◇ K Q 7
♣ Q J 7 4

Your first response must be 2◇ but your holding is only one point under a positive response. Raise 2♡ to 4♡ or 3♣ to 5♣. Raise 3◇ to 4◇, and to 2♠ bid 3 N.T.

♠ Q 10 8 7 6 3
♡ 7
◇ 8 6 2
♣ 7 5 3

Respond 2◇ to 2♣, and then go on repeating spades until a game contract is reached.

♠ K Q J 10 8 6
♡ 8 2
◇ 8 4
♣ 10 9 8

Respond 2◇ to 2♣, and then whatever opener rebids, make a jump bid in spades, showing the long, solid, though Aceless suit.

REVISION QUIZ ON CHAPTER 11

1. What opening bid would you make on the following hands?

  (a) ♠ A K J 9 6: ♡ A 10 4: ◇ K Q 10: ♣ A 4:
  (b) ♠ A K: ♡ K Q 9 4: ◇ A K Q 9 6: ♣ 8 3:
  (c) ♠ A K 9 6 3 2: ♡ A 4: ◇ 5: ♣ A J 6 2:
  (d) ♠ K 3 2: ♡ —: ◇ A K 10 9 6: ♣ A Q 8 3 2:
  (e) ♠ A 5: ♡ K Q 10 9 5: ◇ A K 4: ♣ K Q 10:
  (f) ♠ A Q 9 4: ♡ A Q 10 5: ◇ A: ♣ A J 6 3:

2. On the following hands you opened 2♣ and partner responded with 2◇. What is your rebid?

  (a) ♠ A K J 9 6: ♡ A 10: ◇ K Q 10: ♣ A Q 2:
  (b) ♠ A 5: ♡ A K 10 9 5: ◇ A K 4: ♣ K Q 10:
  (c) ♠ A 9: ♡ K Q 9 4: ◇ A K Q 9 6: ♣ A 3:
  (d) ♠ A K: ♡ A K Q J 9 6 3: ◇ A K 9: ♣ 8:
  (e) ♠ A J 9 6 4: ♡ A 10 8 6 3: ◇ A K: ♣ A:

3. Your partner has opened the bidding with 2♣. What is your response on the following hands?

  (a) ♠ 8 6 3: ♡ K 10 6 4: ◇ K 9 6 3: ♣ 4 3:
  (b) ♠ 8 3 2: ♡ 9 6 4: ◇ A K J 9 5: ♣ J 7:
  (c) ♠ J 10 9 8 6 3: ♡ A 4 3: ◇ K 10 3: ♣ 6:
  (d) ♠ K 10 5: ♡ Q 10 4: ◇ J 10 7 4: ♣ Q J 2:
  (e) ♠ Q 10 9 6 3 2: ♡ Q 3 2: ◇ 4: ♣ J 3 2:
  (f) ♠ K J 5 4: ♡ Q 10 4: ◇ J 10 7: ♣ Q J 2:

4. Your partner opened the bidding with 2♣ and you responded 2◇. Partner now rebids 2♡. What is your own rebid?

  (a) ♠ 9 5: ♡ Q 10 6: ◇ K 9 5 4 3: ♣ K 9 6:
  (b) ♠ Q 4: ♡ Q 10 5 4: ◇ K 10 3: ♣ J 9 4 3:
  (c) ♠ K 10 9 5 3: ♡ K 4: ◇ 10 9 2: ♣ J 8 4:
  (d) ♠ Q 5 3: ♡ 10 5 2: ◇ 9 8 4 3: ♣ J 10 6:
  (e) ♠ —: ♡ Q 9 6: ◇ A 9 8 4 2: ♣ 10 9 6 4 3:

ANSWERS TO REVISION QUIZ
ON CHAPTER 11

1. (a) 2♣   With five quick tricks and enormous playing strength this is the only opening bid you can make.

   (b) 2♣   Again, you have five quick tricks and do not want to find yourself left in anything less than a game contract.

   (c) 1♠   Only $4\frac{1}{2}$ quick tricks and not quite an opening Two bid, so start with 1♠.

   (d) 1♦   Only 4 quick tricks and clearly not a Two Bid.

   (e) 2♣   There's no doubt about this one—a perfect 2♣ bid.

   (f) 1♣   The hand has five quick tricks but precious little playing strength so you don't want to force a game contract if partner is very weak. Open with a simple one bid in the suit below the singleton.

2. (a) 2♠   You certainly want to play in a game contract, and your good suit is spades.

   (b) 2♡   The same story, except that your suit is hearts.

   (c) 3♦   Show your long suit before the shorter hearts and await developments.

   (d) 3♡   This is a case for the jump rebid and asking partner to cue-bid if he holds the missing ♣A. If he bids 3 N.T. just remove to 4♡.

   (e) 2♠   The higher ranking of two equal and adjacent suits. You can show the hearts on the next round.

3. (a) 2♦   You have none of the requirements for a positive response on the first round.

I   129

(b) 3◇   2◇ would be "negative" and you have the "positive" requirement of an Ace and a King, plus a biddable suit.

(c) 2♠   Another positive response, but you make it in your long suit.

(d) 2 N.T.   With nine points and no biddable suit, you must make the positive response of 2 N.T.

(e) 2◇   The negative response first, and then show your spade suit on the next round.

(f) 2♠   You have the requirements, with 10 points, for a positive response, and it is more economical in bidding space to show your biddable 4-card spade suit than it would be to bid 2 N.T.

4. (a) 3♡   With trump support as good as Q 10 6 it is better to give the direct raise than to show your rather miserable diamond suit.

(b) 4♡   The direct raise to game is indicated here as you have particularly good trump support, eight points, and no Ace or void.

(c) 2♠   As you cannot give immediate trump support, the best you can do is offer your five-card suit.

(d) 2 N.T.   Partner's heart bid does nothing to raise your enthusiasm for this hand. A second negative is all you can offer.

(e) 3◇   Although you have heart support, five to the Ace in diamonds is well worth showing.

CHAPTER 12

Two, Three and Four No Trump Opening Bids and Responses

♠♡♣◇♠♡♣◇♠♡♣◇♠♡♣◇♠♡♣◇♠♡♣◇♠♡♣◇

W E come now to the big No Trump hands, that is, the ones coming beyond the scope of the 12-14 and 15-17 point hand already covered in Chapter 5.

Evenly balanced hands with high point counts are opened with a bid of 2 N.T. or with 2♣ coupled with the appropriate rebid, and they fall into this same group because the same "fit-finding" sequences are available for use with them, though these sequences differ from the ones used over 1 N.T. opening bids.

Using "weak throughout", the top limit for an opening bid of 1 N.T. is 14 points, and hands containing between 15—19 points must be opened as suit bids and rebid in No Trumps, and these will largely be amongst the hands discussed in Chapter 7 in relation to the "Prepared" minors. There are, however, many stronger hands which come into the category of Two No Trump Openers.

Three and Four No Trump openers are specialised Acol conventional bids, and are covered at the end of this Chapter.

TWO NO TRUMP OPENERS

An opening bid of 2 N.T. may be made on an evenly balanced hand of between 20-22 points. There is no question of vulnerability and the same distributional limits as in the case of 1 N.T. openers apply. There is no Acol law against making the bid with a five-card suit in the hand and, indeed, this often proves invaluable.

Two No Trumps as an opening bid is not forcing, and responder may pass on a worthless hand. On the other hand, opener will not require much assistance to make game and, with any luck in the world, as little as five points should be enough, so the yardstick for responder is to raise 2 N.T. to 3 N.T. on five points, or on four points if the hand contains a five-card suit.

A take-out into three of a major suit by responder, though a bid at the lowest available level, is not the weak take-out that a two-bid over 1 N.T. would be. It is, therefore, an inferential force which will result in at least a game contract, either in the suit or in No Trumps, and must not be passed by the 2 N.T. opener. The only complete sign-off bid that responder can make to the original bid is to pass.

You will not, perhaps, be surprised by this time to learn that a simple take-out into three of a suit *excludes* the club suit, a bid of 3♣ being conventional. *So also is a bid of 3♦ over an opening 2 N.T.* We shall go into these two bids presently, but meanwhile, let us look at some examples of Two No Trumps opening hands and responses. The hands below all qualify, under our terms of reference, as Two No Trump openers, being well-balanced and containing a point count of 20—22.

♠ A K 7	♠ A Q 10	♠ K J 10	♠ A 10 4 2
♡ K 9 8 3	♡ K J 6 2	♡ A Q 8 2	♡ A J 8
◇ K 10 3	◇ K Q 5	◇ K 5	◇ A Q 4
♣ A K 4	♣ A Q 7	♣ A Q J 8	♣ A Q 5
20 points	21 points	20 points	21 points

♠ K J 10
♡ A Q 8
◇ K 5
♣ A Q J 8 7

On this hand, the 20 points are far too good and too nearly well-balanced to make anything but a 2 N.T. opening bid. The five-card club suit, and particularly the fact that the opening lead will come up to the hand at No Trumps, makes the bid acceptable.

The responder to an opening Two No Trump bid cannot work on quite the same principles that he would use over an opening One No Trump bid as, for one thing, he has no immediate weak take-out available.

♠ Q 5 4
♡ 6 5 4
◇ J 9 8
♣ Q 8 6 2

This hand is quite as evenly balanced as opener's can be and, therefore, suitable for a No Trump contract. Raise to 3 N.T. in the hope that its few high cards will fill the necessary gap for your partner.

♠ 5 3 2
♡ 6 4
◇ K J 8 6 5
♣ 8 6 2

On this hand again, responder should raise to 3 N.T., this time in preference to bidding 3◇ which would be conventional. He has the requisite 4 points plus a 5-card suit and is certain that opener will have at least one high honour in diamonds. With any luck at all the suit can be brought in for four tricks at No Trumps.

♠ K 9 8 6 5
♡ Q 6
◇ 9 7 6
♣ 8 5 4

With five points and a five-card biddable suit you can afford to respond 3♠ to 2 N.T. If partner rebids 3 N.T., pass.

♠ Q J 10 8 7 5 4 2
♡ 9
◇ 8 6
♣ 9 7

Bid 3♠ over 2 N.T. and 4♠ over 3 N.T. In fact, continue repeating spades until partner gets the idea! Strengthen the hand a bit, though, say by the inclusion of an outside Ace, and you should bid 4♠ direct. This will be taken by partner as a mild slam try on a hand which *must* be played in spades.

NO TRUMP HANDS OPENED WITH 2♣

Well-balanced hands even stronger than these 2 N.T. openers are bid by way of the 2♣ "cipher bid" which, as you will remember, bears no relation to the actual club holding. When the 2♣ opening bid is made responder does not, of course, know whether the hand is well balanced or otherwise, and must make his correct response, either positive or negative. We dealt with the unbalanced type of 2♣ opener in Chapter 11, so now let us confine ourselves to the well-balanced No Trump type of hands containing a point count of over 22, which is the upper limit set for the 2 N.T. opening bid.

On 23 or 24 balanced points you should open the bidding with 2♣ and rebid 2 N.T., which pin-points your hand very exactly for your partner. You have already learned that an opening 2♣ bid carries with it a guaranteed minimum of five quick tricks. This rule may be slightly relaxed on these 23—24 points hand, though you will find it difficult to achieve one *without* five quick tricks.

A 23 or 24 point hand which you intend to rebid with 2 N.T. may, of course, change its character in the light of the unexpected, a positive response. If, for example,

♠ A K 8   you open 2♣ on this hand, and
♡ A Q J 4   partner responds with 2♡, you
◇ A J 6   would be foolish indeed to rebid
♣ K Q 7   2 N.T. You would set the trump
suit by raising to 3♡ and wait to hear partner's next offering, which would doubtless be a cue-bid of the ♣A if he has it. However, had hearts not suited your hand as trumps your 2 N.T. rebid would have carried exactly the same significance, that

is, that you hold a well-balanced hand of 23—24 points, which leaves responder free to judge his own next best action.

The usual course of the bidding over an opening 2♣ is for partner to respond 2◇. Now, if opener rebids 2 N.T., responder may pass on a completely worthless hand. This is the only opener's rebid below the level of the game that he may pass, but it is obvious that an evenly balanced 23—24 points opposite to an equally well balanced Yarborough is unlikely to produce game.

On an evenly balanced and still stronger hand containing 25 or more points, opener's rebid after the initial 2♣ is 3 N.T. This itself being a game bid, responder is at liberty to pass or, of course, to bid on if he thinks his hand worth a try.

The 2♣—2◇—2 N.T. sequence can, as already stated, be passed by responder, as too can the opening 2 N.T. bid. Responder can, in fact, treat opener's bid exactly as he would do a slightly stronger 2 N.T. bid, that is to say, as if the requirements for an opening 2 N.T. bid were 23—24 points. Instead of needing five points to raise to 3 N.T., he needs only 3 points. His suit take-out bids remain the same except that they too, of course, can be slightly down-graded in value. In other words, what we have here is a simple distinction between a weak (20—22 points) opening 2 N.T. and a strong (23—24 points) opening 2 N.T.

♠ Q 6 4
♡ 10 9 8
◇ J 8 2
♣ 10 9 8 2

Respond 2◇ to 2♣ and if opener rebids 2 N.T., raise to 3 N.T. In addition to your three points, you have some possibly helpful intermediate values in your tens and nines.

135

♠ 8
♡ Q 10 9 8 7 5
◇ 7 4 2
♣ 9 6 4

Respond 2◇ to 2♣ and if partner rebids 2 N.T., take out into 3♡. Take 3 N.T. out into 4♡.

♠ 9 8 6
♡ 9 7 5 2
◇ 6 5
♣ J 6 4 2

Respond 2◇ to 2♣ and if partner rebids 2 N.T., pass. You will be lucky indeed if your ♣J is the only card partner needs to make the game!

THREE CLUBS OVER TWO NO TRUMPS

We come now to the important conventional 3♣ bid, which responder can use equally well over either an opening 2 N.T. or the 2 N.T. bid in the sequence 2♣—2◇—2 N.T. This 3♣ bid is no more "Stayman over Two No Trumps", as you will almost always hear it called, than is the 2♣ over 1 N.T. Never let it be said that the Acol system steals its bids without acknowledging the source. 3♣ over 2 N.T. owes its inception to the Baron system, to which grateful thanks are due.

As in the case of 2♣ over 1 N.T., though not used in exactly the same way, this 3♣ is a fit-finding bid and is, it goes without saying, unconditionally forcing. At the lower level, you will remember, opener's response can be passed for a part-score contract. Here, of course, any bid by responder other than a pass or 3◇ must produce a game contract, either in No Trumps or in a suit. With these big hands you are not so much afraid of going down as anxious to explore further possibilities.

Used at this higher level, the 3♣ response requests opener to show his four-card suits *in ascending order*, that is, the lower ranking first. If his *only* four-card suit is clubs, he rebids 3 N.T., as a bid of 4♣ would block a possible 3 N.T. contract. Holding two four-card suits, one of which is clubs, opener should bid his other suit first, letting his actual holding and his partner's subsequent bidding dictate his further action.

Interpreting these rebids over 3♣, then:

1. 3 N.T. promises a four-card club suit, and no other four-card suit.

2. 3◇ promises a four-card diamond suit, possibly also a four-card club suit, and possibly, alternatively, four cards in one of the majors.

3. 3♡ promises a four-card heart suit and denies a four-card diamond suit, though clubs or spades may also be held.

4. 4♠ promises a four-card spade suit and no other four-card suit except, possibly, clubs.

How exceedingly well this method works can be seen by looking at a few examples. Suppose you had picked up this hand, on which you would, of course, have opened 2 N.T.:

♠ A K 9 2   and responder holds this: ♠ Q J 6 3
♡ A Q 6   ♡ J 7 5 3
◇ A J 9 2   ◇ 8 7
♣ K 8   ♣ 9 6 5

The bidding would go:

2 N.T. — 3♣   Responder can see as soon as he hears the
3◇   —3♡   2 N.T. opening bid that a major-suit
3♠   —4♠   contract, if a fit can be found, would be
                 the safest but, in reply to his 3♣, hears
3◇. Now this is the *lowest* available four-card suit and it costs responder nothing, still at the three-level which does not block 3 N.T., to show his own next-ranking suit with a bid of 3♡. Over this opener can, still at the three-level, show that he holds four spades in addition to four diamonds. This is just what responder wants to hear and he raises to 4♠, a much better and safer contract than 3 N.T.

♠ Q 6 5   Take the same opening 2 N.T. hand and give
♡ K J 8 5   responder this. Now the bidding might well
◇ K Q 8 4   go 2 N.T.—3♣   Opener, knowing that one
♣ 9 3   3◇ —4◇   Ace is missing but that
           4 N.T.—5♣   responder is otherwise good
           6◇   with a diamond fit, bids
                       this otherwise unreachable
                       slam.

♠ A Q 6   Opener bids 2 N.T. on this   ♠ K 5 2
♡ A J 8   hand and responder holds: ♡ 6
◇ K Q J   ◇ A 8 7 3
♣ K J 4 3   ♣ A Q 7 6 5

The bidding:

2 N.T.—3♣   The 3 N.T. bid, of course, shows four
3 N.T.—4♣   clubs, and responder's 4♣ agrees the
4 N.T.—5♡   suit as trumps.
5 N.T.—6◇
7♣

The same type of sequence occurs if opener is just
that little bit stronger so that he opens 2♣ instead of
2 N.T. Take these two hands:

♠ A K 9   opposite   ♠ 7   2♣ —2◇
♡ A Q 6   ♡ K J 9 3   2 N.T.—3♣
◇ A Q 9   ◇ 8 6 3 2   3 N.T.—5♣
♣ K J 5 4   ♣ Q 10 9 8

The following hand is from a duplicate pairs event:

♠ K Q 2   opposite   ♠ 8 7 4   2 N.T.—3♣
♡ Q J 2   ♡ A   3◇ —4◇
◇ K Q J 6   ◇ A 10 9 8   5♣ —6◇
♣ A Q 4   ♣ K 10 9 7 2

THE "FLINT" 3◇ TRANSFER BID

Basically, this is a device to allow the partnership
to stop below game level in a suit contract after an
opening bid of 2 N.T., or in the sequence 2♣—2◇—
2 N.T. As a natural bid over 2 N.T., 3◇ is so seldom

needed that it is used as an artificial transfer request to opener to bid 3♡. If responder's suit is hearts he passes this, or, alternatively, he converts to 3♠, 4♣ or 4◇, which opener is expected to pass unless his hand is particularly suitable for the game contract.

Note the last words above—unless his hand is particularly suitable for a game contract. This he must determine for himself, and he must at all times be prepared to face his partner's wrath if the three-level contract would have been a "top" whilst the game goes down! However, having decided to take matters into his own hands and go for a game, here are the sequences shown against possible example hands:—

♠ A K 9 8	Responder bids 3◇ over this maxi-
♡ A J 6	mum 2 N.T. opening hand, and
◇ K 7	opener, as requested, bids 3♡. When
♣ A K 7 3	responder converts to 3♠, with this
	spade fit, even if his partner's only

holding is a weak five-card spade suit, opener fancies the chances for the spade game, and so goes to 4♠.

♠ K 7	This is the same maximum hand as
♡ A K 9 8	the one above, except with the suits
◇ A J 6	reversed and, if when responder bids
♣ A K 7 3	3◇, his suit happens to be hearts, 3♡
	will be passed and the play for 4♡

missed. Instead, therefore, of bidding 3♡ as requested, opener bids 3♠. This guarantees a maximum hand with a strong *heart* fit. If responder's suit is spades he passes 3♠, and if it is hearts, bids 4♡.

♠ A K 9 8	The same hand again, but containing
♡ A K 7 3	the powerful fit for *both* major suits.
◇ A J 6	Instead of the requested conversion to
♣ K 7	3♡ opener rebids 3 N.T., this time
	guaranteeing a maximum hand with a

strong fit for both hearts and spades, leaving responder to select the suit at the four-level.

From responder's side of the table, the 3◇ response to

2 N.T. can be a natural bid if it is followed by anything other than a minimum suit bid—or a pass of opener's rebid, and a responder's rebid of 3 N.T. shows a genuine diamond suit plus mild slam ambitions.

♠ K 7
♡ A J 9
◇ Q J 9 6 5
♣ 10 9 7

Opposite to a 2 N.T. opening bid this is a powerful hand, but it does not justify either a "Gerber" 4♣ or a quantitative raise to 4 N.T. Opener's most probable rebid is the requested 3♡, whereupon responder rebids 3 N.T., putting opener fully in the picture, and he is free to pass 3 N.T. or explore further with a view to either a No Trump or diamond slam.

It goes without saying, I think, that there may be many hands on which responder will have to take the responsibility of bidding on for a slam. Although a very strong one, a Two No Trump opening bid is still a limit bid, the strength of which has been announced. Suppose, for instance, you as responder to this opening bid held something like:—

♠ Q 7 5
♡ A K 9 7 6 2
◇ J 6
♣ 8 3

You would respond 3♡ to 2 N.T., and whether opener rebid 3 N.T. or 4♡, the onus would be on you to make another try. This is a hand from a duplicate event and opener did, in fact, raise the 3♡ response to 4♡, whereupon, at one table, responder passed! The missed slam was neither the fault of the Acol system nor of opener, who could not know what his partner's hand was like, but responder should have realised that a minimum of 20 points, not more than three of which could possibly be in hearts, really must add up to a slam.

"GERBER" OVER TWO NO TRUMPS

The immediate bid of 4♣ over an opening 2 N.T. is again the "Gerber" convention, as it was over 1 N.T., calling for Ace-showing from opener and is, of course, a valuable means whereby responder, with a good hand, can not only elicit information, but show his interest in a possible slam contract. The convention may also be used where a 2♣ opening bid has been followed by a rebid in No Trumps, for example:—

$$2♣ \quad —2♡$$
$$2 \text{ N.T.}—4♣$$

This 4♣ bid is "Gerber", requesting opener to show Aces on the same step principle as before. It cannot be a "force" in clubs, as such a bid could not conceivably be necessary in the circumstances.

ACOL OPENING THREE NO TRUMPS

In most systems an opening bid of 3 N.T. shows the usual balanced hand, but with 25—27 points. In Acol, as we have already seen, such a hand would be opened with 2♣ and rebid 3 N.T., which releases the 3 N.T. bid for another purpose.

Three No Trumps as an opening is used as a tactical bid on a hand containing a long and strong minor suit with protection in at least two other suits, and one of the main purposes of the bid is to discourage partner from bidding either of the major suits. In response to a 3 N.T. opening bid, therefore, even a six-card major suit should be suppressed. Such hands as the following would be typical of this opening bid:

♠ J 7	♠ K 5
♡ K 9	♡ A 3
◇ K J	◇ A K Q 10 9 2
♣ A K Q 10 8 4 2	♣ Q J 8

As a third-in-hand opener the bid is particularly valuable, as you already know that partner does not even hold an Acol Light Opener in either major, and unless fourth hand is enormous, he will almost certainly be blocked from making any attempt to enter the auction.

Recently a 'new' version of the opening 3 N.T. has been publicised, coupled with an elaborate series of conventional responses to guard against a possible double. If you face the fact that all opening three-bids are pre-emptive, whether in a suit or No Trumps, and are made with no real anticipation of succeeding in the contract, then for my money I'd rather play where

♠ 7 6
♡ 7
◇ A K Q J 7 3
♣ 7 6 5 4

I have a chance of making some tricks. To open 3 N.T. on a hand like this, as is suggested, seems to me to be the height of folly. Open 3 ◇, where you will at least make six tricks.

ACOL OPENING FOUR NO TRUMPS

This bid is quite a different cup of tea and one which, if it comes but rarely, is invaluable when the suitable occasion does arise. It is used on the rare type of hand where opener is interested in Aces only. It is unconditionally forcing and partner's responses are as follows:

(a) Holding two Aces, he responds 5 N.T.
(b) With the ◇A, ♡A, or ♠A, he bids five of the suit in which the Ace is held.
(c) With the ♣A he bids 6♣.
(d) With no Ace, he bids 5♣.

♠ A
♡ A
◇ K Q J 10 7
♣ K Q J 8 7 5

This would be a good hand on which to use the bid, though it must be used with special care if the hand contains a void. If partner responds 5♣ showing no Ace, that bid can be passed. 6♣, showing the Ace of that suit, would be a highly acceptable response, and would also be left in as the final contract. 5◇, showing the diamond Ace, you would raise to 6◇, and if the miracle of a 5 N.T. response occurred, I leave the choice of the final contract to you!

There is one other point to note about this bid, and that is that, having given his correct response, responder must leave the choice of the final contract to his partner, whose only need is to know the Ace position before making his decision.

♠ A   On this hand, opener intends to play
♡ 8   in 6◇ whether or not his partner
◇ A K Q J 10 7 6 5   has a Yarborough, but if he holds the
♣ A K Q   ♡A the contract will be 7◇ at
                     rubber bridge, to gain the 150 for
honours, and 7 N.T. at duplicate for the Match Point score.

For another example of this bid in action, look back to the Introduction.

If you are ever lucky enough to be in the position of wondering whether to open a direct 4 N.T. or to start with 2♣ and follow the almost certain negative with a jump suit bid as described earlier, remember that the 2♣ opening will ensure a lower contract if one vital Ace is missing. The direct opening of 4 N.T., on the other hand, means that you cannot in any circumstances play in anything lower than the five-level. The bid, therefore, should be reserved for hands on which the risk of a positive response to 2♣ might confuse the issue, or when opener wants to make it clear to responder immediately that his only interest lies in Aces. Kings and Queens by the dozen will be of no use whatsoever.

REVISION QUIZ ON CHAPTER 12

1. Assume that your partner has opened 2 N.T. What do you respond on the following hands?

(a) ♠ K 8 4: ♡ Q 9 6 3: ♢ 10 4 2: ♣ 9 7 6:

(b) ♠ Q 10 8 4: ♡ K 7: ♢ Q 4 2: ♣ K 10 9 4:

(c) ♠ Q 10 9 7 4 3: ♡ Q 4: ♢ J 9 3: ♣ J 4:

(d) ♠ 8 7 6: ♡ 9 8 7 5 4 3: ♢ 6: ♣ 7 5 4:

2. Assume that your partner has opened 2♣. On the first three hands above, what do you respond?

3. Partner opened 2♣ to which, on the following hands, you responded 2♢. Partner now rebids 2 N.T. What is your next bid?

(a) ♠ J 7 3: ♡ 10 7 2: ♢ 9 8 7 4: ♣ J 3 2:

(b) ♠ J 7 3: ♡ Q 10 7 2: ♢ 9 8 7: ♣ Q 3 2:

(c) ♠ Q 10 9 6 5 2: ♡ J 4: ♢ J 9 3: ♣ J 3:

(d) ♠ J 10 6 3 2: ♡ Q J 6 5 :♢ 8 4 3: ♣ 6:

(e) ♠ K 10 9 2: ♡ 9 8 7: ♢ K 3 2 : ♣ Q 3 2:

(f) ♠ 8 7 6 5 4 3: ♡ 7: ♢ 9 4 3: ♣ 6 3 2:

4. What opening bid would you make on the following hands?

(a) ♠ Q 5: ♡ K 7: ♢ K 9: ♣ A K Q 10 8 6 4:

(b) ♠ K J 9: ♡ Q J 6: ♢ A K 10 4: ♣ A Q 9:

(c) ♠ A K 10: ♡ K Q 9: ♢ A 10 6: ♣ K Q 10 8:

(d) ♠ A K Q J 9 7 4 : ♡ 5: ♢ 6: ♣ A K Q J:

(e) ♠ A K J: ♡ K Q 9 6: ♢ A Q 4: ♣ A K 10:

(f) ♠ K 4: ♡ Q J 5: ♢ A K Q 9 7 5: ♣ A 4:

(g) ♠ K 10 9 6: ♡ K Q 8: ♢ A Q 4: ♣ A Q J:

ANSWERS TO REVISION QUIZ
ON CHAPTER 12

1. (a) 3 N.T. With five points opposite to a minimum of 20 points you want to be in game, and your hand is evenly balanced.

    (b) 3♣ You would prefer a 4♠ contract, but will settle for 3 N.T. if partner cannot show spades.

    (c) 3♠ A simple matter of showing your long suit, and whatever opener rebids, you will merely repeat spades—unless, of course, he raises your spades, in which case you will pass.

    (d) 3◇ This requests opener to convert to 3♡ which you will pass.

2. (a) 2◇ A normal negative response. Your next bid of course, will be conditioned by opener's rebid.

    (b) 2 N.T. A positive response showing at least 9 points and no biddable suit.

    (c) 2◇ A negative response to start with, after which you will show your spade suit.

3. (a) 3 N.T. Horrible as it may seem, two Jacks , a ten and that 9-8-7 sequence just make this worth the raise.

    (b) 3 N.T. The same raise, though this time without a qualm.

    (c) 3♠ Having "denied" with 2◇, you will show your spades on the next round.

    (d) 3♣ Obviously you hope for a major suit contract here.

    (e) 3 N.T. You are too evenly balanced to want to bother with anything but the obvious contract.

K

(f) 3♢ Partner will convert to 3♡ and you in turn will convert to 3♠ *which opener will pass.*

4. (a) 3 N.T. The typical type of hand for this opener, with the long club suit.

(b) 2 N.T. Evenly balanced, 20 points. A "book" bid.

(c) 2 N.T. Again, though just one point stronger, a typical 2 N.T. opener.

(d) 4 N.T. The conventional bid asking partner to show Aces immediately. If he shows one Ace, you will bid 6♠ and if he shows both, you will bid 7♠.

(e) 2♣ This you will follow with a rebid of 3 N.T.

(f) 3 N.T. As in (a) above, only with the long diamonds.

(g) 2 N.T. Well balanced, 21 points. What better bid could you find?

The Acol Opening Two Bids
and Responses

♠♡♣◇♠♡♣◇♠♡♣◇♠♡♣◇♠♡♣◇♠♡♣◇♠♡♣◇♠♡♣◇

THE Acol Opening Two Bids are no less fundamentally important to the system than the bids which have formed the theme of the previous chapters. They are an integral part of it, and to play "Acol with weak two's" is to undermine one of its main foundation stones. It changes the whole range of Acol opening bids and makes nonsense of the Acol theory of pre-emptive bidding—in fact, the system will no longer be Acol and weak two's, therefore, do not come within the range of possible reasonable alternatives.

As we have already seen, the opening Two Club bid is conventional, so that these opening Two Bids can be made only in the other three suits. They, as well as their responses, are also conventional, though in a wider sense. They must only be made on hands of a certain power and quality and, furthermore, on hands which do not qualify for an opening Two Club bid. Though a Two Club bid might also easily qualify for an opening Two Bid, a Two Bid must not be made on hands which honestly can be opened with a Two Club Bid, as this opening should be preferred to any other if it is available. The opening Two Bids are *unconditionally forcing for one round* and in all cases are made on hands promising high hopes of a game with the barest minimum of assistance from partner. The weakness response is Two No Trumps.

Opening Two Bids fall into three classes:

(1) Prospective game hands containing a long and powerful suit with at least eight playing tricks at the suit bid. The three examples which follow all come within this category.

♠ A K Q J 8 6
♡ 8
♢ A 10 9
♣ A 6 4

♠ K Q 7
♡ A K J 10 8 7 2
♢ K 6
♣ 8

♠ —
♡ K 5 4
♢ A Q J 9 7 6 4 2
♣ A 5

If you look at them you will see that, if they are opened as one-bids, they present insuperable problems when it comes to the question of your rebid, and you will be unable to find any bid which will do justice to your holding without risk. A jump to three of your long suit might well be passed out by your partner with a minimum hand, whereas only very slight help is needed to make game. On the other hand, an immediate jump to a game contract might be equally disastrous.

So announce your strength by an opening bid of two of your long suit, and give your partner a chance to judge what he should do himself.

(2) A powerful two-suiter so strong that, played in the suit which fits your partner best, it is likely to be worth eight tricks or more. The opening two bid is made in this case, not because the hand holds eight playing tricks at that suit, but to ensure that opener is given the opportunity of showing both suits. Here are three examples of hands which come into this class:—

♠ A Q J 9 7 2
♡ A K J 7 6 3
◇ —
♣ 6

♠ —
♡ A
◇ A K J 9 6 2
♣ A Q 10 9 6 3

♠ A K Q 5 4
♡ A K Q 5 4
◇ 5 4
♣ 4

With all three of these hands you want, at all costs, to be given the chance to show your second suit in order to find the best available fit. On each of them you would, of course, open the higher ranking. Unless you make a jump rebid or reverse, the Two Bid is forcing for one round only, so that the bidding may be dropped at the three level if you don't force and partner holds a "blizzard". Recognising that you have power as well as "shape", though, he will not pass if he can offer any assistance at all.

(3) Now we come to the third and most difficult class of opening Two Bids. This covers hands of great strength containing 20 or more points which, because of their shape or actual content, are unsuitable for either a Two Club or a Two No Trump opening bid. They fall into a number of distributional classes, and are opened as Two Bids only because there is a danger that they may be passed out when game is "on" with only the most slender support from partner. This type of hand is, without doubt, the most difficult to judge, as it appears at first to fall between the upper limit of a one bid and the lower limit of a two bid. The best yardstick you can apply is the urgency of your need for a reply from partner, even if he has less than the minimum of five or six points with which he would respond to a one bid.

♠ A J 9 3 2
♡ A K J 4
◇ 8
♣ A Q J

On this hand you have 20 points and the remaining 20 points in the pack may be so divided that, if you open 1♠, the hand will be passed out, but to find a 4-4 fit in hearts would

produce at least a useful part-score. Open 2♠ and make sure
that you gain yourself a second bid.

♠ 6
♡ A Q 9 2
◇ A K Q 7 4
♣ K Q 3

♠ K J 10 8 5 2
♡ 8
◇ A K 4
♣ A K 7

♠ A 10 7 5 4 3
♡ A K J 3
◇ A Q J
♣ —

Look at these three hands. On
none of them do you want the
bidding to die below the game
level if your partner has "the smell
of an oil rag", so tell him so by
opening with a Two Bid, in each
case in the longest suit.

Exponents of other systems
claim to have improved on the
Acol Two Bids saying that they,
but not Acol players, would open
2♠ on such a hand as: ♠ A J 10
6 3: ♡—: ◇ A Q J 6 3: ♣ A K 4.
True it has only 19 points, and
true also that it has no pre-
dominating suit, but it is powerful, and it also has two
good suits. Surely, then, played either in spades or
diamonds, it is more than probable that it will develop
eight playing tricks. Make no mistake about it—players
who really know their Acol will open 2♠ on this hand.

To sum up, the main points to remember when
learning these Acol Two Bids are:

1. They are reserved for hands of a type and *not*
   for hands of a specific strength or point count.

2. They are not glorified one bids, as hands which
   require time for the development of the bidding
   are better opened at the one level.

3. The Two Bids must only be used when opener
   sees prospects of game in his hand with the
   minimum of support and when he can afford
   to skip one level of bidding to show his partner
   this immediately.

There is one point which I should like to make quite sure is clearly understood here, as it is one about which there has been some confusion in the past. The specific requirements for an opening Two Bid falling into the first class we discussed is that the hand should contain a minimum of eight playing tricks at the suit named. A hand with eight spades to the five top honours or seven to the A K Q and an outside Ace both fulfil these requirements and not only may, but should, be opened as Two Bids. This applies very particularly third-in-hand after two passes, on account of the pre-emptive value of the bid. Little trouble is likely to result as, if partner has a completely worthless hand, the bidding will be dropped at the three level, and even with no trick at all developing from the dummy, opener should not be more than one down while, very possibly, having obstructed a fourth-hand opening.

THREE CLUB OPENING BIDS

A powerful two-suiter qualifying for a Two Bid when one of the suits held is clubs presents no special problems, as the higher-ranking suit can be bid first followed by a rebid in clubs in the normal way. When, however, the hand belongs to Class 1, with a long club suit predominating for the eight playing tricks, the hand cannot be opened as Two Clubs which, as we already know, is a specialised and conventional cipher bid. Different players have different views as to how to deal with these big club hands, but one accepted method is to open 3♣ with hands of this particular type. In other words, you keep 2◇, 2♡ and 2♠ for strong distributional opening bids such as we have already discussed, and 3♣ for hands of the same type when clubs predominate.

You already know that a Two Club opening bid can be slightly under value when the predominating suit is clubs and the intended rebid is 3♣. From this it will be clear that if you elect to use the strong 3♣ opener, the limits of the bid will be very narrow. It can be made on a hand:—

(a) Too strong for a 1♣ opening.

(b) Not strong enough for a 2♣ opening with a 3♣ rebid.

(c) Single-suited in clubs, or the higher-ranking suit could have been bid first.

This 3♣ strong opening bid, therefore, *can be passed by responder*, unlike the other strong Two Bids, on a complete bust. This is logical if you consider that responder knows his partner is not going to offer a second suit, and that he is also not strong enough to open with 2♣ and rebid 3♣.

It must be pointed out that the use of this strong 3♣ opening bid automatically eliminates the use of 3♣ as a weak pre-emptive opening bid (see Chapter 14), but the suit is the one of least value for a pre-emptive opening as it can be more easily overcalled than any other. 4♣, therefore, takes the place of 3♣ as a pre-emptive opening bid in that suit. Before we go on to the responses to Opening Two Bids, compare these two examples:

♠ A
♡ —
♢ K Q 10 9 6 5
♣ A J 10 5 3 2

Here the hand is obviously a powerful two-suiter coming into Class 2, and the opening bid should be 2♢ with a rebid of 3♣, which gives no problems to anyone.

♠ A 3   This is a typical example of a strong
♡ —   3♣ opener. The only, and pre-
◇ K J 8   dominating suit, is clubs, but the
♣ A K J 10 6 5 3 2   hand won't develop game without
                              some very slight help from partner.
Partner would respond to 1♣ on 5 points, so he will respond
to a strong 3♣ on a good deal less. Notice, by the way, that
this hand is only fractionally weaker than the one quoted
on p. 120 as an opening 2♣ bid with a 3♣ rebid.

This use of 3♣ as a strong opening bid, the
equivalent of an opening Two Bid in the other suits,
and 4♣ taking the place of 3♣ as an opening pre-
emptive bid, may be regarded as a "reasonable alternative". If you prefer to keep to the 3♣ pre-emptive
bid, then disregard this last section and deal with your
big club hands as described in Chapter 11.

RESPONSES TO OPENING TWO BIDS

There are three points which must be stressed before
we go into the particular holdings required for the
responses. Firstly, as already stated, an opening Two
Bid is unconditionally forcing for one round.
Responder's negative response is 2 N.T. and this he
must make however little he admires his hand. A force
is at all times a force, and responder is not at liberty
to judge whether or not to take it upon himself to pass.

♠ 8 2   Opposite a 2♠ opener such a
♡ J 8 6 5   hand as this could prove a gold-
◇ J 9 8 6 4   mine if partner has a second suit
♣ 8 4   of hearts or diamonds. In any
                      case, opener's hand may be so
good that he wants to play in game whatever his
partner's weakness and his only reason for opening
2♠ was that he did not qualify for 2♣ though he has
game "cold" in his own hand.

Secondly, if responder gives a positive answer to an opening Two Bid, it is inconceivable that the bidding should be dropped short of game. A positive response, therefore, must be treated as a force to game at least.

Thirdly, if trump support can be given when making the initial positive response, this should be preferred, as it will inevitably be the most welcome news opener can hear.

The bidding, then, will be kept open by responder with a bid of 2 N.T. if his hand does not qualify for a positive response, and responder is at liberty to pass any rebid by opener other than a jump bid in a new suit. He would not, however, do so unless his hand were a complete blank.

♠ 8 7
♡ Q 7 2
◇ 10 7 5 2
♣ 9 8 5 4

If partner opens 2♠, respond 2 N.T. and pass if he rebids 3♠. If he rebids 3♡, however, showing a strong two-suited hand, you can raise to 4♡.

♠ Q J 7 5 4
♡ 10 9 6
◇ Q 8 4
♣ 7 2

If partner opens with any Two Bid, respond 2 N.T. If he opens 2♠ raise to game in spades after your original 2 N.T., whatever his rebid. Over a 2♡ opening bid 2 N.T. first, and then raise in hearts if rebid in preference to showing such a moderate spade suit.

♠ 8 5
♡ K 10 9
◇ 10 9 8 5
♣ Q J 8 3

If partner opens 2♠ respond 2 N.T. If he rebids 3♠ bid 3 N.T. on your distributed strength. If, however, he shows a two-suiter by a rebid in a second suit, support the second suit.

♠ K J 10 9 7 5 2
♡ 7
◇ 6 5 2
♣ 9 4

Respond 2 N.T. to either 2♡ or 2◇ then, whatever opener rebids, bid 3♠.

So much for the negative responses. The positive

ones are vitally important and must be fully understood if proper use is to be made of this valuable Acol
weapon.

DIRECT SUIT RAISES

If you have studied the examples thus far you will
have realised that moderate trump support and other
very modest values should first be bid as a 2 N.T.
negative, with the appropriate raise after hearing
opener's rebid. This negative response, of course,
denies the holding of the values to make a positive
response and if you learn your positive responses,
you will automatically know when you cannot make one.
These two "positive" replies are very important:

1. **A single raise** of opener's trump suit is a
    constructive and unlimited bid. It guarantees
    a hand containing trump support in the suit
    opened and at least one ace or void.

2. **A direct raise to four** (2♠—4♠, 2♡—
    4♡, or 2♦—4♦) shows good trump support,
    a certain amount of high card strength, **and
    no ace or void.**

It follows from this that a single raise may be a
stronger bid than a double raise. The first gives room
to develop the bidding towards a slam by means of
subsequent cue bids or the use of your chosen slam
convention. The second informs partner immediately
that responder has **no first round controls,** though
he has an otherwise good supporting hand. In the light
of this information, opener can decide whether or not
to go "slamming".

♠ K 10 8
♡ 8 6 2
♦ J 8 7
♣ A 8 5 3

If partner opens 2♠ raise to 3♠,
a positive response confirming trump
support and at least one Ace or void.

♠ Q J 9 4
♡ K 9 7 2
◇ K 8 7 6
♣ 5

This hand holds a responding raise to four in either spades, hearts or diamonds. It has good trump support for any of these, but no Ace or void. Don't make the error of giving a single raise in any of these suits, which would promise at least one first round control.

Obviously, as opener, you must not go "slamming" when your partner has raised your opening Two Bid to four unless you yourself hold at least three first round controls in the form of Aces or voids. Responder, by his bid, has specifically denied that he has any first round control which, therefore, means that you must be in a position to supply these yourself. Missing two Aces—or compensating voids—you must not try to bid a slam that can only make against a "lucky" lead.

RESPONSES IN A NEW SUIT

To take out an Acol Opening Two Bid into another suit at the same level, (i.e., 2♡ over 2◇ or 2♠ over 2♡), responder should hold a fairly good biddable suit and at least one honour trick. If the take-out is in a suit which raises the level of the bidding (i.e., 3◇ over 2♡), responder should have at least one and a half honour tricks in addition to his biddable suit. With trump support for opener and only a moderate suit of his own, responder should prefer a raise of his partner's suit.

♠ J 10 9
♡ K Q 10 9 7
◇ 7 6 2
♣ 8 7

Respond 2♡ over an opening 2◇, but 2 N.T. over an opening 2♠. Strengthen the hand by the inclusion of the ♣A, though, and 2♡ should be bid over 2◇ or 2♠ raised to 3♠.

♠ Q 8 7   If partner opens 2◇, respond 2♡,
♡ A J 10 7   which does not raise the level of the
◇ 6 2   bidding. If he opens 2♠, raise to 3♠
♣ K 8 7 5   in preference to showing the heart suit.

It might be as well here again to touch on the modern interpretation of the phrase "biddable suit", although this has already been discussed in Chapter 11 in connection with the positive responses to 2♣ opening bids.

It is customary nowadays to regard any four-card major suit, if headed by a high honour, and if this can be shown without raising the level of the bidding, as "biddable", the object of which is to facilitate the finding of a four-four fit for game or slam contracts. Here is a hand from tournament play on which the "top" went to the only pair who found 6♡ as the final contract. In response to North's opening 2◇ bid, South said 2♡. South, in fact, has practically a "text

♠ A
♡ A Q 7 6
◇ A Q J 8 7 6 2
♣ A

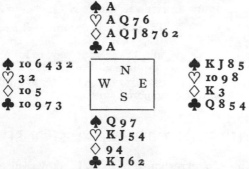

♠ 10 6 4 3 2   ♠ K J 8 5
♡ 3 2   ♡ 10 9 8
◇ 10 5   ◇ K 3
♣ 10 9 7 3   ♣ Q 8 5 4

♠ Q 9 7
♡ K J 5 4
◇ 9 4
♣ K J 6 2

book" response of 3 N.T. (see the next section) but it costs nothing to notify his partner of his "positive" holding en route.

Nowadays no one expects a change-of-suit response at the one-level, such as 1♡—1♠, or 1◇—1♡, to promise any better holding that would be required to bid 1 N.T. in this position. What it does promise is that responder has at least enough points to make his bid and that he also has at least four cards in the suit named, so why should responses at this higher level be unable to show even this much of their "shape" and content?

Over an opening 2♠ bid South, on the hand above, would *not* bid 3♡, raising the level of the bidding on this weak suit. He would, in fact, give the double raise to 4♠, which is the only reasonable positive response. The logic of this is quite clear if you consider South's hand in relation to a response to a normal one-bid. Over 1◇ he would respond 1♡.

One other bid comes into this category of responses in a new suit, and that is a jump take-out by responder. This shows a solid suit, self-supporting, and with no losers. It should be as good as six cards long to the four top honours or seven to the A K Q.

♠ 5 3
♡ A K Q J 7 6
◇ Q 3
♣ 9 4 2

To partner's opening 2◇ respond 3♡, showing the long and solid suit. In the same way, to his opening 2♠ respond 4♡. He will know exactly what you have, and that you are not seeking trump support from him.

THREE NO TRUMP RESPONSE

An immediate response of 3 N.T. shows an evenly balanced hand with no biddable suit, about 10—12 points **and no Ace or void.**

♠ Q 6 5
♡ 7 6
◇ K 10 8 3
♣ K Q 5 2

If partner opens 2♡, respond 3 N.T. If he opens 2♠ raise to 4♠.

158

♠ 9 5   If partner opens 2♠, respond 3 N.T.
♡ K 9 6 5   If he opens 2◇ respond 2♡, and if
◇ K Q 7   he opens 2♡, respond 4♡.
♣ K 9 8 2

OPENER'S REBIDS

If responder signs off to an opening Two Bid with
the negative 2 N.T. and opener has a hand of game-
going strength, he should bid the game direct himself.
On a two-suiter such as the ones covered in Class 3,
he makes a simple rebid of three of his second suit.
Responder may pass, give simple preference to the
first bid suit, or raise one or other suit. On the powerful
two-suiters explained in Class 2, opener can make a
jump rebid in his second suit, forcing his partner to bid
again, unless the jump rebid is already at game level
(i.e., 2♠—2 N.T.—4♡).

♠ 8   Open 2♡. If responder bids 2 N.T.,
♡ A K Q 10 6 5 4   rebid 4♡. If he bids 2♠ or 3◇,
◇ 10   rebid your hearts before showing the
♣ A Q J 6   clubs as the bidding will continue to
                 game level now anyway. If responder
gives an immediate direct raise to 3♡ you know he has at
least one Ace or a void, so cue-bid your ♣A as a slam try,
and he will show the diamond or spade Ace if he holds it.
If he gives a direct raise to 4♡ in the first place, pass—you
know he has no Ace or void and that you have, therefore,
two Aces missing which may be cashed against you on the
opening lead.

As a final footnote to this Chapter may I just add
that far too many players miss the opportunities of
making these opening Two Bids, particularly on the
type of hand coming into Class 3. Try to get into the
habit of looking for these bids, and you will find yourself with fewer missed games and slams than in the past.

REVISION QUIZ ON CHAPTER 13

1. What opening bid would you make on the following hands?

    (a) ♠ A K Q 9 6 4 3: ♡ A 10 4: ◇ 6 5: ♣ 3:

    (b) ♠ 9 6: ♡ A K Q 10 6 4: ◇ J 10 9: ♣ A K:

    (c) ♠ A J 9 6 4 3: ♡ A K 8: ◇ K J 9: ♣ 5:

    (d) ♠ 7: ♡ A K J 9 6: ◇ A Q 10 8 4: ♣ A 4:

    (e) ♠ K Q 10: ♡ K 9: ◇ 4: ♣ A K Q 7 5 4 3:

    (f) ♠ A K 3: ♡ A K Q 9 6 2: ◇ Q 2: ♣ 10 4:

    (g) ♠ Q J 4: ♡ K Q J 10 4 6: ◇ A K J: ♣ 4:

    (h) ♠ 8: ♡ 7: ◇ A K Q J 9 7 4: ♣ A 10 9 6:

    (i) ♠ A Q 4: ♡ K J 9 6 4 3: ◇ K 8: ♣ A 4:

    (j) ♠ 9: ♡ A Q J: ◇ K 10 4: ♣ A K Q 10 9 5:

    (k) ♠ A Q 9 6 4: ♡ A J 10 8 4: ◇ —: ♣ A Q 6:

2. Assume that partner has opened 2♠. What is your response on the following hands?

    (a) ♠ K 9 4 3: ♡ Q 7 3: ◇ J 9 8 2: ♣ Q 4:

    (b) ♠ K 9 2: ♡ A 7 4: ◇ Q 7 3: ♣ 10 9 4 2:

    (c) ♠ 4 2: ♡ Q 10 9 6 4 3: ◇ 8 3: ♣ J 9 6:

    (d) ♠ 4: ♡ K 9: ◇ Q 10 9 6 5 4 3: ♣ 8 7 6:

    (e) ♠ A 4 3: ♡ K 3 2: ◇ Q 10 9 6 5 4: ♣ 7:

    (f) ♠ Q 10: ♡ Q J 4 3: ◇ K 9 2: ♣ Q 6 3 2:

3. You opened 2♠ and partner responded 2 N.T. What is your rebid on these hands?

    (a) ♠ A K Q 10 9 8: ♡ A K 4: ◇ 6 3: ♣ 5 4:

    (b) ♠ A Q J 9 8 4 3: ♡ A 10 5: ◇ A 8 4: ♣ —:

    (c) ♠ A K Q 10 6: ♡ A K Q 9 5: ◇ Q 4: ♣ J:

    (d) ♠ A J 10 9 8 6: ♡ K J 10 9 7 4: ◇ —: ♣ A:

ANSWERS TO REVISION QUIZ
ON CHAPTER 13

1. (a) 2♠   This hand contains exactly eight playing tricks at spades.

(b) 2♡   With these six hearts the hand just qualifies for a two bid. It is too strong for a one bid.

(c) 1♠   This hand does not qualify under any of the three classes and must be opened 1♠.

(d) 2♡   This is the two-suiter type where you want to be certain of a chance to show the diamonds.

(e) 1♣ or 3♣   If you prefer to keep 3♣ as a pre-emptive bid your alternative is 1♣.

(f) 2♡   Eight playing tricks at hearts should be safe.

(g) 1♡   You can only count seven playing tricks here.

(h) 2♢   There are definitely eight playing tricks in diamonds.

(i) 1♡   This hand is just a normal strong 1♡ opener.

(j) 1♣ or 3♣   Here again, 1♣ is the alternative, if 3♣ is your pre-emptive bid.

(k) 2♠   You must be sure of a chance to show the hearts in case partner doesn't like spades.

2. (a) 4♠   A double jump, showing good trump support and no Ace or void.

(b) 3♠   Here you have an Ace as well as trump support.

(c) 2 N.T.   An obvious negative response.

(d) 2 N.T.   This too is a negative response in spite of the seven card diamond suit. Show this on the next round if expedient.

(e) 3♠   Though your diamond suit is biddable, trump agreement is far more likely to help opener.

(f) 3 N.T.   Evenly balanced—10 points—no Ace.

3. (a) 3♠   With just your eight playing tricks make the minimum rebid.

    (b) 4♠   This time you want to try for game however little partner has, so bid it direct in case he passes 3♠.

    (c) 4♡   Bid your second suit at game level.

    (d) 3♡   Here again, offer your second suit. Partner may pass, bid 3♠ or raise either suit to game.

CHAPTER 14

Pre-Emptive Bidding

♠♡♣◊♠♡♣◊♠♡♣◊♠♡♣◊♠♡♣◊♠♡♣◊♠♡♣◊♠♡♣◊

ALL bidding systems include some form of pre-emptive or shut-out bidding so Acol is not alone in this, using, as the basis for pre-emption, weak opening bids of three in a suit. A surprising number of people favour the weak opening two bids, but this cannot under any circumstances be considered as one of the "reasonable alternatives" for use with Acol. To play Acol with Weak Two's is a contradiction in terms, as it changes one of the basic features of the system, the Strong Two's. This in turn upsets the balance of the opening bids and allied responses and the bidding becomes, quite clearly, no longer Acol. For our purposes, then, we need consider weak two's only in the light of how to counter them when bid by the opposition, and we shall go into this, and into the countering of the weak three's by the opposition in detail later. Every bid known in the game can produce its successes, and weak two's cannot be excepted from this rule. There can be no doubt, however, that weak three's are an infinitely superior weapon, and that the Acol Strong Two plays a big part in the success of Acol players.

A pre-emptive bid has one object, and one object only, and that is to obstruct the opposition to the limit. Opening at the three-level deprives the opposition of two rounds of bidding space, and may well make it impossible for them to find their fit and certain game contract, let alone a slam.

A pre-emptive opening bid is made on a hand that:

(a) Is virtually useless in defence.

(b) Is unlikely to be of any value to partner as a supporting hand.

(c) Is worth six or seven tricks if played in a particular suit. Vulnerable, seven playing tricks should be expected, but six suffice if not vulnerable, expecially against vulnerable opponents.

The bid is, in effect, an immediate sacrifice as opener, if he finds himself facing a worthless dummy, expects to be defeated by two or three tricks.

The best position at the table for making an opening pre-emptive bid is third-in-hand after two passes. As neither your partner nor second hand has opened and you as third hand have a typical pre-emptive holding, the chances are extremely high that fourth hand has an opening bid, and a good one at that. To open with a three-bid just before him may put him in such a quandary that he is unable to make the best use of his hand. An opening three bid is never made fourth-in-hand, as there can be no object in trying to shut out three players who have already passed. Neither should a pre-emptive Three-bid be made on a hand containing two or more honour tricks, as such a hand has constructive as well as defensive value, and it should normally be opened as a one-bid.

Another very important "don't" is to open three on a hand containing four cards in a major suit in addition to its own long suit, as there is a grave danger of preventing your partner from showing a suit for which you have very adequate support. Here are two examples which illustrate these last two points:

♠ 7
♡ K Q J 8 6 5 3
◇ A 7
♣ Q 8 5

This hand is far too strong for an Acol three bid, yet not strong enough for an Opening Two Bid. The correct opening is 1♡ with a rebid of 3♡.

♠ A Q J 6 4 3 2
♡ Q 10 5 4
◇ 3
♣ 7

The correct opening bid on this hand is 1♠. If you open 3♠ you may well prevent partner from making a response in hearts, for which you have invaluable support.

You will, of course, want examples of hands which *do* qualify as Opening Three Bids. The following are typical. Note that they contain virtually nothing outside their own suit:

♠ 9 6	♠ A Q 7 6 5 3 2	♠ 9
♡ 9 3	♡ 8	♡ K Q J 8 7 6 5
◇ K Q 10 9 5 4 2	◇ J 7 2	◇ 8 7
♣ Q 6	♣ 8 6	♣ Q 8 5

If you will look back to Chapter 13, you will be able to refresh your memory on what has already been said about pre-emptive opening bids in clubs, and one of Acol's "reasonable alternatives" is the use of 4♣ in place of 3♣ as an opening pre-emptive bid. Here, perhaps, the guiding factor—if one dare say it— should be the quality of the opposition. The weaker the players, the more easily will they be out-manoeuvred by an opening three bid, which means that an opening four bid may well be at a higher level than is necessary, thus costing an extra trick "off". Be guided, therefore, by your own preference and judgment. If using the opening weak 4♣, then partner must judge his possible responses accordingly.

RESPONDING TO OPENING THREE BIDS

There are two possible situations which may arise when you are responding to an opening three bid. One is a raise, or bid in a new denomination with a view to a game or slam contract in spite of the opening bid, and the other is further bidding with the "sacrifice" position in view. If opener is third-in-hand, then the first position virtually cannot occur as, if you had to pass originally, you cannot possibly hold enough to do anything constructive, and the only bidding you will do will be towards further sacrifices.

So let us assume that partner, as either dealer or second-in-hand, has opened with a three bid, that is, before you have had time to pass in which case, for all he knows, you may hold the earth. As responder you must recognise at once that opener has virtually nothing except length in the suit he has named and that he has, at best, seven tricks if allowed to play in that suit, so whatever action you decide to take will be on your own head. You will need some general rules to guide you in this situation.

Firstly, opener has told you his whole story with his first bid. To raise his bid to game you will have to provide him with at least three or more certain tricks, and you must raise directly to game yourself. Opener will not bid again unless put in a forced position, such as we shall come to in a moment, or towards a sacrifice.

♠ A 10 9   If partner opens 3♡, raise to 4♡.
♡ J 5   True you have not got much heart
◇ A Q 8 7   support for him, but he will have at
♣ K 10 9 6   least seven himself and your outside
strength is enough for the raise. If
he opens 3◇ or 3♣ (or the alternative 4♣) raise to 5 of that
suit.

A cardinal rule is never to "rescue" a pre-emptive opening bid. Opener has already announced his desire to play in one specific suit and you must not take him out unless you have something really superior to offer.

♠ 8
♡ K J 10 9 8 4
♢ A Q 8
♣ Q 7 6

If partner opens 3♣ (or, of course, 4♣) don't be tempted to take him out into hearts. You have excellent support for his suit. Likewise don't disturb 3♠ on the grounds that you have a singleton. Nor must you try 3 N.T. over any opening he makes.

♠ A 9 8
♡ A K Q J 10 7
♢ Q
♣ K Q 6

Now you take 3♢ out into 4♡. Your suit is quite certainly better than your partner's and you need very little assistance indeed to make a game on this hand.

Any response to an opening three bid below the level of game is a slam try in the suit opened and must be treated as such by opener. It is forcing to game and the bid itself shows control of that suit. This, of course, is the forcing situation mentioned above. If you held our last example opposite to a 3 or 4♣ opener you would undoubtedly visualise a slam in clubs. Similarly, with a hand such as this:

♠ A Q 8 7
♡ K J 7
♢ 9
♣ A Q 9 7 5

Bid 3♠ over an opening 3♡, and over opener's inevitable 4♡ response, bid 4 N.T. Note that the 3♠ bid agrees hearts as trumps.

A take-out by responder into 3 N.T. gives a guarantee of support for the suit opened and high honour strength in at least two of the other suits. The guaranteed fit is essential as opener is already known to be almost devoid of anything except his own long suit, and must be assured that responder feels himself to be in a position to make use of it without the assistance of outside entries.

♠ K Q J 5　　　Respond 3 N.T. to 3◇ on this hand.
♡ 6 2　　　　With any luck you may be able to
◇ K J 10　　　run nine tricks before the opposition
♣ A Q 4 3　　discover your weakness. If the hand
　　　　　　　which will be on lead doubles, you
can be sure it is on the heart suit, and can "escape" into 4◇.
But he is unlikely to double you for just that reason. The hand
on your right is unlikely to double as his partner's lead will
be "blind".

Now we come to another aspect of responding to a
pre-emptive bid, and that is an "anticipatory sacrifice".

♠ J 4 3 2　　　As dealer or second-in-hand you will
♡ 5 3　　　　doubtless have passed on this hand,
◇ K J 9 5 4 2　or you may hear your partner in one
♣ 10　　　　of these positions open 3◇. In any
　　　　　　　case it is quite obvious that you have
nothing between you except diamonds, diamonds, and more
diamonds, and that the opposition will have virtually the
choice of slam contract. Raise partner's opening 3◇ immediately to 5◇, or even to 6◇ if you are brave enough,
which with any luck, will leave your opponents completely
groping, for their right contract.

This last example is one from actual play, and the
opposition bid 3 N.T. for a take-out over the dealer's
opening 3◇. Responder jumped to 6◇ and fourth
hand, on a guess, bid 6♠. This was one down when
there was no defence whatsoever to 7♡—a very useful
gain for the diamond holders! So don't pass on a
hand like this and allow opponents time to find their
fit. Your judgment should tell you that it is a typical
case of the less you have, the more they have, so try
to bid them out of it.

PRE-EMPTIVE OPENING FOUR BIDS

Whether you have decided to use 3♣ or 4♣ as your pre-emptive opening in this suit, both 4♣ and 4◇ can be used as effective opening bids on exactly the same type of hand but with a little added length in the suit concerned. Say, for instance:

♠ 8 7 ♡ 6 ◇ K J 9 8 6 5 4 3 ♣ 10 7	This hand should be opened with 4◇ and, if you switch the suit to clubs, it makes an equally good 4♣ opener whether or not you have decided to make that your only club "pre-empt".
♠ 8 ♡ K Q J 10 7 6 5 2 ◇ 9 ♣ A 9 8	Made in the major suits, opening four-bids are pre-emptive. They show however, game-going hands containing *not more than two honour tricks* and partner, if he has already

passed, will not make any sort of slam try on less than two Aces. This hand offers a typical 4♡ opening, if third or fourth in hand. As first or second hand, open 2♡.

PRE-EMPTIVE OPENING FIVE BIDS

Direct opening bids of 5♣ or 5◇, that is, in the minor suits, may be made on better quality hands containing eight or nine playing tricks.

♠ 6 ♡ 8 ◇ A K J 9 7 6 4 3 ♣ K 6 2	In this hand the lack of major suit cards is so marked that an opening bid of 5◇ is the best and probably the only—method of obstructing the opposition from finding their own fit.

COUNTERING PRE-EMPTIVE OPENING BIDS

We have now seen what damage an opening pre-emptive bid can do to the opposition, but all too frequently you will find that *you* are in the opposition seats, so it becomes very necessary to use some suitable machinery to prevent yourself from being too much damaged. There is a variety of conventional calls which can be used over opening three bids as a request to partner to take action. No method is perfect, and which ever you decide to use, you will inevitably meet hands where one of the others would have proved more satisfactory on the particular cards. We will look at all the operative conventions, but only the last three can be considered as "reasonable alternatives" and of these three, the ultimate choice lies between the last two.

1. **The Informatory, or Take-Out Double:** The great disadvantage of this is that it removes the business double from the operative list of bids. Suppose the opposition opens 3♡ and you hold this hand:—

♠ A 4
♡ Q 10 8 5 3
◇ A K J 3
♣ 10 5

If, using the Take-Out double, you double 3♡, there is no chance in the world that partner can hold enough strength to leave the double in. He will, as the bid orders him to do, take out into his least repulsive suit, whereupon *you* will probably go down instead of the opposition. So you pass, and get a few measly fifties for it.

2. **The Optional Double:** This is a bid which announces some strength and asks partner to decide from his hand whether to take out or to leave the double in for penalties. It puts far too great an onus on partner who will, for more often than not, make the

wrong decision. If an opening 3♠ is doubled, partner would take out into 4◇ on a hand such as:

♠ 8 3	only to find that his	♠ A Q 9 4
♡ J 5 4	partner had doubled	♡ A 3 2
◇ J 9 7 5 4 2	on . . .	◇ 10 6
♣ A J		♣ K Q 8 4

Some players use a combination of conventions, with the optional double in the protective position, but this has many drawbacks.

These two conventions we can, therefore, discount completely, and they are not included in the "reasonable alternatives". Let us take next:

3. **The Fishbein Convention:** This convention has become almost universally known as "Herbert", and is a bid in the next higher ranking suit as a request for a take out. That is, 3◇ over 3♣, 3♡ over 3◇, 3♠ over 3♡ and, by agreement, either 3 N.T. or 4♣ over 3♠.

The disadvantage of this convention is that it eliminates a natural bid of the next higher ranking suit with hands on which you do not wish to ask for a take-out. Thus, over an opening 3♡ bid you hold:

♠ A Q J 9 5 4	Using Fishbein, you must either bid
♡ 7 5	4♠ at once, or bid 3♠ and follow
◇ A Q 3	it by 4♠ over your partner's take-
♣ 8 3	out, a level which you do not want to
	be forced into on this hand. It is,

however, a widely used and popular convention, but one which I prefer to class as a possible alternative rather than a reasonable one, the real choice lying between Nos.: 4 and 5 which follow.

4. **Lower Available Minor:** This means that over an opening bid of 3♣ you bid 3◇ to request a take-out, and over 3◇, 3♡ or 3♠ you bid 4♣. This leaves free for normal natural bidding the majority of the bids you may wish to make. Any suit bids, other than those in

the minors as set out above, are normal suit bids on hands unsuitable for a take-out request. 3 N.T. can be treated as a natural bid with a desire to play in that contract, and the double can be used as business. All in all this method has a very great deal in its favour, the only natural bids that are sacrificed being 3 ◇ over 3 ♣ and 4 ♣ over any other three-bid.

5. **Three No-Trumps:** This was the original Acol convention, remains popular amongst a very wide field of players, and is still my own choice. It has the merit of simplicity and, in addition to that, it only eliminates one single bid from the range of natural overcalls and that, of course, is the Three No-Trump bid itself which you might possibly want to make on the type of hand suitable for an Acol Opening Three No-Trump bid, expecting to run out on a very long minor suit with sundry "stops" elsewhere. Nor does this bid of Three No-Trumps, used as the take-out demand, stop an ultimate Three No-Trump contract because the responder to it, knowing that the bidder *is strong in the other three suits,* can himself leave it in as the final contract if he holds the necessary stops. If, also, when using this convention, you double an opening three bid, this obviously guarantees a good holding in the suit in addition to other strength, and partner to the doubler, knowing this, can convert the double to 3 N.T. if this appears a more profitable chance at the vulnerability existing.

There may be other very rare types of hand which you would genuinely like to play in Three No-Trumps over an opening three-bid, but in the majority of these cases you will find that you have either a natural suit bid as an alternative or can make a business double of the suit opened. In any case the incidence of these hands is very low. I freely concede that none of these methods is infallible, but I recommend that No: 5, Three No-Trumps for a take-out, should be used, with Lower Available Minor running it a close second.

It goes without saying that with a long and powerful suit in your hand you would bid your suit rather than ask for a take-out.

Let us finish this section by our usual selection of examples, the answers to which are based on the use of 3 N.T. for a take-out.

♠ K 9 7
♡ A K Q 9 5 4
◇ 7 6
♣ J 9

Overcall 3♣ or 3◇ with 3♡. You should always call to the limit of your hand, making a direct game bid if you can. In this case the hand is only worth 3♡ and points an example of how you might be "fixed" against an opening 3◇ playing Fishbein.

♠ K Q 5 2
♡ A 7 3
◇ K J 9 2
♣ A Q

Using 3 N.T. for a take-out you can most certainly double 3◇ or 3♠ for penalties.

♠ A K Q 8 6
♡ A K J 9 3
◇ K 10
♣ 7

On a strong two-suiter like this, bid 3 N.T. for a take-out over 3♣ or 3◇. If partner responds with the other minor you can bid 4♡ which, by inference, asks for preference between the major suits.

♠ A K 8 6
♡ A K Q 4
◇ K Q J 4
♣ 10

Bid 4♣ over 3♣—you don't care what partner's best suit is as long as he has one! Double any other three-bid for penalties.

COUNTERING OPENING WEAK
TWO BIDS

As with the pre-emptive threes, there are a number of ways of dealing with weak opening Two Bids. Any one of the five methods already outlined for dealing with pre-emptive threes can be applied, though the same strictures hold good. For this lower level, however, there is another method available in addition to simple natural bidding, and that is one which was publicised in *The Field* by M. Harrison Gray. It has been tried out and proved very effective, and I offer it to you as the best alternative to natural bidding.

Apart from the full range of natural bids over an opening weak two bid, there are just two bids which are conventional under this method. Both are two-way, or optional for partner to take out or to pass, and both carry with them the requirement of a strong hand, one with four quick tricks or more, good enough to stand a contract at the three or four level:

(a) **A Double** guarantees a minimum of two of the opponent's suit, plus the four or more quick tricks mentioned. Partner, with this knowledge, can very well judge whether to leave the double in for penalties, whether to make a simple take-out, or whether to go for game in his own suit.

(b) **A Bid of Two No-Trumps** guarantees either a singleton or void in opponent's suit plus, again, the quick tricks. The bid may only be left in (or raised to 3 N.T.) on responder's own holding in opponent's suit, or another suit can be bid or jump-bid, according to strength.

In both these cases, partner has the sure knowledge about the opponent's suit and the tricks he can expect from his partner. All other overcalls of an opening two bid are natural and carry their own significance of suit length or strength.

REVISION QUIZ ON CHAPTER 14

1. What would you open, as dealer, on the following hands?

    (a) ♠ K J 9 7 6 4 2: ♡ 9 6: ◇ 10 4: ♣ J 3:
    (b) ♠ J 9 6 3: ♡ K Q 10 9 5 4 3: ◇ 3: ♣ 5:
    (c) ♠ J 4: ♡ 9 6: ◇ A J 9 6 4 3 2: ♣ 6 4:
    (d) ♠ 9 8: ♡ K J 10 9 7 4 2: ◇ 5 4: ♣ 10 6:
    (e) ♠ 4 2: ♡ 9 6: ◇ 8: ♣ A J 9 8 6 5 3 2:

2. If your partner opened the bidding with 3♣ (weak),
what would you bid on the following hands? Your opponents
only are vulnerable, and passed over your partner's 3♣.

    (a) ♠ A Q 10 9 6: ♡ A Q 3 2: ◇ 9: ♣ K 10 4:
    (b) ♠ 8: ♡ A K J 10 8 4 3: ◇ A 6 4: ♣ 9 4:
    (c) ♠ K J 10: ♡ A Q 4: ◇ K 10 9 7: ♣ Q J 3:
    (d) ♠ Q 6 3: ♡ A 10 4: ◇ K 9 6: ♣ J 10 6 3:
    (e) ♠ 8 6: ♡ 9 5 3: ◇ 10 9 8: ♣ K 10 9 6 4:
    (f) ♠ A 10 3: ♡ K 10 5: ◇ Q J 4 2: ♣ K 6 4:

3. Your right-hand opponent deals and opens the bidding
with 3♡ (Acol weak). What would you bid on the following
hands?

    (a) ♠ A K 10 4: ♡ K J 9 6: ◇ A 6 4: ♣ 8 3:
    (b) ♠ A K Q 9 6 5 2: ♡ 5 4: ◇ A 4: ♣ Q 4:
    (c) ♠ 6: ♡ 4 5: ◇ A K Q J 8 4: ♣ K J 4 3:
    (d) ♠ A K Q 6: ♡ 4: ◇ A K 10 8: ♣ A K 6 3:
    (e) ♠ A J 6 4: ♡ K J 9: ◇ Q 9 4: ♣ K 3 2:

4. Your right-hand opponent deals and opens the bidding
with a weak 2♡ bid. What would you bid on the following
hands?

    (a) ♠ A K 9 6: ♡ 8 4: ◇ A 10 6 3: ♣ A 4 2:
    (b) ♠ A K 9 6: ♡ 8: ◇ A 10 6 3: ♣ A 8 4 2:
    (c) ♠ K Q 10 9 6: ♡ A 3 2: ◇ Q 4: ♣ 10 9 6:
    (d) ♠ K 4: ♡ K J 9: ◇ A K Q J 9 6: ♣ A J:
    (e) ♠ A Q 10 9 7 6 4 2: ♡ —: ◇ Q J 3: ♣ K 2:

ANSWERS TO REVISION QUIZ
ON CHAPTER 14

1. (a) 3♠ A perfect pre-emptive opening bid with no support for any other suit or any defensive values.

   (b) No. The four spades rule this out for a pre-emptive opening in hearts, as your support for spades, if partner bids them, is so good.

   (c) 3♢ Here again, you have nothing but the diamonds and are uninterested in anything except getting your obstructive bid in as quickly as you can.

   (d) 3♡ Another typical opening three bid.

   (e) 3♣ Or 4♣, of course, if you have decided on that variation.

2. (a) 3♠ This bid is a slam try in clubs, not a take-out into spades. It agrees clubs as trumps.

   (b) 4♡ An immediate take-out into a game contract in your own suit is your best bet here.

   (c) 3 N.T. With three suits well stopped and a fit in clubs, this contract should be well worth trying.

   (d) No. Just hope that with your support he may even make 3♣!

   (e) 5♣ This is a clear case of the less you have, the more they have. As your right-hand opponent passed the opening 3♣, fourth hand is morally certain to hold a big hand.

   (f) 3 N.T. Again here you have a very good chance of bringing in nine tricks at No-Trumps. Note the club fit.

3. (a) Double. This, of course, is a business double which should be more profitable than trying to find a contract for yourself.

(b) 4♠   Bidding to the limit of your hand, 4♠ is a very reasonable contract on this hand. If he is strong and can envisage a slam, your partner will not consider this as a shut-out bid.

(c) 4◇   It is to prevent the bidding of such a suit that the opening three-bids were developed. This is a hand from actual play. Those who overcalled with 4◇ reached the "cold" 7♣ contract, and those who didn't allowed the 3♡ opening bid to do its full damage.

(d) 4♡   This immediate overcall of opponent's suit means what it would mean at the lower level. In this case you don't care what your partner's best suit is as long as you can find out what it is and play in a game contract in it.

(e) No.   This is the lesser of two evils. If you miss a good contract, well, that's just why Acol advocates the use of pre-emptive opening three bids, and in this case it is your tough luck that you had Acol opponents.

4. (a) Double. Four quick tricks and at least a doubleton of the suit bid. Partner can take what action he sees fit with this knowledge.

(b) 2 N.T. Four quick tricks with not more than a singleton of the suit opened. Again, partner should be able to judge how to bid and will only leave in or raise No Trumps on his own holding in the suit.

(c) 2♠   A normal and natural overcall.

(d) 3 N.T. Here your own stop in hearts plus your long and solid diamonds make this an excellent proposition.

(e) 4♠   A natural bid—in fact, a pre-empt of your own.

CHAPTER 15

Intervening Bids

THERE are no special conventions or bids which belong solely to the Acol system when it comes to defensive and intervening bidding. Such bids, therefore, cannot be classed as basic Acol, though no book on the subject could be complete without mention of the Acol player's policy in this respect.

In general, Acol players continue to carry out their policy that the best form of defence is attack and, if the opposition has gone into the attack first, to counter-attack as often and as freely as possible. The more you intervene, the more opportunities you create for the opposition to go astray, but this does *not* mean that you should stick your neck out and risk incurring huge penalties when there is no possibility of gain to your side.

A SIMPLE OVERCALL

When the opposition opens the bidding you have to decide whether or not to make an overcall, so you must make a quick estimate of your hand for playing strength. It is a trifle easier to estimate the position at duplicate than it is at rubber bridge because at duplicate each board is a separate entity, and a disaster incurred on one board at Match Pointed Pairs carries with it no worse than a "bottom", whereas at rubber bridge it will have to be added to any further disasters, or opportunities for recuperating may not occur. Broadly speaking, though, you should not risk incurring a penalty greater than the points the other side can gain. A non-vulnerable game is worth 300 bonus points and a vulnerable game 500 bonus points, so 3 N.T. bid and made will score 400 if not vulnerable and 600 if vulnerable. Obviously, then, to risk being doubled and going down more than these amounts is idiotic if you are not vulnerable and the worst sort of insanity if you are.

To make a vulnerable overcall at the one-level you should be able to see five playing tricks, and four if not vulnerable. In other words, you should have not more than two playing tricks short of your bid if vulnerable and three short if not vulnerable. If you are contemplating bidding at the two-level, you should be at least one trick stronger in either case.

It is important, too, to make your overcall in the suit:

(a) In which you can afford to play

and

(b) Which you would like your partner to lead if you become the defenders.

Remember, too, that if you allow the bidding to get too high before making your intervening call, you may miss the opportunity of bidding altogether.

Another point I should like to make is the stupidity of suddenly coming into the auction with a bid at too high a level when you are not even strong enough to make an Acol Light Opening. With North-South vulnerable, I heard this sequence the other day:

N.	E.	S.	W.
No	1♠	No	2♡
3♣	?		

With the opposition both bidding in the majors, with partner having passed, and at adverse vulnerability, why should

179

North feel able to produce a 3♣ bid at this stage when he could not open 1♣, let alone 3♣? A major-suit game would have scored 420 points for East-West whereas the double, which East did not need much imagination to make, netted 800 points. This sort of bidding is sticking your neck out with a vengeance. This is, however, a digression, so let us return to the simple overcalls and their indications.

An overcall may be made with the express intention of contesting the auction yourself, or it may be to suggest a lead to partner. It may be merely of nuisance value, to deprive the opponents of a round of bidding. If you intervene with 2♣ over 1◇ for example, you stop opener's partner from responding in hearts or spades at the one-level, but to overcall 1♠ with 2♣ does not upset their bidding at all, as it would have had to be carried to the two-level in any case. Remember this, and try to strike a happy medium between the risks of your losses and the chances of your gains.

With length or strength only in the suit opponents have bid, your best course is to pass. If opener's partner passes, your partner may be able to take some action, and you may well get the opportunity of making a penalty double if opponents bid higher in their suit. To overcall in No Trumps implies a strong hand containing at least 15 points with a good stop in the suit opened, and an immediate double would be taken as a request for a take-out by your partner. (See Chapter 17).

♠ K Q 9 8 7 ♡ 7 5 ◇ Q 8 6 ♣ A 9 2	If opponent bids 1◇ or 1♡, overcall with 1♠. This does not raise the level of the bidding.
♠ 9 7 ♡ K J 7 ◇ K Q 10 9 5 3 ♣ A J	If opponent opens either 1♡ or 1♠ you are strong enough to intervene at the two-level with 2◇.

180

♠ K 10 7
♡ A J 7
◇ Q 6 5
♣ Q 8 6 5

Whatever opponent may open, don't be tempted into making a call on this balanced type of hand. It will make a good defensive hand but not an attacking one. Keep quiet and hope that they will bid too high. To intervene would probably only *prevent* them from bidding too high.

♠ A 8
♡ K J 7 6 5
◇ Q 9 5
♣ 9 6 2

If opponent opens 1♡, *pass*. A bid of 1 N.T. would imply a 16—18 point hand, and a double is asking partner for a take-out—the last thing you want. You can make a penalty double later if they call on in hearts.

Finally, here are two hands which make an interesting comparison. The first qualifies for an opening bid but not an overcall, and the second qualifies for an overcall but not an opening bid.

♠ A 7 2
♡ A 6 4
◇ J 9 5
♣ A 10 9 3

Here you have 13 points, a "must" for a weak 1 N.T. opening, but an overcall would be quite unacceptable. To overcall in clubs at the two-level, bid either 1 N.T. or make an informatory double would be insane.

♠ K J 9 7 5 3
♡ A 6 2
◇ 9 4 3
♣ 6

This hand is not even worth an Acol light opener, but it has all the qualifications for an overcall of 1♠ over any suit bid. Note the difference between these two examples. For an overcall, the point count is less important than the playing strength.

BALANCING BIDS

If you are sitting fourth-in-hand when the dealer opens and both your partner and the opener's partner pass, you are justified in re-opening the bidding on a very moderate hand. Opener's partner is now known to be so weak that he could not raise even a bid of

1 N.T. and if, for example, the dealer opened 1 ♡, your partner may have passed holding something like the hand in our last example. As we have seen, he could not overcall the opening 1 ♡ and to hear a balancing double from you, which he can pass, will be just what he is praying for!

This type of bidding position is known as balancing because your own bid is made to *balance* your partner's pass in the light of the knowledge that opener's partner is exceedingly weak. The values required for a bid in this position are largely a matter of partnership understanding. They differ, however, from ordinary second-in-hand overcalls and the following can be considered as more or less standard practice.

A 1 N.T. balancing bid may be made on as little as 10—11 points provided this includes a stop as good as Q J x x or K 10 x x in the opponent's suit. A double in the balancing position should always be a strong bid containing a minimum of 11 + or 12 points. The reason for this is more fully discussed on p. 226 of Chapter 17 on doubling. The weakest balancing bid is a simple overcall in a new suit, and this may be made on as little as 8—9 points.

The partner of a player who makes a bid in the balancing position should bear in mind the possibly limited values and should slightly underbid his own hand to compensate for this.

♠ A J 9 6 4
♡ J 5 2
◇ J 7
♣ Q J 9
East

Bidding:
S. W. N. E.
1♡ — — ?

On this hand East, as fourth caller after two passes, can make a simple take-out into 1♠. Change the hand slightly though, say by the inclusion of the

◇ K in place of the fifth spade, and he would double, sincerely hoping that his partner's pass was based on strength in hearts. If this should be the case, West will leave the double in, and very profitable it should prove!

JUMP OVERCALLS

If you have a strong hand and are contemplating making an overcall with a view to securing the contract for your own side, it is not enough to make a simple overcall. One method of dealing with this type of hand is to make an Informatory or Take-Out Double, and we shall be discussing this bid later. Meanwhile let us confine ourselves to the hands where this method is not satisfactory.

When the bulk of your strength is concentrated in one or two suits, you should make a Jump Overcall, that is, a bid of one more than is necessary for a simple overcall. 1♡—2♠, or 1♡—3◇ are both jump over-calls, and to make such a bid you should hold at least one strong and long prospective trump suit and the promise of eight playing tricks. The bid is not forcing but is obviously highly encouraging and your partner, knowing that you are strong, will make every effort to respond.

You can make a jump overcall on a good two-suiter as well as on single suited hands. It is better to do this than to use a Take-Out Double, as this can often lose you time, apart from allowing the opposition—who may also be playing Acol!—to obstruct you with a high limit bid in their own suit. A few examples should make this position clear.

Whatever suit opponent opens, you are too strong for a simple overcall and should make a jump bid of 2♡ over 1♣ or 1◇, or 3♡ over 1♠.

♠ 7
♡ A K 10 8 4 3
◇ A Q J 9 7
♣ 8

Over opponent's 1♣ make a jump bid of 2♡ and later, if the opportunity occurs, show your diamonds, and your partner will give you preference.

A jump overcall in a minor suit may encourage your partner to try a No Trump game contract if he has suitable stops in the opponent's suit. This last hand is an example

♠ 8
♡ K J 7
◇ A Q 5
♣ A K Q 10 8 6

where you should bid 3♣ over an opening 1♠, and don't start saying you can't leave a No Trump contract in on this hand—partner, if he bids it, will have done so in the light of his

knowledge of your hand. You have not promised him any guard in spades. You have promised at least one long and strong suit and some outside strength, and this you have got.

PRE-EMPTIVE OVERCALLS

Pre-emptive overcalls are made for exactly the same purpose as pre-emptive opening bids, that is, to deprive the opposition of bidding space. Just as with the opening pre-emptive bids, partner should recognise that the hand is weak except in the suit bid. A single jump in a suit is, as we have seen, a strong bid, and a pre-emptive bid is made by a jump of at least one more level than is necessary for a strong bid.

♠ K Q 8 7 5 4 3 2
♡ 9
◇ 5 2
♣ 6 4

Overcall any opening bid with 3♠, not 2♠. You have none of the requirements for a strong jump over-call, yet all the requirements for a pre-emptive opening bid of 3♠ if

you had been allowed to get it in first.

Just as you were told to open with 4♡ or 4♠ on stronger hands of the same character, so you may make a similar pre-emptive jump overcall to four, which there is no chance of your partner misunderstanding.

♠ K Q J 10 8 6 4 3
♡ 7
◇ 9 5
◇ 7 4

Overcall any opening suit bid made
by the opposition with a jump to 4♠.
What have you got to lose? You have
a hopeless defensive hand, very little
risk of going badly down, and you
may well prevent their game or even slam contract.

NO-TRUMP OVERCALLS

You may only use the bid of 1 N.T. as an immediate
overcall on one specific type of hand, and that is a
balanced hand containing *at least* one good stop in
opponent's suit, and as strong as 15 points as a minimum. You must not make the bid merely to show your
partner that you have a stop in opponent's suit, but
also to tell him of your strength and willingness to play
in No Trumps, either at a part score or in game if he
is strong enough to raise. On either of these two hands
you can overcall 1♠ with 1 N.T.

♠ A J 3
♡ K 10 8
◇ K Q J 8
♣ Q 8 7

♠ K Q 5
♡ Q 10 9 6
◇ Q J 8 7
♣ A Q

Never be tempted into de-valuing this bid or you may
easily find yourself caught and helplessly trapped by a
double from opener's partner on your left.

FORCING OVERCALLS

The use of an immediate overcall in the suit opened
by an opponent has been modified in recent years. It
is now a strong bid, forcing for at least one round, and
partner must respond as he would to a take-out double
on the first round. Thereafter he must use his own
judgment, subject, of course, to his knowledge of the

strength of his partner's hand and that it is unsuitable for a take-out double. A minimum rebid by the original forcer may be passed on complete weakness unless the forcer makes a repeat bid in the opponent's suit.

An advantage this bid has over a take-out double on some types of hands is that it avoids the danger of a penalty pass from responder.

♠ A K 10 9 8 6 3
♡ 9
♢ A J 9
♣ K 8

Overcall an opening 1♡ with 2♡ and, over partner's probable 3♣ or 3♢ response bid 3♠, the minimum level. This *may* be passed but won't except on extreme weakness.

♠ K J 10 9 6
♡ A Q J 6 2
♢ K Q 3
♣ —

Bid 2♣ over an opening 1♣. If partner bids 2♢ make the repeat force of 3♣, indicating a major two-suiter. If he can't go direct to game, pass his rebid.

♠ A K 9 8 7
♡ 5
♢ A
♣ K Q J 9 8 6

Bid 2♢ over 1♢ or 2♡ over 1♡. To partner's probable reply in the other red suit, bid clubs, indicating a black two-suiter. He should give preference to spades if that suits him best.

TWO NO-TRUMP OVERCALL

An overcall of Two No-Trumps over opponent's opening One No-Trump is a conventional one. It is a specialised Acol bid, forcing to game, and demands that partner should show his best suit. If he holds two suits of approximately the same strength he bids the lower ranking one first, to facilitate the bidding.

The type of hand on which to make this Two No-Trump over-call is one which it is extremely difficult to bid in any other way. A double of a One No-Trump opening bid is always for business and will only be taken out by the doubler's partner on weakness or distribution—or when the partnership has slam expectations. A double, therefore, cannot be used to ask for information from partner and the immediate Two No-Trump overcall takes its place, with the difference that it is forcing to game. Strong two-suiters are virtually impossible to handle in any other way.

♠ A   If your right-hand opponent opens
♡ A K J 9 7 4   1 N.T., overcall with 2 N.T. Partner
◇ —   will now show his best suit but, being
♣ A Q 10 7 3 2   obliged to keep the bidding open to
               game, you can now bid this wonderful
two-suiter at leisure, with time to discover the best fit.

RESPONSES TO OVERCALLS

This is a department of bidding where a very great many errors are made, and it should be well worth your while to make sure you fully understand the Acol attitude of mind on the matter. This is based—as indeed the whole of the system is—on the fact that Acol players bid their cards to the full and do not wait for their partners to bid them.

In the first place, if you have read the earlier pages of this chapter, you will have realised that there are a number of ways in which your partner, in the over-caller's position, can announce that he has a particularly good or strong or distributional hand. He can double or bid One No-Trump. He can make a jump overcall, a "pre-empt", or an immediate overcall in opponent's suit. If, therefore, he has done none of these things but has merely made a simple overcall, he has none of the appropriate hands and there is not the same urgency for you to "find a response" on minimum values as there would be if you were responding to an opening bid. It may be expedient to find a response, of course, as obstruction to the opposition, but you must never lose sight of the fact that, in making only a simple overcall, partner is using one of the basic principles of Acol and is denying the strength to make a better bid.

Another fact to remember is that an overcall, generally at the one-level, (1♡—1♠) and always at the two-level (1♡—2◇) will be made on a minimum of a five-card suit, so that a direct raise in partner's suit can be given on three-card trump support—always provided, of course, that you have the necessary playing strength outside. The only objects in responding to a simple overcall are either to obstruct, or if the hand offers a reasonable chance of a game or part-score to your own side.

Do not, however, fall into the error of *underbidding* in response to an overcall. Your partner's overcall will be at least the equivalent of an opening bid or will have compensating features, so if you have values equivalent to a reasonable response to an opening bid, show them.

A point which cannot be emphasised too strongly is that *a change of suit on the part of responder who has passed originally is not forcing*, and opener need not bid again as he would have to do if it were a response made to an opening bid before an original pass. Once you have got this into your head you will see that the use of the Limit Bids, that is, the direct raises in partner's suit, are vitally important in this position. Suppose you dealt and passed originally on this hand:—

♠ K 8 7 5 4
♡ 7
◇ A 8 6 4
♣ Q J 6

You are North and the bidding goes:

N.	E.	S.	W.
No	1♡	2◇	2♡
?			

If you had not already passed, and if partner had been the opener, you would have bid 1 ♠ over his opening 1 ◇, hoping to find a major suit contract in spite of your diamond fit. Now, having once passed, you dare not show your spades. Partner may pass, feeling quite unable to bid to 3 ◇ unsupported. Give instead a direct raise to 3 ◇—your hand is well worth it. Furthermore, never "rescue" your partner in this position if he has not been doubled, just for the sake of bidding a suit of your own. If you have something really worth showing, show it, of course. Acol never says that you should sit silent if you have a good bid. But settle first and foremost, in this position, for a direct raise in partner's suit if you have it.

REVISION QUIZ ON CHAPTER 15

1. At score Love All, assume that your right-hand opponent, the dealer, has opened the bidding with 1♡. What would you bid on the following hands?

   (a) ♠ A Q J 7 4 2: ♡ 9 4: ◇ K 8 2: ♣ 5 4:

   (b) ♠ K J 9 8 7 4 2: ♡ 5: ◇ A 9 6: ♣ 10 4:

   (c) ♠ Q J 10 9 7 4: ♡ A 3 2: ◇ Q 9 6: ♣ 4:

   (d) ♠ A 10 9 :♡ K J 9: ◇ K Q 6 4: ♣ A 10 4:

   (e) ♠ K Q J 10 7 4 2: ♡ A: ◇ A 10 4: ♣ K 3:

   (f) ♠ 7 4: ♡ 8: ◇ A Q J 9 6 5 3 2: ♣ K 4:

   (g) ♠ A 10 9 7 4 2: ♡ —: ◇ Q 4 3: ♣ K 10 6 3:

   (h) ♠ A 4: ♡ A K Q: ◇ K Q 10 9 6 4: ♣ K 3:

   (i) ♠ K Q 10: ♡ K 10 5: ◇ A 4 2: ♣ K J 6 5:

   (j) ♠ K 10 4: ♡ 8 4: ◇ A K J 9 3: ♣ Q 4 3:

   (k) ♠ A K Q 6 5 4 3: ♡ K 3: ◇ 8 4: ♣ 3 2:

   (l) ♠ A K Q 10 7 5: ♡ —: ◇ A K Q 4 3: ♣ 6 3:

   (m) ♠ A 4 3: ♡ 9: ◇ K 9 8 7 4: ♣ K 10 6 3:

   (n) ♠ A J 6: ♡ Q J 4: ◇ A Q 4: ♣ K J 3 2:

   (o) ♠ 5: ♡ 6: ◇ 7 6 5: ♣ A Q J 9 7 5 3 2:

   (p) ♠ K 7 3: ♡ —: ◇ K Q 10 7 4 3 2: ♣ Q 9 6:

2. With North the dealer, the bidding has gone:—

         N.   E.   S.   W.
         1♠ No No ?

What would you, as West, bid on the following hands?

   (a) ♠ 9 4: ♡ A K J 9 4: ◇ J 10 6: ♣ Q 6 4:

   (b) ♠ K J 9: ♡ Q 9 6 4: ◇ A J 4: ♣ 10 9 8:

   (c) ♠ 10 6: ♡ K Q 9 5: ◇ K J 9 4: ♣ A 4 3:

   (d) ♠ —: ♡ K 10 9 6: ◇ K Q 8 6 4: ♣ K J 9 6:

   (e) ♠ 7: ♡ Q 10 6: ◇ A K 10 9 4 3: ♣ Q 10 5:

   (f) ♠ Q 10 6: ♡ K 9 4 2: ◇ K 10 6 2: ♣ J 5:

3. Assume that your right-hand opponent has opened the bidding with 1 N.T. (weak). What would you bid on the following hands?

    (a) ♠ A 4: ♡ K Q J 9 6 3: ◇ K Q 10 9 4: ♣ —:

    (b) ♠ A K Q J 9 8 4: ♡ 8 7: ◇ 9 6: ♣ 6 3:

    (c) ♠ J: ♡ 8: ◇ A K Q 7 6 4: ♣ A K Q 9 5:

    (d) ♠ K J 8: ♡ A Q 7 2: ◇ K 10 6: ♣ Q J 10:

    (e) ♠ A K J 7 6 4: ♡ A Q 10 9 3: ◇ 5: ♣ 7:

4. The bidding, with North the dealer, has gone :—

        N.   *E.*   *S.*   *W.*
        1♠   2◇   No   ?

What do you, West, bid on the following hands?

    (a) ♠ K J 3: ♡ J 9 6 4: ◇ K 10: ♣ Q 10 4 3:

    (b) ♠ 9: ♡ K 4 3: ◇ Q J 7 6 2: ♣ 10 9 8 2:

    (c) ♠ Q 9 4: ♡ Q 4 3: ◇ J 7 4 2: ♣ 10 6 2:

    (d) ♠ A: ♡ K Q 8: ◇ Q J 9 7 5: ♣ 9 8 7 6:

ANSWERS TO REVISION QUIZ
ON CHAPTER 15

1. (a) 1♠ A simple overcall at the one-level on a hand which would make an opening bid of 1♠ in any case.

(b) 3♠ A weak pre-emptive "interference" bid.

(c) 1♠ Another perfectly normal overcall at the one-level.

(d) 1 N.T. An evenly balanced 17 points with a good stop in the suit opened.

(e) 2♡ A forcing overcall on a hand which is unsuitable for a take-out double.

(f) 4♢ Pre-emptive on a hand completely worthless in defence.

(g) 1♠ A simple overcall on a hand just worth an opening bid of 1♠.

(h) 2♡ Forcing again.

(i) 1 N.T. Another evenly balanced hand typically suitable for this bid.

(j) 2♢ A hand just strong enough for a simple overcall at the two-level.

(k) 2♠ A jump overcall, for which the hand just qualifies as it holds the ♡K over the opening bid.

(l) 2♡ Forcing, to give yourself the certain chance to show both these beautiful suits.

(m) No. Not strong enough to bid diamonds at the two-level, as even not vulnerable this could cost you a packet.

(n) 1 N.T. By far the best bid on this hand.

(o) 4♣ Having no defence to either of the major suits and no interest in any other suit as trumps, make the maximum possible interference bid at once.

(p) 4♢ Here again you want to interfere to the limit

before the opposition finds its own best
contract.

2. (a) 2♡   A simple take-out into a new suit.

(b) 1 N.T. You are justified in re-opening the bidding
on a lower point count than normally
required for this bid.

(c) Double. If your partner passed with a good holding
in spades and can leave the double in, it
should prove most profitable.

(d) Double. You do *not* bid 2◇ on a hand like this. If
partner passed on good spades, defending
should at least be good fun, and you like
any suit if he makes a take-out.

(e) 2◇   A take-out into your own good suit.

(f) No.   Here your best bet is to pass. It is unlikely
that your partner passed on good spades
and a 2♣ take-out would be embarrassing
on your hand.

3. (a) 2 N.T. The Acol game-forcing overcall. A double
would be "business", and you want to play
this in hearts or diamonds.

(b) No.   You will be on lead if the opposition play
in 1 N.T. and should take the first seven
tricks in spades. If you double they will
almost certainly escape into a suit contract.

(c) 2 N.T. Another example of this forcing bid, designed
to give you time to show both diamonds and
clubs.

(d) Double. Your 16 points all lie over the opening
bidder who will probably find it quite
impossible to make his contract. Your
partner will only take out on complete
weakness or if he thinks you have a slam on
yourself.

(e) 2 N.T. You don't want to defend a No Trump
contract on this sort of hand, but you *do*
want to play in spades or hearts.

4. (a) 2 N.T. If partner can overcall at the two-level, you must tell him that your own hand is far from worthless. You would not make this bid without a good stop in the suit opened and some fit with partner's suit.

(b) 3♢ Your hand is worth this raise and North will probably find it impossible to rebid 3♠ unsupported, whereas he might well bid 2♠ if left to himself. When you then come in, South may be able to compete.

(c) No. Pass and hope that partner is allowed to play in 2♢. If North bids 2♠ you can come in with 3♢ on the next round.

(d) 2♠ A cue bid, "setting the suit" as diamonds. (It might also be a Directional Asking Bid—see Chapter 20).

Forcing Responses

WHEN your partner makes an opening bid you immediately have to look at your hand, not with a view to opening the bidding, but as responder with the knowledge that your partner has sufficient strength, even if only an Acol Light Opener, to start the auction. You may see that you have so little that you can only just bid 1 N.T.—or even pass— but, on the other hand, you may say to yourself: "Well, if partner can open the bidding, we must have *at least* a game on between us." Apart from a direct raise to game in your partner's suit, for which your hand may be quite unsuitable, none of the Limit Bids will be any good to you now because, as you know, they are not forcing and partner, with an Acol Light Opener, is at liberty to pass. So now it is necessary to find a new bid, one which will compel your partner to keep the bidding open at least to game however weak his opening bid, and this is done by way of a Forcing Take-Out. This is a bid of a new suit at a level of one higher than is necessary. 1♠—3◇, or 1♣—2♡ are examples, and these responses are *unconditionally forcing until at least a game contract has been reached*. Opener, hearing such a force, should not immediately take fright if he has a weak hand. Playing Acol, his partner is well aware of just how weak it may be, and all opener need now do is to keep the bidding open as commanded while concentrating on telling the truth, the whole truth, and nothing but the truth, about his hand.

This Chapter is primarily about forcing take-out bids, but this seems a good moment to expand just a little on opener's actions. Too many slams are missed because opener, having a weak hand, refuses to revalue it in the light of partner's force which comes well and truly under the heading of telling the truth.

♠ Q 7
♡ Q 9 5
♢ 6
♣ A K 8 7 5 4 3

Suppose for instance that you have, as all good Acol players should, opened the bidding with 1♣ on this hand. Your partner forces with 2♠ and you rightly rebid 3♣, which confirms length in clubs at any rate. It was because of your major suit holdings, of course, that you refrained from opening 3♣ (or 4♣) in the first place. Well, after your 3♣ rebid, partner rebids 3♡—what do you do now? Sign off with a further rebid in clubs? Not on your life you don't! You have already made a truthful opening bid and rebid, so now the least you can do, holding Q 7 of one of your partner's suits and Q 9 5 of the other, is to tell him of his luck. Raise his heart bid to 4♡. Again, before we leave this example, change your hand by just one card:—

♠ Q 7
♡ Q 9 5
♢ 6
♣ A K Q J 5 3 2

You will, of course, open 1♣, and once again you hear your partner force with 2♠. You remember this one, don't you? A jump rebid in a forcing situation such as we have here guarantees a long and solid trump suit of your own, self-supporting and with no losers. Tell partner at once that he need have no fears about his probable lack of support for your clubs by making the jump rebid of 4♣.

After that little diversion, let us return to responder's forcing take-out. Obviously there must be more than one type of hand calling for the use of such a bid but these cannot be tied to arbitrary rules and point counts. To say that you must *always* force on 17 points, or *never* force on less than 16 points is only to impose the straight-jacket which Acol seeks to avoid, and although there are guiding indications, the final decision must be left to judgment of the individual situation. The one emphatic rule which can be given without equivocation is **always force on a hand where game is certain and slam is possible.** The delayed game raise dealt with later in this Chapter is not a contradiction of this as it is made on hands where, although responder is determined to try for game, he is not certain which way the hand is going, and wants to hear opener's rebid.

A typical forcing response situation arises when you have a hand with good support for your partner's suit plus a strong side-suit of your own which can be used for discards of partner's losers and which, subject to his holding certain controls, may well be worth a slam bid. Take, for example, this hand, when partner opens 1 ♠ :—

♠ Q 8 6 5
♡ K 7
◇ A K Q 9 6 4
♣ 5

Although this hand contains only one Ace (and many of the old school would refuse to force with less than two Aces) and it only has 14 points, it would be madness not to force.

Partner only needs to hold the ♡A in addition to his spade suit to make a small slam in spades an odds-on certainty while, even if he has opened on the lightest of light openers, you will reach your contract for the sure game in spades.

Here is a hand from actual play which illustrates a forcing situation as well as our point regarding opener's rebids. It occurred in a Duplicate Pairs, and only two of the nine pairs bid the slam in diamonds. With East-West vulnerable, West

	West		East
♠	9	♠	A K Q J 2
♡	9 7 2	♡	A Q
◇	A Q 10 6 5 2	◇	J 9 4
♣	A K 4	♣	9 7 3

opened 1◇ and North butted in with 1♡. At only two tables did East visualise the possibilities of the situation and force with 2♠. East has 17 points, it is true, but two of these are not very fruitful ones—at least for the moment. The staringly important feature of the hand is the spade suit. Over 2♠ West rightly rebid 3◇. Now, of course, East's J to three diamonds becomes valuable support. At one of the two tables where the slam was bid East took matters into her own hands and bid 4 N.T., following with 6◇ when opener showed two Aces but, provided partner can be trusted, there is no need to take this action at this point. Opener has heard a force and has made a rather neutral 3◇ bid which at least affirms length in diamonds, so anything further he can now show will not be misleading. Over his 3◇ at the other table East, knowing that the bidding was safe for a game contract, merely raised to 4◇ whereupon, the bid costing nothing at all, West cue-bid his ♣A, after which East bid a direct 6◇.

Let us, however, look at another aspect of this situation.

♠ 5
♡ A K 10 6 3
◇ K Q 10
♣ K Q 5 3

Here, when partner opens 1♠, still with 17 points, it would be as mad to force on the first round as, in the previous case, it would be mad not to. Why? Because that all-important fit is missing, at least as far as you know at the moment, and if partner's hand is an Acol Light Opener based on spades, you are not going to get very far. Bid a quiet 2♡ and await developments. Change the hand very slightly, though, by moving just one Queen. Make the spades Q 5 and the diamonds K 10, thus:—

♠ Q 5
♡ A K 10 6 3
◇ K 10
♣ K Q 5 3

The same 17-count, but now the hand is by no means a mis-fit. If partner has an Acol Light Opener based on spades, then this time you can well stand a sign-off into 3♠ which you

will raise to 4♠, so you can afford to force. Opener's almost certain six-card suit supported by your ♠ Q 5 and the rest of your honour tricks makes game as nearly sure as any contract can be.

There are occasions when you should force with even a mis-fit. It goes without saying, of course, that

198

you may pick up a hand so big that you don't care how light partner's hand is, or how little fit he has for your suit, and your only query is whether to play in a small or a grand slam. But these hands come once in a blue moon, and you can want to force on a much lesser hand—a strong two-suiter, for instance. Suppose you find yourself holding:

♠ 9
♡ A K 8 6 3
◇ A K 9 7 5
♣ K 10

You may well be surprised to hear your partner open the bidding but, alas, he chooses the almost inevitable 1♠, your singleton suit. However, if you can find even a *slight* fit with one of your suits you can feel certain of game and possibly of slam. Unless his spade suit is solid, you most certainly have grave misgivings about allowing this hand to be played in spades, either at a game or a slam contract, so don't force on the first round. Take it easy again, and bid 2♡. If partner signs off with 2♠ you can bid 4◇, which is still a force even if it were not bid on the first round. You have a count of 17 points and partner should now have a complete picture of your hand — at least nine and probably ten red cards, with high honours in both suits, and certainly no more than a singleton spade. If partner, with this knowledge, can still only repeat spades then, even though reluctantly, you can still abandon the bidding at 4♠. At least you know that your winners will take care of a number of his losers, and surely the less support he has for your suits, the more spades he will have himself. Let us suppose, though, that his hand is this:—

♠ K Q 10 8 6 5 3
♡ 9 5
◇ Q 10 6
♣ A

Even anyone who is only a faintly imaginative bidder, having once shown the nature of his hand by his first rebid, must at some stage come to life and realise that three small cards of either of partner's suits must have strong playing value, and that he must give preference for one or the other, as a game contract in that suit is almost certain to be safer than one in his own suit, even though it is six or seven cards long. Having, however, not only three, but three to the Q 10, the position becomes even stronger, and you should learn to look at such holdings with the eyes of hope. Always, too, place a value on an additional King or Queen, even if it is only a singleton (let alone a card that the other side have not got) as a strong filling-in card, if you are able to give preference with three of the other suit.

You may well pick up a two-suiter even stronger than the one we have just discussed, with which we did not feel strong enough to force on the first round. Suppose you held:

♠ —
♡ K 10 7
◇ A K Q 9 5
♣ A K J 8 4

Partner—needless to say—opens 1♠. Fit or no fit, and it's certainly no fit on this occasion, you can force on the first round with 3◇, and show your clubs on the next round. A game you must, and intend, to bid, however weak your partner's opening.

If the bulk of your values lies in one long strong suit you should force on the first round whenever you can, as otherwise you may find yourself in difficulties on the next round, being unable to find a bid which expresses your values properly. Just for the sake of being different, let's have partner opening 1◇ this time, and you hold:

♠ 10 7
♡ A K Q J 7 4
◇ 6 2
♣ A 8 6

14 points and no real support for partner's diamonds yet, if you only bid 1♡ and partner rebids 1♠ or 2◇, what bid can you possibly make to get yourself out of trouble? 3♡ only

means good long hearts, and may be passed by opener, and if you jump directly into 4♡ you may well find that you have missed a certain slam. If you try 4 N.T. you may equally well find yourself playing in 5♡ one off, so make your force at once.

Here is another hand from actual play which illustrates this particular point. It comes from a Duplicate Pairs, and all the

♠ 4
♡ A Q J 10 9 6
◇ K 5 4
♣ K 3 2

players who made an immediate force in hearts over partner's 1♣ ended in 6♡ making all thirteen tricks. Those who made a simple take-out of 1♡ ended in 4♡, missing the slam. Opener's hand, though minimum, contained three Aces which, in view of the force, he was confidently able to see as three first-round controls, meriting the 6♡ contract.

The conclusion we arrive at from these last two examples is that if you have a mainly single-suited hand with enough values elsewhere to give good promise of game, force even without support for partner. The yardstick here should be in the region of 13 or 14 points.

Similarly, with good support for partner's suit and a reasonable suit of your own, the fewer cards you will have in the other two suits so again, you can force at once. The force does not, in fact, lose time, but gains it, because once it has been made you can explore at leisure, without fear of being passed out below game. A couple of examples here should make this clear. Back to partner opening 1♠, and on either of these two hands you should force in your own suit, not make a jump bid in spades:

♠ K Q 8 5 3   ♠ A 9 6 3 2
♡ A K Q 7 4 2   ♡ —
◇ 9   ◇ A Q J 10 8 6
♣ 6   ♣ K 5

Without the fit, be careful. You may need to force to be sure of reaching your game contract, but you may well be better off making just a simple over-call to begin with.

On a balanced hand you should generally choose to force on about 16 or 17 points or, later on, you may find it difficult to persuade your partner that you are as strong as you are. This does *not*, as I have already pointed out, mean that you should force on all 16 or 17 point hands, and a mis-fit with the opening bid is the exception, as in this example:—

♠ 6
♡ A Q J 7 5
◇ A Q J 7
♣ K 8 3

Consider what happens if you force with 3♡ over 1♠ and partner rebids 3♠. You cannot bid 4◇ without giving up the chance of playing the hand in 3 N.T. and, for all your 17 points, the hand may not run to game in either of the majors, and 5◇ is an awful lot to make! So don't force. Bid 2♡, and over a weak sign-off of 2♠ you can now bid 3 N.T. which is probably all the hand will be worth. If partner makes anything other than a weak rebid, you are in a position to take very much stronger action.

Sometimes you may find yourself holding a hand with all the qualifications for a force and no suit to force in. This can happen when your only suit is the one partner has opened. This is one of the moments when you cannot—*dare* not—use a Limit Bid which partner may pass. Suppose partner opens the bidding with 1♡ and you hold:—

♠ A K 8
♡ K J 9 5 6
◇ J 8
♣ A Q 6

This is a thing that can happen to all of us. You have 18 points and, far from being allergic to the opening bid, you are enthusiastic about it, but clearly you cannot risk making a direct raise in hearts. In these circumstances you "manufacture" a force in a suit in which you have some good holding, in this case clubs. You must *never* make this type of force in a suit in which you have no good cards: on this hand you must not even consider forcing in diamonds. You must also avoid, apart from the most exceptional circumstances, forcing in a suit which is higher ranking than the one opened by partner. The reason for this is that opener, with a liking for the suit you choose to force in, may insist on putting you back into it, in which case the situation may develop where you are being given preference to a suit you do not, in fact, prefer, which might occur on this hand if you forced in spades. If, however, you force in clubs, you can return partner to hearts every time he tries to insist on clubs, until he gets the idea.

Just once in another blue moon you may get caught with a hand like this when partner opens 1♣:—

♠ Q 6   This is a horrible situation—if it
♡ A K 8   is ever horrible in any circum-
♢ A Q 6   stances to hold 20 points!—
♣ K Q 9 6 5 because you cannot find a suit
             lower-ranking than clubs in which
to make your force. So you force in diamonds, and try to go straight into 4 N.T. on your next bid. Make your spades A Q 6 and your diamonds Q 6 on this hand, though, and there is nothing you can do except force in a major you haven't got, in which case probably the safest thing you can do is to make a direct bid of 4 N.T. You can, however, force in a non-existent major suit provided that your hand is such that you don't mind the prospect of removing all your partner's enthusiastic raises in your major, including the final slam contract, into No Trumps.

To sum up, it is impossible to set rigid standards for a hand on which to force, but you should always do so when game is certain and slam is possible. Likely situations are:

(a) Hands containing good support for partner plus a strong side-suit which may be used for discards of losers.

(b) Mainly single-suited hands, containing one long suit and some outside values, which will be difficult to rebid otherwise.

(c) Hands with outstanding support for partner's

suit and a good side-suit, giving shortages in the other two suits.

(d) Two-suiters strong enough to demand a game contract whether or not a good fit can be found.

(e) Hands with 16 or more balanced points where there is, *ipso facto*, support for partner's suit.

(f) Any hand on which, for these or any other reasons, you know where you are going and are determined to play in at least a game contract and possibly a slam.

THE DELAYED GAME RAISE

Whilst not a direct game force, there is one other responding bid which falls into place here, and that is the Delayed Game Raise. The indications for this bid are good trump support, good honour strength, and yet not quite enough for an immediate game force. The main feature to be borne in mind is that responder, although he intends the hand to be played in a game, is not yet sure just where it is going and wants first to hear his partner's rebid. Thus the first response is strictly an exploratory bid, and two sequences to illustrate the delayed game raise might be:

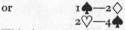

This is a 13-point hand which does not justify a force opposite a 1♠ opener on the first round, on any of the grounds we have considered. On the other hand, it is not the type of hand on which you want to make a Limit Bid. If you temporise with a bid of 2♣ he may rebid 2—or even 3◇, whereupon you are virtually certain a slam will be "on". If, however, he rebids either 2♠ or 2♡, you now make a direct raise to game in spades—a delayed game raise because in these circumstances you meant the hand to be played in spades anyway, but at least in game, the possible slam depending on his rebid. Nothing is lost because the game contract has been reached anyway.

This delayed game raise does away with the necessity to force lightly, and allows a slow approach where it will do the most good. It may be used whenever the suit you bid is not very big and the support for partner's suit is not overwhelming. The yardstick is in the region of 13—15 points, and the qualifications mainly good trump support yet not a strong enough hand on which to force immediately whilst fearing, on account of some feature in the hand, that a better contract may be missed if a direct raise to game in the suit opened is made.

THE 4♣ — 4◇ CONVENTION (SWISS)

There is one modern development which falls into place here, and that is the 4♣—4◇ Convention. There are a number of variations, developed from the original Swiss Convention, but Acol advocates the one set out below which is valuable as well as having the merit of simplicity.

The convention may be used on hands on which partner has opened one of a major suit and responder is strong enough to make a direct raise to game in this suit. As explained in Chapter 4, the direct raise to game in a major, which used to be used as a very strong Limit Bid, has been replaced by a pre-emptive bid in this position, and the 4♣—4◇ Convention takes its place. In practice it was found that, when responder's hand contained two or more Aces, opener was likely to be short of first-round controls and, therefore, frequently felt disinclined to take the bidding beyond game level in search of a slam. So using this convention responder, instead of making the direct raise to game for which his hand is strong enough, bids 4♣ if holding two Aces and 4◇ if holding three Aces. These bids both agree opener's suit as trumps and leave opener free to sign off in four of his suit, himself make a cue bid, or take any other strong action his hand suggests in the knowledge of his partner's trump support and Ace holding. Take as an example the fol-

♠ A J 7 6
♡ 7
◇ A 10 8 6
♣ A 7 5 3

lowing hand opposite to partner's opening 1♠ bid. Responder has the full values for a raise direct to 4♠—he dare not, in fact, bid less, as his hand is not strong enough to force. Now, however, he can bid 4◇, announcing the values for the raise to game, a fit in spades, and three Aces. Since a natural bid of 4♣ or 4◇ in this position would be meaningless, this special conventional meaning cannot cost the partnership anything and may, instead, greatly facilitate the bidding of an otherwise difficult slam.

Note also the logical extension of "Blackwood", the Acol Direct King Convention explained fully in Chapter 19. The 4♣ or 4◇ bid *already having shown the number of Aces held by responder*, opener has no need to ask this question again. If opener rebids 4 N.T., therefore, this asks responder immediately to show his Kings, if any.

It is important to remember that these bids do *not* take the place of a normal force if the hand is strong enough to make one. Either of them, in fact, *denies* the strength to force. The convention is, therefore, a valuable additional weapon but not a replacement one.

OPENER'S REBIDS

We have already touched on two of opener's rebids over a game force, but other positions arise about which you should know.

A rebid in the suit opened is a neutral bid, confirming length but denying a long *solid* suit, a second biddable suit, or immediate support for the forcer's suit. The subsequent bidding will show whether opener's hand is maximum or minimum.

♠ Q 10 6   A rebid in No Trumps following
♡ K J 4   a force, when the rebid is made at
◇ A 8 2   the lowest possible available level,
♣ A J 5 2   indicates a minimum hand with no rebiddable suit. Playing "weak throughout" you would open 1♣ on this hand, intending to rebid 1 N.T. over any simple change-of-suit response. If partner forces, say by bidding 2◇, you would sign off by bidding 2 N.T.

As at the lower level, 1♠—2♣—2♡, so after a force, 1♠—3♣—3♡, the 3♡ is not a strong bid, merely offering an additional spot in which to play the hand. As a corollary to this, if opener's hand contains a possible alternative trump suit, he should take his earliest opportunity—his rebid after partner's force—to show it.

A jump rebid to 3 N.T. by opener, in a sequence such as 1◇—2♡—3 N.T., when the force is at the two-level, shows the same sort of balanced hand of 16+ to 18 points which opener would have for a 2 N.T. rebid after a response at the one-level.

* * * * *

As you go through the revision quiz for this Chapter, note the great difference your "shape" and the disposition of your points makes to your decision as to whether to make a simple change-of-suit bid preparatory to a delayed game raise, or a second round force, or to use the 4♣—4◇ Convention or an immediate forcing bid.

REVISION QUIZ ON CHAPTER 16

1. Your partner, North, opens the bidding with 1♠. East does not intervene. What would you, South, bid on the following hands?

    (a) ♠ K J 8 6: ♡ A Q 5: ◇ K 7 5 3: ♣ Q 4:

    (b) ♠ K 10 8 4: ♡ K Q 7: ◇ A 9 7 6: ♣ A J:

    (c) ♠ A 9 7 6: ♡ 7: ◇ K J 10 8: ♣ K J 5 3:

    (d) ♠ Q 10 9 8: ♡ A 10 8 6: ◇ A 6 5 2: ♣ 8:

    (e) ♠ A 9 6 2: ♡ 6: ◇ A Q 10 9 5: ♣ A Q 8:

2. As dealer you open the bidding with 1♡ and your partner forces with 3◇. What would you rebid on the following hands?

    (a) ♠ K 7: ♡ A Q 10 9 4: ◇ Q J 4: ♣ A 4 2:

    (b) ♠ K 7 4: ♡ A Q J 10 9: ◇ Q 10: ♣ A J 5:

    (c) ♠ A Q 10 4: ♡ K Q 10 9 7: ◇ K 4: ♣ A 6:

    (d) ♠ 9 5: ♡ A K Q 10 7: ◇ A 3: ♣ K Q 10 4:

    (e) ♠ A J 10: ♡ K Q 10 7: ◇ A 8: ♣ Q 10 5 3:

    (f) ♠ 7: ♡ A K Q J 10 4: ◇ A 6: ♣ 9 7 5 3:

    (g) ♠ 7 5 3: ♡ K J 10 9 6 5: ◇ Q 8: ♣ A 3:

3. Your partner, North, opens the bidding with 1♡. With no intervention, what would you bid on the following hands?

    (a) ♠ 8: ♡ J 7 6: ◇ A K Q 10 9 7 5: ♣ K 2:

    (b) ♠ K 9 3: ♡ Q 9 5: ◇ K Q 10 7: ♣ K Q 4:

    (c) ♠ A K J 9 5 2: ♡ Q 9: ◇ A 8 3: ♣ J 9:

    (d) ♠ K 7: ♡ Q J 9: ◇ A J 9 5: ♣ K Q 7 4:

    (e) ♠ K Q 5: ♡ Q 9 5: ◇ K Q 10: ♣ K Q 4 2:

    (f) ♠ 9 2: ♡ 7: ◇ A K Q 9 4: ♣ A K J 9 3:

    (g) ♠ A K Q 10 6 4: ♡ 6: ◇ A 8 6 2: ♣ 5 3:

    (h) ♠ A 4: ♡ K Q J: ◇ J 9 6 5 4 3: ♣ A Q:

    (i) ♠ A 9 5 4: ♡ 10: ◇ A Q 9 8: ♣ A Q J 6:

    (j) ♠ 10 9: ♡ A 9 7 6: ◇ A J 9 5: ♣ A J 8:

ANSWERS TO REVISION QUIZ
ON CHAPTER 16

1. (a) 2♦   This is a delayed game raise hand—not quite strong enough to force on the first round but intending to put partner straight to 4♠ if he merely rebids 2♠. Of course, if he takes stronger action, you will be fully prepared to join in the fun!

(b) 3♦   Now you must force immediately, as you are far too strong for any other action.

(c) 2♣   This time again you delay your raise, although you have no intention of stopping out of game. You want to hear partner's rebid.

(d) 4♣   This is the conventional bid showing full values for a direct raise to 4♠, including two Aces.

(e) 3♦   An immediate force is in order here. Game is certain and slam is more than merely possible.

2. (a) 4♦   With 16 point opposite your partner's force, you are far too strong to make a neutral rebid and there is no reason to suppress your diamond fit. If partner has forced on a short minor he will be telling you so by returning to hearts.

(b) 3♥   This time your hearts are stronger and your diamond support weaker. Make a waiting rebid, and see what happens next.

(c) 3♠   You have an enormous hand of your own, on which you are quite strong enough to 'reverse'. Don't panic because you only have K 4 of partner's diamond bid—he very probably means you to play a heart slam anyway!

(d) 4♣   Take this first opportunity to show your second suit, which you had every intention of bidding whether partner forced or not.

(e) 3 N.T. Over a simple change-of-suit to 2♢ you would have shown your 'shape' and count by bidding 2 N.T., so now the forced higher level carries the same significance.

(f) 4♡ The Acol conventional bid in a forcing situation, which shows a long and solid suit with no losers, needing little or no support.

(g) 3♡ You had a near minimum opener in the first place, so all you can do is confirm that at least you have heart length.

3. (a) 3♢ You will be in great difficulties to find a suitable rebid if you don't make an immediate force on this hand, especially as you have a fit with hearts.

(b) 2♢ This time you don't want to force on the first round. You have, in spite of your 15 points, no first round controls, so you would like to hear partner's rebid before giving a delayed game raise of some sort.

(c) 2♣ As in (a) above, you will be in hopeless difficulties for a rebid if you don't force at once.

(d) 3♢ With 16 points and a heart fit, you force in a suit ranking below partner's suit and, having two, select the better one of the two.

(e) 3♣ Again, with 17 points you really must force, or later you will find it impossible to make your partner believe how good your hand is. Force in clubs which, though the same in point-count, are longer than the diamonds.

(f) 3♢ This is a case of no fit for partner but two suits of your own, both so good that you feel sure game must be on somewhere between your hand and partner's opening bid.

g) 2♠ Even with no fit at all for partner's hearts, you can't afford not to force with such a good suit plus an outside Ace.

(h) 3♦   17 points and a good fit for partner's hearts, so you must force, but don't fall into the trap of doing this in clubs. With a six-card suit of your own and, above all, so many of partner's heart honours isn't there a very strong chance that his bid was partly based on diamond honours?

(i) 1♠   Definitely a hand on which *not* to force on the first round. You have only a singleton heart and no long suit of your own, so take it slowly, you'll get another chance to bid. If partner signs off with 2♥ your best bet will probably be a direct bid of 3 N.T.

(j) 4♦   Using the same convention as in 1 (d), you show a hand strong enough for an immediate raise to 4♥, containing three Aces, and with insufficient strength to force.

CHAPTER 17

The Double

ASS with the intervening bids, Acol lays no claim to the exclusive use of doubling conventions. Acol, however, exploits the use of this valuable bid to the full, and students of the system should make sure that they understand and recognize the situations where the double is called for and miss no opportunities of using it where it would pay dividends.

Doubles can be divided into four main classes, Penalty or Business doubles, Lead-Directing doubles, Tactical doubles, and Informatory or Take-Out doubles, and each has its own important part to play in good bidding. Sometimes one class may be allied to another as, for instance, when a player announces a certain amount of strength by making a take-out double which, in turn, enables his partner to make a penalty double. We shall see how these work if we consider the various types in turn.

PENALTY OR BUSINESS DOUBLES

These are doubles made in such a position that partner knows the doubler thinks that the opposition's contract can be broken. If partner has bid, or if the doubler has missed a chance to double the same suit on a previous round of bidding, a double will be intended primarily for penalties, and the doubler's partner should only take out if his hand is unduly weak for his bid, highly unsuitable distributionally, or good for a more profitable contract for his own side.

N.	E.	S.	W.	
No	1♠	2♡	x	

Here West's* double, being made after East has made an opening bid, is intended as a penalty double which, particularly if North-South are vulnerable, may well prove highly remunerative.

There are certain requirements for a double in this position, and these are a damaging holding in the enemy's trump suit, some honour strength (generally about 8—9 points should suffice) and, most important of all, a poor fit for partner's suit. In fact the mere act of doubling in such a position should warn your partner immediately of your lack of fit for his suit. The logic of this is that the better your support for your partner's suit, the fewer tricks you are likely to take in it as defenders. Vulnerability is another factor to be taken into account. To defeat non-vulnerable opponents by a mere two tricks, scoring 300 points when doubled, is poor compensation for a vulnerable game of your own, whereas to defeat them by two tricks doubled and vulnerable, 500 points, is far more attractive than the 400 points you would score for a non-vulnerable No Trump game at duplicate.

♠ 8
♡ K J 9 7 5
♢ A 8 7 6
♣ 10 5 3

On the bidding sequence quoted, a double of the 2♡ bid would be called for at any vulnerability. The hand is unlikely to produce a game unless a heart stop is the only thing required by partner to bid 3 No Trumps—in which case you will be assisting him by your double rather than hindering. On the other hand, if he is as good as all that, then the penalty you can hope to exact from the double should be all the greater.

* A popular innovation drops the "business" aspect of a double in West's position in favour of a "Sputnik Double", requesting opener to bid a different suit.

Another of these part-score doubling positions is when partner has missed a previous opportunity of doubling a bid in the same suit.

N.	E.	S.	W.
1♥	No	1♠	No
2♥	No	2♠	x

West's double in this position is a business one. He missed doubling or taking any other action over South's 1♠, so his double now is intended for penalties, and he doubtless feels competent to deal with the opponents should they try to "escape" into 3♥. If West were competing, and wished to be taken out into another suit at this point, he could employ the "Unusual No Trump" convention, explained in Ch. 20.

Still another double which is always intended as a business one is a double by a player who has himself opened the bidding with a No Trump bid. It does not matter if this is weak or strong—the mere fact that he opened in No Trumps makes his double a penalty one.

N.	E.	S.	W.
1N.T.	2♥	No	2♠
x			

Doubtless here, as in the previous case, North would not double if he did not feel capable of doubling an "escape" into 3♥.

The most usual moment, however, for making a penalty double is when the auction has been competitive and you are in a position to judge that the opposition has bid beyond its depth.

N.	E.	S.	W.
1♣	1♥	2♦	No
3♣	No	3♦	x

♠ Q J 7 4
♥ 3
♦ A J 9 2
♣ K J 8 7

As West, with this hand, your double is a business one. Your partner has bid—the suit of which you hold a singleton—and the opposition's sequence fairly shouts of a misfit. Any attempt to escape you can double equally well.

Don't double just for the sake of doubling when the opposition has bid up freely and easily either to a game or to a slam without any intervention from your partner or yourself. This does not, of course, mean that you should refrain from doubling if you are for some reason certain that they have reached a contract they cannot make. It is not entirely unknown for even experts to bid to a Grand Slam missing the Ace of trumps! But be very ware, when doubling game or slam contracts, that you do not give away the disposition of the few resources you hold. If your partner has not bid and your opponents have reached their contract with unembarrassed ease, then probably all the strength left outstanding against them lies in your hand and to double may well be to give away this vital information.

Here is another point. If the opponents have been bidding, for example, in hearts and spades, and have settled for a game contract in hearts which you are certain you can defeat, don't double, which may only tip them off to switch to spades, unless you can take care of a spade contract too. It is silly to persuade them out of a contract they can't make into one they can, when you have no reason to believe that your partner can double the change of suit.

Be careful, too, of doubling for a penalty when you have a highly distributional hand and when, from the bidding, it appears that the other hands too may be distributional. A six or seven card suit, even if headed by K Q J, cannot be reckoned as worth one winner from a doubling point of view, and if it has been supported by partner during the auction, it becomes of even less value. Apart from exceedingly quick-looking quick tricks, strength in the opposition's suit is your best bet for doubling unless, of course, you know that they have been trying to push you beyond your own depth or are in any other way competing unwisely.

If you keep to the policy of doubling part-scores you will at times, inevitably, double the opposition into a game on some unforeseen distribution. I remember one disastrous evening when, playing against a very weak team, both I and the other member of our team who held my hand at another table, doubled a vulnerable 2♡ over-call by the opposition when partner had opened 1♠. My hand was:—

♠ 5
♡ K Q 10 9
♢ A Q 6 3
♣ K 9 7 4

Believe it or not, we made three heart tricks and the ♢A. It was a very highly distributional hand, declarer holding seven hearts to the A.J. At the other two tables, where the weaker players held this hand, neither thought of doubling, which made this a somewhat expensive board for us! This kind of disaster, though, must not be used as an argument against doubling when all the indications are there, and in the long run you will inevitably gain more than you will lose by these tactics.

There are two more "don'ts" in this section, both of them important. Don't double when you have only a slender chance of defeating the contract because, if it is made, you stand to lose more than you can gain by the double.

The other "don't" is to double because it is what is often cheerfully called a "free" double, of which there is actually no such thing. What is meant, of course, is a double which, even if the contract doubled is not broken, does not give the opposition game, or when making their contract will give them a game whether or not they are doubled. Again, if the opposition make their doubled contract, they will score more than you would have gained had you defeated them by one trick, and if they are able to re-double, the cost to yourself and your partner will be even greater.

DOUBLING AN OPENING ONE
NO TRUMP

In Acol, the double of an opening One No-Trump bid is always intended as a penalty double, and it should not be taken out by the doubler's partner except on extreme weakness or as set out below. From this it follows that the doubling hand must be strong—at least the upper limit of the opposing opening bid, or have some compensating feature such as a suit which can be easily set up to run off against declarer with damaging effect.

Partner of the doubler should be guided by the following rules when deciding when or not to take the double out:

(a) When holding fewer points than can possibly produce the balance.

(b) When opener's partner has redoubled and the doubler's partner has a pointless hand or near "bust". He must then take out into his "best" suit on weakness. A pass would indicate values sufficient to defeat the redoubled contract.

(c) When holding a very unbalanced hand, of little or no use defensively, but giving promise of game for the doubler's side.

As an additional counter to the obstructive opening bid of a weak One No Trump, the "Sharples Two Club" was developed by these famous twins, and is now being widely used. Its application is described in Chapter 20.

TAKING OUT A PENALTY DOUBLE

Here again, it is possible that occasionally the wrong decision will be reached, but the lack of defensive values in an Acol Light Opening Bid must be allowed to sway opener in his decision as to whether or not to leave in a double of an intervening bid at a low level.

♠ 8 2 On a hand such as this, having opened
♡ K Q J 8 7 5 1♡ and been overcalled with 2♣, if
◇ A 8 7 6 partner now doubles the 2♣ for
♣ 7 penalties, opener would be well
advised to remove the double to 2♡.
He has a near minimum light opener and outstandingly poor assistance for defending a club contract. His own heart suit, however, is solid enough to stand up without much support from partner, who has already stated his lack of fit for it by his double.

LEAD-DIRECTING DOUBLES

Many players think only of lead-directing doubles in terms of high contracts, but this is a very great mistake, and doubles of low level conventional bids can often be made to ask partner for a lead in that suit.

Doubles of No Trump game contracts by the partner of the player who will be on lead should generally be taken to be lead-directing and the leader should respond to whatever request he reads into the double unless he has some especially good reason of his own for making another lead. Broadly, the rules to follow are these:

(a) If the doubler has himself bid a suit, his double confirms that it is the suit he wants led.

(b) If the doubler's partner has bid a suit, the double confirms willingness for that suit to be led.

(c) If neither defender has bid during the auction, the double suggests the lead of the first suit bid by the dummy.

The Lightner Slam Double comes into this

category of lead-directing doubles. Unless the slam bid is an obvious sacrifice one, in which case the Lightner inferences do not apply, the double is used to indicate the possible best defence to the contract, and asks for some lead which would not normally be made. A lead of a suit bid by either of the defenders would be a normal one, so must be ignored. A trump lead would be neutral and harmless, so this too must be ignored, as, too, should the lead of an unbid suit when it seems that this would ordinarily be a normal lead. In the majority of cases, a lead of the first side-suit bid by dummy or, failing that, a side-suit bid by declarer, will be the best choice. It may well be that the Lightner double was made by partner because of a void in that suit.

From this it follows that there are, as usual, "don'ts" to apply. Don't make a Lightner double if you want, and hope for, a normal lead unless, of course, you are certain of defeating the contract in any case. And don't make the double if it seems likely to produce the one "unusual" lead that you *don't* want.

TACTICAL DOUBLES

Although lead-directing doubles are, strictly speaking, tactical ones, there is yet another class which operates mainly when the bidding is high and competitive. Both sides are fighting for the contract, and it appears to you that it is time a decision was reached. In this position you may double the opposition *in order to tell your partner to stop bidding*.

N.	E.	S.	W.
1♡	2♡	4♡	5♣
x			

North, if he is playing Acol, already knows a lot about his partner's hand. He also knows a lot about his own hand, and his decision is that he does not want to be put into 5♡ in spite of his partner's bid, though it goes without saying that he would not make the double without some assurance of defeating 5♣. This same bidding sequence, varied just a little by substituting a pass for North's double, imposes on South the obligation to take action, either by himself doubling 5♣ or, if he cannot do this, by bidding 5♡. It is known, by the way, as a Forcing Pass, as it forces the decision, when some decision is obviously necessary, onto South.

Before leaving this section I should like to quote a hand which comes from the 1961 final of the London Pairs Championship, on which there was some interesting bidding on both sides.

With East-West vulnerable West, the dealer, opened the bidding with 1♣, and North made the pre-emptive over-call of 3♠. East somewhat boldly came in with 4♡ and South countered with 4♠. West now made the master-bid of 6♡, a psychologically perfect move. He knew that either North or South would feel unable to stand the vulnerable slam contract and would take out

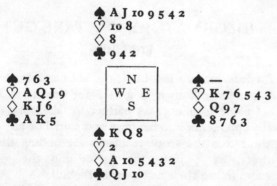

into 6♠ which he could double. This, in fact, is what happened. Over 6♡ North made a forcing pass. Quite obviously the onus was on South to take some action. North had bid his hand to the full already, and Acol does not ask you to bid your cards twice. Remembering North's pre-emptive 3♠, South was doubtful about defeating 6♡ (though, in fact, East-West have an inescapable loser in clubs and diamonds in addition to North's diamond ruff) and duly took out into 6♠ which West, as he had planned to do, doubled. This would have been the best available result on the hand once North-South had effectively blocked the heart game. The only thing that went wrong was that East did not trust his partner's opening bid to be good enough to break 6♠, and took the double out into 7♡ which South now doubled. This, on the lead of ♢A and another, went quietly three down. Incidentally, one wonders why West, with 18 points, chose to open 1♣ instead of 1♡.

This, however, is a digression, put in because I thought it might amuse you. Let us now return to doubles in general and in particular to:

INFORMATORY OR TAKE-OUT
DOUBLES

An Informatory Double is the old name for what is now generally known as a take-out double and this, as its name implies, asks partner to take out the suit bid by opponents into his own best suit. The advantage of the bid is the scope it affords for finding the best contract, as it gives the partnership the greatest freedom to use their resources to the full.

An ordinary overcall, whether a simple bid in a new suit or a jump bid, definitely points to where the strength of the bidder's hand may be expected to be found. A double as an immediate over call, on the other hand, announces that there is strength, though not exactly where it lies, and asks for information from partner. The overcall of a suit, therefore, *informs* partner of your choice for trumps. A take-out double asks him for his opinion on the matter.

It is important to remember when considering whether or not your hand qualifies for a take-out double that you *must be prepared for any response your partner is likely to make*. This establishes that you must have strength in the suits *not* called by the opposition which, in turn, immediately indicates the type of hand suitable for the bid—one with little or nothing, including few, if any, small cards, in opponent's suit, and something in the other three. Alternatively, a good holding in two of the other three suits, especially if one of these is an unbid major, qualifies the hand for a double. In this case, if partner responds by bidding the one in which you are weakest, you have your own good suit to fall back on.

Don't forget, either, the importance of "shape" in making this bid. Three little cards in the opponent's suit are as good as three losers, and you would have to have some outstandingly good honour count to double with such a holding.

Another thing to remember is that if you make a take-out double, and as you must be prepared, in doing so, for any response your partner may make, *you must also be prepared for him to make a penalty pass*, that is, leave the double in for penalties because he thinks that his trump holding plus your honour strength will make the penalty worth while. For this reason alone, strong unbalanced hands should be shown by means of a jump overcall in preference to a take-out double.

♠ 7
♡ K 10 6 5
♢ K J 8 4
♣ A Q J 6

Double an opening bid of 1♠. No absolute rule as to the point count required for a take-out double can be given as this, like all other bids, must be conditioned by "shape", but 12—13 points minimum should be your rough guide. On this hand you have not only 14 points but perfect distribution for the bid. Whichever suit your partner bids, you can give him more than adequate support, and even should he choose to make a penalty pass, your honour strength is such that you will be undismayed.

♠ A Q 8 5
♡ K 10 4 3
♢ 8 6
♣ A J 9

Double an opening bid of 1♢. You have both major suits well held, from which a game contract may develop, and even should partner respond with 2♣, you will again be undismayed.

♠ K 10 6 3
♡ A K J 9 8
♢ 8
♣ A 6 4

Double an opening 1♢ in preference to making an overcall in hearts. Your four-card spade suit would make this ideal for trumps should partner bid that suit, but if he in fact, bids 2♣, you can now bid 2♡.

♠ 6 2
♡ Q J 10 7 6
♢ A J 5
♣ A Q 8

Double an opening 1♠ in preference to overcalling 2♡. This might well "catch a packet" if next hand makes a penalty double, whereas the double gives you the opportunity, which would have been lost for ever, of finding a resting place in two of a minor.

You now have your general rules. Double on about 12—13 points (required in case partner makes a penalty pass) and "shape", which should include a good holding in any unbid major. On hands lacking these requirements, make the appropriate overcall, either simple, jump, or forcing as the case may be.

It is very possible for the partner of the doubler to make a penalty double on the strength of his partner's take-out double.

N.	E.	S.	W.	
1♦	No	No	x	Here West's double is a protective take-out double but
2♣	x			East, knowing his partner will have at least 11—12 points, makes a penalty double of North's 2♣.
1♦	x	1♠	x	Here again, West is able to make a penalty double of South's

1♠ in the knowledge of his partner's holding.

We must not leave these take-out doubles without making one other point, and that is the *negative inference* of not making such a double. Examine the following sequence:—

N.	E.	S.	W.	
1♣	1♦	2♣	No	One might well use this as an illustration of the age-old children's game of "What is wrong
No	2♠	No	3♥	
No	No	x		with this picture?" Study it carefully before you look at what

is really a very simple solution. Well the wrong, quite simply, is West's bid of 3♥. North clearly has either a weak or a difficult hand—one of the sort on which Acol players feel the bidding must be opened but, having had such minimum support from partner, are glad to pass thereafter. East, on the other hand, though he has bid strongly, *did not double the 1♣ opening bid*. The inference which West should have drawn from this was that East's hand was unsuitable for a double. From his subsequent bidding he was clearly two, or semi-two suited, thus holding little or no support for a sudden heart bid at this level. The inference would have been correct, and failing to make it resulted in a neat penalty of 500 points to North-South who had nothing at all "on" for themselves.

BALANCING TAKE-OUT DOUBLES

Take-out doubles in the balancing position, already touched on in Chapter 15, must not be overlooked.

They are, of course, doubles made when two passes have followed the opening bid. Once opener's partner has passed, he is known to be very weak, and it is always possible that the player on opener's left has passed on account of a strong holding in the suit opened and that he may be eagerly awaiting the opportunity to make a penalty pass of a double. For this reason a balancing double should only be made on a strongish hand containing 11 or more points.

♠ K J 10 7	*N.*	*E.*	*S.*	*W.*
♡ K J 9 5	1♣	No	No	x
◇ 9 4 2				
♣ A 8				
West				

On this hand you, as West, would be willing to defend 1♣ doubled. You know that South is hopelessly weak and, therefore, unlikely to provide declarer with the necessary entries to lead through your major suits. On the other hand, you can stand a take-out by North into any of the other three suits.

Here is one other take-out doubling position before we go on.

♠ A Q 10 9 2	*W.*	*N.*	*E.*	*S.*
♡ A J 8 7 6	1♣	No	1◇	x
◇ 8				
♣ 6 3				
South				

Here South's partner has not bid, and South has not missed any previous opportunity of doubling either clubs or diamonds. North will, therefore, know that the double is for a take-out and will show his best major suit. 1 N.T. by South in this sequence would be a natural bid showing strength (16 or more points) as well as a good stop in both clubs and diamonds.

RESPONDING TO A TAKE-OUT DOUBLE

As the partner of a player who has made a take-out double, it is very necessary that you should know how to give the right information about your hand. If there is an intervening bid or a re-double on your right, the situation changes, and we shall deal with these two positions later. Meanwhile, however, in the simple situation of the opening suit bid being doubled by your partner and next hand offering no intervention you should proceed as follows:

1. **On an exceedingly weak hand,** that is, one containing not more than 4 points, you should bid your longest suit at the lowest available level. With no five-card suit, bid your best four-card suit, always provided that this is not the suit doubled, when you should bid whatever three-card suit keeps the bidding at its lowest possible level. The hand given on the last page of this chapter is a good example of what West should bid, although it is actually given to illustrate the possible danger of a "trap pass" by opponent. In this case West's only four-card suit in his completely pointless hand is diamonds, the suit opened, so he is forced to bid 1♡. Over 1♠ doubled, on a worthless hand bid 2♣ of which, if your only four-card suit is spades, you must hold three. You must **not,** on this type of hand, be tempted to bid 1 N.T., as this would have a different meaning, as explained in No: 2.

♠ 8 7 6 4	♠ Q 9 3	♠ J 8 5 3
♡ 9 3	♡ 8 5 3 2	♡ 9 6
◇ J 7 5 4 3	◇ J 9 8	◇ J 8 4 3
♣ 8 5	♣ 7 6 3	♣ 8 6 5

| If partner doubles 1♣, bid 1◇. If he doubles 1♡, bid 1♠ not 2◇. | If partner doubles 1♡, bid 1♠. If he doubles 1♣ or 1◇, bid 1♡. | If partner doubles 1♣, bid 1◇. If he doubles 1◇ or 1♡, bid 1♠. If he doubles 1♠, bid 2♣. |

The general rule to remember is that, on very weak

hands, the bidding should be kept at its lowest possible level. Provided the level of the bidding can be kept at one on these very weak hands, a 4-card major suit should be preferred to a 5-card minor.

♠ 9 8
♡ Q 8 6 4
♢ 7 3
♣ 10 8 6 4 2

If partner doubles 1♢ when you hold this hand, bid 1♡, not 2♣. If you are forced to bid at the two level to respond to a double of 1♡ or 1♠, bid 2♣. If your take-out cannot be kept at the one-level, prefer a response of 2♣ to showing any weak 4-card suit.

♠ Q 7 6
♡ 8 6 5 4
♢ 9 6 3
♣ 10 7 6

If partner doubles 1♠, take out into 2♣ rather than 2♡ on this dreary lot, though over a double of 1♣ or 1♢ you would certainly offer 1♡.

2. **On Moderate Hands** (4—8 points) you should generally take out into your longest suit but, if you have the choice, prefer a 4-card major suit to a weak minor. Remember that your partner's double will almost certainly include good support for any unbid major suit.

3. **A Balanced Hand** with a minimum count of 8 points should be bid as 1 N.T. This does not, repeat **not,** promise a guard in the opponent's suit, but only the minimum of 8 points, and the doubler must not proceed with a No Trump contract unless himself holding a guard. If you find yourself with the choice of bidding 1 N.T. or one of a major suit, bid the major.

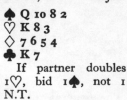

♠ 9 7 6
♡ Q J 9
♢ K J 5
♣ J 7 6 2
If partner doubles 1♠, bid 1 N.T.

♠ Q 10 8 2
♡ K 8 3
♢ 7 6 5 4
♣ K 7
If partner doubles 1♡, bid 1♠, not 1 N.T.

228

4. **On Stronger Hands** of from 9—10 points, jump
the bidding by one step in your longest suit. If you have
two suits of equal length, keep to the normal rule of
bidding the higher-ranking first.

On a balanced hand of this count, *but provided you
have two stops in the opponent's suit*, bid 2 N.T.

♠ 8 6 5	♠ K J 9 6	♠ K 8 6
♡ J 9 7 5 2	♡ A Q 8 2	♡ Q 8 3
◇ A K 8	◇ 8 3	◇ A J 8
♣ K 9	♣ 8 7 5	♣ Q 7 6 2
If partner doubles	If partner doubles	If partner doubles
1♣, bid 2♡.	1♣ or 1◇, bid 2♠	1◇, bid 2 N.T.

5. **On A Very Strong Hand** which offers a choice of
contract, your response is to make a bid in the opponent's suit. This, of course, creates a forcing situation
and your partner must now keep the bidding open to
game. It also, as it were, tosses the ball back to him,
asking him to show his own best suit because your
hand is such that you feel his choice will provide the
best contract.

♠ K Q 10 5   If partner doubles 1♣, bid 2♣. The
♡ A 10 9 6   doubler is almost morally certain to
◇ A J 8   show hearts or spades in response,
♣ 9 2   and you would obviously prefer to
               play in whichever suits him best
rather than make the choice yourself.

RESPONDING AFTER AN INTERVENING BID

N.	E.	S.	W.
1♣	x	1♡	?

In this sequence your
partner, East, doubled the
opening bid of 1♣, after
which South put in an intervening bid of 1♡. What
difference does this make to the responses you have

just learned? Quite a lot. Whereas without the intervening bid you were forced to respond, however miserable your hand, now the intervening bid relieves you of this responsibility and you may take the opportunity to pass if you have nothing worth showing. On the other hand, the intervening bid was quite likely made with just the object of obstructing your natural bid, so you must not allow yourself to be blocked if you hold anything your partner is likely to be glad to hear about.

♠ Q J 7 5 4
♡ 8 6 2
♢ K 7
♣ 9 5 3

After the bidding sequence shown you, as West, should bid 1♠. The suit is well worth showing, and may lead to at least a part-score for your side. Your hand must be far from worthless opposite a double.

♠ Q 6 5
♡ K 9 8 6 5 4
♢ 9
♣ 8 4 2

This time your partner doubles an opening 1♢ bid and opponent intervenes with 1♠. Here you are too good, with your six-card suit, to allow yourself to be shut out and should bid 2♡. You are not strong enough, however, to make a voluntary jump bid if, for instance, the sequence had been 1♣—x—1♢—?. You should then only bid 1♡.

IF OPPONENT REDOUBLES

N.   E.   S.   W.
1♡   x   xx   ?

The intervention of a redouble by your right-hand opponent again relieves you from the responsibility of replying to your partner's double, and once more you may use this as an opportunity to pass if you have a worthless hand. Partner himself has now been given a further opportunity of bidding so there is no necessity to rescue him if you are very weak. With any five-card suit, however, you should at least tell him that you can offer this much assistance, particularly if it is a major, or a suit which can be shown at the one-level. This may be of great help to your partner who, very possibly, has no five-card suit of his own, and will have to guess which of his own suits to bid when he holds three, or even four card support for you. If by any odd chance you happen to have a reasonably good hand in West's position, you will realise that there are not enough points in the pack for the bidding thus far and that someone at the table is "psyching", and you will have to take appropriate action.

IF OPPONENT DOUBLES

One other important point, and that is if an opponent doubles your partner's opening bid.

N.   E.   S.   W.   As South, what line should
1♡   x   ?   you take? First and fore-
                         most, if you have any sort
of a limit bid as a raise for your partner you should make it, to the full and over. You should, in fact, devalue your limit bid responses to obstruct the doubler's partner to the fullest possible extent. Particularly if your opponents are vulnerable and you are not, get in their way as much as you can.

On a moderate hand bid naturally. Show a suit or bid 1 N.T. if you would have done so without the double, which will not have detracted from your hand. Indeed, it may even have strengthened it, as any cards you hold will lie over the doubler's holding.

If you have a reasonably good hand there are various courses you can take according to how it is made up.

You have, for instance, the choice between passing and redoubling and it is, I think, as well to have both these gambits up your sleeve, letting the score and your actual holding decide your course. On a hand of 9 or more points outside your partner's suit you can certainly redouble, telling him that you will be able to take action on the next round and that he should not let the double scare him off.

Your redouble, of course, ranks as a bid, which lets the doubler's partner off the hook of having to bid on what may well be a completely worthless hand, leaving him at liberty to pass. This, therefore, is where a pass by you—a trap pass—may be used to advantage at favourable vulnerability.

If your partner has opened the bidding and next hand has doubled while you hold 9 or more points without much of a fit for your partner, you will have something worthwhile in the other suits. It also seems probable that poor fourth hand will hold the well-known "blizzard" or collection of garbage, *and if you pass, he will be forced to respond to his partner's double.*

N.	E.	S.	W.	
1◇	x	No	1♡	Not, of course, knowing that you, South, have so much power, your partner North is more than

likely to pass West's 1♡ and now you can come into your own. Especially if East-West are vulnerable, a most attractive doubling position may arise. I give you an example from actual tournament play, where the luckless West got helplessly caught for a penalty of 800—doubled, vulnerable, and three down.

The bidding was:

N.	E.	S.	W.
1◇	x	No	1♡
No	No	x	

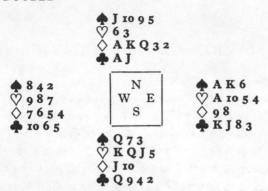

♠ J 10 9 5
♡ 6 3
◇ A K Q 3 2
♣ A J

♠ 8 4 2
♡ 9 8 7
◇ 7 6 5 4
♣ 10 6 5

♠ A K 6
♡ A 10 5 4
◇ 9 8
♣ K J 8 3

♠ Q 7 3
♡ K Q J 5
◇ J 10
♣ Q 9 4 2

True, at Game All (and at all other tables) North-South made a vulnerable No Trump game, but this was not as valuable as the 800 they picked up at this table. If East-West had not been vulnerable South could not have afforded to make this trap pass but, at the score, and with his poor support for partner's opening diamond bid, it paid handsome dividends.

Finally, a response of 2 N.T. in this position, that is, when your partner's opening bid has been doubled for a take out, is conventional. It shows a hand suitable,

N.	E.	S.	W.
1♡	x	2NT	

in ordinary circumstances, for a limit bid of three of the suit opened, i.e., 10—12 high card and distributional points including primary trump support. The object of this is to make it clear to your partner that you are not bidding pre-emptively, showing the distinction between full values for the raise and the de-valued limit bid of three. Apart from being highly pre-emptive in itself, as the 2 N.T. bid agrees the trump suit, opener is free to take any further action his hand suggests.

REVISION QUIZ ON CHAPTER 17

1. The opponent on your right opens the bidding with 1♡. What action would you take on the following hands?

   (a) ♠ K Q 10 7: ♡ 9: ◇ A Q 8 4: ♣ A 10 3 2:
   (b) ♠ J 10 7 4: ♡ 3: ◇ A J 10 9: ♣ A 4 3 2:
   (c) ♠ K Q J 10 9 7: ♡ 4: ◇ A Q J: ♣ A J 7:
   (d) ♠ Q 10: ♡ J 10 8 7: ◇ A K 5 4: ♣ A 10 6:
   (e) ♠ Q 10 9 7: ♡ 4 3: ◇ K Q 10 6: ♣ A K J:
   (f) ♠ A 4: ♡ 6 3: ◇ K Q J 10 7 2: ♣ A 4 3:

2. Your partner, North, has opened the bidding with 1♡ and next hand doubles. What do you, South, bid on the following hands? East-West are vulnerable.

   (a) ♠ Q 10 9 7 4: ♡ J 4 3: ◇ 6 4: ♣ 10 9 7:
   (b) ♠ Q J 9 6: ♡ 4 3 2: ◇ K J 9: ♣ K 8 4:
   (c) ♠ Q 10 6 4: ♡ 10 3: ◇ J 4 2: ♣ Q 9 6 2:
   (d) ♠ A 4: ♡ Q 10 9 6: ◇ 6 3: ♣ K J 6 5 4:
   (e) ♠ 9: ♡ Q 10 8 4 3: ◇ J 9 5 3 2: ♣ K 3:
   (f) ♠ K J 9 6: ♡ 4: ◇ A 10 9 5: ♣ K J 8 4:

3. West, the dealer, has opened with 1◇. North, your partner, has doubled, and East has bid 1♠. What do you, as South, bid on the following hands?

   (a) ♠ J 4: ♡ J 10 9 6 4: ◇ Q 4 2: ♣ K 7 3:
   (b) ♠ Q J 8 6 4: ♡ 10 7: ◇ K 6 2: ♣ 10 9 4:
   (c) ♠ A J: ♡ K 10 9 8 4 3: ◇ 4: ♣ Q 8 4 2:
   (d) ♠ K J 9: ♡ J 10 9 8: ◇ A Q 10: ♣ 6 4 3:
   (e) ♠ Q 10 9 8 4: ♡ J 6: ◇ 9 8 3: ♣ A Q 10:

4. Again West, the dealer, has opened 1♦ and North has doubled. This time East had redoubled. What do you, as South, bid?

(a) ♠ Q J 10 7 4: ♡ 10 7 4: ♦ 9 8 4: ♣ K 3:
(b) ♠ 10 7 4: ♡ K Q 10 9 7: ♦ Q J 4: ♣ K J:
(c) ♠ 7 4 2: ♡ 9 3 2: ♦ 7 6 5 3: ♣ 8 4 2:
(d) ♠ Q 4 3: ♡ K 7 4: ♦ K 10 9: ♣ 10 9 6 3:
(e) ♠ J 10 9: ♡ K 4: ♦ Q J 9 4: ♣ Q J 4 3:

ANSWERS TO REVISION QUIZ
ON CHAPTER 17

1. (a) Double. Here you have a typical doubling hand—strong in every suit but the one opened and you want to ask your partner, rather than tell him, which suit to play in.

(b) No. Exactly the same shaped hand, but not enough playing strength to take action on your own. Pass, and hope to be able to support partner if he can bid.

(c) 2♡ The forcing bid described on p. 185 which avoids the danger of partner making a penalty pass of a double.

(d) No. Although you have 14 points, too much of your "shape" is in opponent's suit. Pass and hope that they will try for a high heart contract which you can double, or that you can bid later in support of your partner.

(e) Double. You have support for any suit your partner may bid.

(f) 3♦ It is better to jump in your long suit, which is the only one you are really interested in playing in. Compare (c) above, for which you are not quite strong enough.

2. (a) 1♠ Your count is only 3 points, but opener will not expect much from you after the double.

(b) Re-double. With 10 points you redouble to tell partner that you can take action whatever the opposition bids, and that he should not allow himself to be put off by the double.

(c) 1♠ You would bid 1♠ over an opening 1♡ from your partner, so bid it now. It may discourage opponents too.

(d) 2 N.T. A typical hand on which, without the double, you would have bid 3♡.

(e) 3♡ An immediate limit bid to the full and even upper limit of your hand. You have so little outside trump support that your object is to obstruct West.

(f) No. This is a very good example of a hand suitable for a "trap pass". If you say No Bid, West will have to speak and you may well get the chance of a highly profitable penalty double when it gets round to you again.

3. (a) 2♡ You have a very far from worthless hand opposite a double and it is probable that South has bid his 1♠ on something like the hand in 2 (c).

(b) No. Without East's bid you would have liked to have bid 1♠ yourself, but are not strong enough to take any action over East.

(c) 3♡ This time both your count and "shape" are good enough to try for a game.

(d) 2 N.T. With 11 points and good stops in both of opponents' suits, this is your honest bid.

(e) Double. Apart from the fact that you would have liked to have bid spades yourself, you hold good defensive values.

4. (a) 1♠ The redouble relieves you from the responsibility of bidding, but you have a good five-card suit, so show it.

(b) 2♡   If you work it out, there are really not enough
            points in the pack for the bidding thus far.
            Tell your partner that you, anyway, are not
            fooling!

(c) No.   Nothing in this hand should induce you to
            bid. The redouble has given your partner
            a chance to speak again.

(d) 1 N.T. This moderate 8-point hand has its values
            scattered and you will not mind what action
            partner may take.

(e) No.   This really amounts to a penalty pass,
            though your partner cannot know it. Some-
            one must be fooling and if it is the opposition
            you may be able to cause great damage. If—
            as is most likely, partner re-opens with a
            bid, you can take the appropriate action.

CHAPTER 18

Responding Over Intervening Bids

IN the previous Chapters we have talked a lot about the various Acol opening bids and the natural and conventional responses to them. We have also discussed what to do if the opposition opens the bidding, but we have touched little at all, except in the previous Chapter where the various types of doubles are involved, on the Acol player's approach to the problem of the opposition putting in a call over partner's opening bid. If North, your partner, opens 1 ♡ and next hand overcalls with 1 ♠, or if North's 1 ♡ is overcalled with 2 ♣, what action should you, as South, take?

Earlier we looked at the penalty double in this position, but all too frequently you find yourself with the bare requirements for a bid. Generally speaking, your aim in this position should be to bid as naturally as possible. If your hand contains a limit bid in your partner's suit, make it just as you would have done without the intervention. If your hand contains a suit you would have shown at the level available to you, show it.

It is assumed that the reader is familiar with the normal approach-forcing responses, for instance that if a suit can be shown at the one-level it need not be more than a four-card one and backed by only as many points as would be required to bid 1 N.T.

A change of suit at the two level, e.g., 1♡—2◇, must not be made on less than 8 points and a five-card suit, and so on. An intervening bid by the opposition makes no difference to these bids. If the opposition has intervened with 2♣ over your partner's opening 1♡ or 1♠, and you would normally have responded with 2◇, you can do so now. If you would have responded with a limit bid of two, three, or four of your partner's suit, do so, though not, of course, forgetting to take into account any revaluation of your hand indicated by the intervening bid. By this I mean that if, for example, you hold the ♣ K J x over an intervening club bid, you can mentally up-grade the value of these four points rather than de-value them as you would have to do if clubs had been bid on your left.

So much, then, for the normal situations, where you can make the bid you had planned on before you heard the intervening bid. Where you will have to think again, and to vary your strategy is when the intervening bid blocks your normal call.

If your partner opens 1♣, and you hold the following hand:—

♠ J 5 4
♡ Q 10 9 7
◇ K J 5 2
♣ 7 6

you would prepare yourself to make the automatic response of 1♡, showing at least a four-card suit, and enough values to justify keeping the bidding open. Suppose, however, that the opponent on your right intervenes with 1♠. You cannot now bid 2♡ and nor can you offer 1 N.T. Pass, and see what happens. If you come into the auction at a later stage, your partner will not be misled as to your strength. Over an intervening bid of 1◇ you would only be over-bidding to the extent of half a point if you bid 1 N.T., and not even that if you consider that the bid of diamonds on your right up-grades the value of your own holding in it. (1 N.T. opposite 1♣ = 8-10 points).

The point to remember here is that a bid of 1 N.T. over an intervening bid now holds a positive message for partner, and that is that while the hand is more or less evenly balanced, it also contains a reasonable stop in the suit bid against you, and is also not strong enough to make a penalty double.

Care must be taken on moderately weak hands not to drive partner too high.

For instance, suppose he has opened 1♡ which has been
♠ 9 2
♡ K 10 6
♢ 9 6 2
♣ A J 8 5 4
over-called with 2♢. On this hand you would have bid 2♣ but now you would be better advised to bid 2♡ than 3♣. Your change-of-suit to clubs is forcing and your partner may well be out of his depth if he now has to rebid 3♡.

In other words, don't force the level of the bidding up unless you feel prepared to stand the higher contract.

This is all just a matter of common, or bidding, sense, and the fact is that, as with your own intervening bids or the use of the double, Acol has no special conventions of its own in this position.

When you have in your hand only what you might think of as a token bid, one made with just sufficient strength to keep the bidding open for one round to give opener a chance to bid again or show a second suit, take the opportunity offered by the intervention to pass. On the other hand you must not allow yourself to be bamboozled out of your own contract by an obstructive intervention and must use your judgement as to possible action. Possible penalty doubles, as described in the previous chapter, must not be overlooked.

A useful bid, incidentally another modification, is what used to be an immediate cue-bid in opponent's suit, used

N.	*E.*	*S.*	*W.*
—	1♡	1♠	2♠

on somewhat rare occasions to show a very strong responding hand with good trump support and no worse than a singleton in opponent's suit. This bid has been modified into a sort of utility bid, game-forcing as before, though it is no longer necessarily a cue-bid, but is used when there is doubt as to the best final denomination. Note that the original use of the bid is not barred, and that West's next bid in the sequence will show whether or not his immediate overcall was more than a mere game force.

In the following examples, if East has opened 1◇ and South has intervened with 1♡, the best overcall for West in each case is 2♡.

1.	2.	3.
♠ A K J	♠ A 10 9	♠ A 9 8
♡ A 9	♡ 9 8 3	♡ K J 9
◇ J 10 8	◇ K Q 10	◇ J 10 7
♣ J 9 8 6 5	♣ K J 9 8	♣ A Q 7 6

On (1) 2♡, the game force, is superior to 2♣, and if East, your partner, can rebid in No Trumps, you can raise to game. In (2), again, if partner can bid No Trumps, this is likely to be the best denomination, and in (3), where East is unlikely to be able to bid No Trumps, you will do this yourself unless his rebid shows added strength.

Competitive bidding, such as may develop when there is intervention, needs even more judgement than straightforward bidding between partners and it is difficult to give more than rough guidance. When wondering whether, for instance, to cover an opponent's 2♡ call over your partner's opening 1♠ with 2 N.T. or to double, the vulnerability must be taken into consideration. 2♠ doubled and two down vulnerable, 500 points, is more than adequate compensation at duplicate for an unvulnerable No Trump game, but 300 if the opponents are not vulnerable is no compensation at all for the 600 points *you* would get for a vulnerable game.

For the most part, bid your cards as naturally as possible, and as always, try to achieve obstruction of the opposition coupled with assistance to your partner.

REVISION QUIZ ON CHAPTER 18

Your partner, North, has opened the bidding with 1♠ at the score of Love All. East has intervened with 2◇. What should you bid on the following hands?

(a) ♠ J 7: ♡ A Q 10 6 5: ◇ K 6 4 3 2: ♣ 6:

(b) ♠ K 8 6: ♡ K Q 10 7 5: ◇ 7 5 2: ♣ J 8:

(c) ♠ Q 8 6 4: ♡ K 7 5 3: ◇ 9 2: ♣ 7 5 4:

(d) ♠ K Q 10 7: ♡ A Q 9 6: ◇ A: ♣ K J 7 5:

(e) ♠ J 5: ♡ A Q 10 8 4: ◇ 8 7: ♣ K 7 3 2:

(f) ♠ K J 6 4: ♡ A Q 9 2: ◇ 5 3: ♣ 7 5 4:

(g) ♠ Q 9 2: ♡ 9 5: ◇ 7 5 4: ♣ A Q 9 7 5:

(h) ♠ 8: ♡ K J 6 4: ◇ K J 9 8 5: ♣ 7 3 2:

(i) ♠ K 6 3 2: ♡ 10 8 6 4: ◇ 8: ♣ K 4 3 2:

(j) ♠ 9 7 4: ♡ K 10 9 3: ◇ K J: ♣ A K J 6:

(k) ♠ K 10 7: ♡ 8 7 6: ◇ 7: ♣ A K J 6 5 3:

(l) ♠ Q J 8 4: ♡ K 7 5 4 2: ◇ 5: ♣ A J 4:

(m) ♠ 7 2: ♡ 6 4 2: ◇ A Q 9 5: ♣ A J 7 4:

(n) ♠ J 7 6: ♡ K 10 3: ◇ A Q 4: ♣ Q 9 6 3:

ANSWERS TO REVISION QUIZ
ON CHAPTER 18

(a) Double. With 10 points, only a doubleton spade and five of the opponent's suit, you must be onto a good thing. If they try to escape into clubs, partner can possibly double.

(b) 2♡ This is the bid you would have made without intervention and you can make it naturally just the same.

(c) 2♠ Again this is a natural bid. Your weak hand is just good for a 2♠ Limit Bid with or without the diamond bid.

(d) 3♢ The forcing bid which gives you time to explore for the best game contract. If partner has the club Ace you will be thinking in terms of the Grand Slam.

(e) 2♡ Here again, you would bid 2♡ without the intervening bid and there is no reason to alter your bid.

(f) 3♠ A natural Limit Bid which the intervention does nothing to alter.

(g) 2♠ On this hand you would just have managed a switch to 2♣ as your response. As, however, the 2♢ call now forces you to the three-level if you want to show your clubs it is wiser to suppress them in favour of a 2♠ raise.

(h) Double. No support for partner, 8 points and five diamonds. This should be your best available contract.

(i) 2♠ Another natural Limit Bid.

(j) 3♢ Either 2♡ or 3♣ would be misleading, as would a raise in spades at this stage, although you want to reach a game.

243

(k) 3♣   This time your club suit is too good to hide
          and you can well afford to hear partner rebid
          3♠, which you will raise to 4♠, risking that
          he holds the hearts covered.

(l) 2♡   You are too strong for a 3♠ Limit Bid
          which you fear partner might pass, so you
          temporise with 2♡. If he only bids 2♠ over
          this you make a delayed game raise to 4♠.

(m) Double. This should be a good bet and is really
          your only possible bid, as you cannot offer
          No Trumps with nothing at all in hearts.

(n) 2 N.T. For all its point count, the hand is too
          evenly balanced, especially with three of
          partner's suit, to double the 2◇, and you
          make, since you hold a double stop in that
          suit, a natural Limit Bid of 2 N.T.

CHAPTER 19

Slam Conventions

THE likelihood of it being possible to make a slam on any two combined hands may be apparent from the outset of the auction, or at any rate immediately the opening bid has been made, when responder sees his own hand in relation to his partner's bid. The three important factors which are required are suit control, honour strength and, above all, the right fit, and it is frequently possible to discover which of these conditions exist before recourse to any slam convention is necessary. You dare not bid a small slam with more than one first round control missing, and you must in any case be sure of second round control of any suit where first round control is missing, or the opposition is likely to step in smartly and cash their two winning tricks before you even get under way. First round control is represented by an Ace or a void, though it goes without saying that a void as a control is only acceptable if one has found a fit in the proposed trump suit, and that a void instead of the Ace is a liability rather than an asset if the contract is to be in No Trumps!

Once the trump suit has been agreed and slam investigations have started, first round controls can be shown, as often as not, by way of cue bids as described in Chapter 10. Frequently it will be clear quite soon that the necessary controls are missing, so that the bidding can be allowed to rest at a lower level than a slam. On many occasions, however, further information will be needed by one or other of the partners, and he will then bring into use whichever slam convention has been agreed between them.

The four most frequently used conventions are "Norman", the "Four-Club Blackwood" (sometimes confused with "Gerber", which is a device for Ace-showing after No-Trump opening bids, as already explained), that good old favourite Blackwood itself, and the Culbertson Four-Five No Trump convention. Of these, the last two are by far the most generally popular, though we will have to look at the mechanics of all four, as well as what is known as the Bowers variation. Many experts still prefer the Culbertson Four-Five No Trump, though Blackwood, because of its greater simplicity, is more widely used by the general run of Acol players.

All conventions have their own victories, as I said when discussing the possible methods of dealing with pre-emptive bids. If you use "Blackwood" you will undoubtedly meet hands on which you wish you had been using one of the others, but my own advice is to know and understand both the Culbertson Four-Five and Blackwood, and to consider these as reasonable alternatives. The others tend to be dangerous outside a regular partnership.

1. THE FOUR-CLUB BLACKWOOD

This convention uses a bid of 4♣ as an enquiry for Aces from partner on a very similar 'step' principle to that employed with the "Gerber" Convention. After the response, a similar bid of 5♣ asks for Kings,

and the convention may even be taken as far as a bid
of 6♣ enquiring for Queens.

A response of 4◇ denies the holding of an Ace, 4♡
shows one Ace, 4♠ shows two, 4 N.T. shows three and,
by arrangement, either 5♣ or 4◇ may show all four.
If the responder to the 4♣ bid shows either one or two
Aces by bidding 4♡ or 4♠, a rebid of 4 N.T. from
opener now asks specifically *which* Aces. When one
Ace is held, it can be identified by a bid of that suit—
that is, over 4 N.T., 5◇ would show the diamond Ace.
To show precisely which two Aces when the response
has been 4♠, Norman Squires suggests the following
method:—

(a) If both Aces are the same colour, i.e., diamond
and heart, or club and spade, bid 5♣.

(b) If both are of the same rank, that is both in the
major suits or both in the minor suits, bid 5◇.

(c) If the two form an odd combination, i.e., one
black and one red, or one major and one minor,
bid 5♡.

Thus a player who has made this 4 N.T. bid,
provided that he has one Ace himself, can tell exactly
which two of the remaining three his partner holds.

This Four-Club Blackwood bid cannot be used
when there is any possibility that it may be taken as a
natural club bid, which is one of its disadvantages,
though on other occasions it gains bidding space for
the partnership. I have, however, seen it come grievously
'unstuck' when one player thought it natural and the
other thought it conventional.

2. THE NORMAN CONVENTION

This is initiated with a bid of 4 N.T., and the responses are given in terms of a point count, covering both Aces and Kings. An Ace counts as one point and a King as half a point, so that there is a total of six points available, and a different form of 'step' principle is used:

With less than 1½ points, i.e., less than one Ace and one King	..	..	bid 5♣
With 1½ points	..	..	..	..	„ 5◇
With 2 „	..	..	..	..	„ 5♡
With 2½ „	..	..	..	..	„ 5♠
With 3 „	..	..	..	..	„ 5 N.T.
With 3½ „	..	..	..	..	„ 6♣

&c., &c.

Long and agonising can be the trances while a player who has initiated the convention and is not very familiar with its workings, seeks to determine just how the 2½ points of a 5♠ response are made up. They may, of course, be one Ace and three Kings or two Aces and one King, and sad will be the day when you need two Aces for your slam.

3. THE CULBERTSON FOUR-FIVE NO-TRUMP CONVENTION

Here again, as with "Norman", the bid of 4 N.T. is a request for information, though this time on a rather more complicated scale. One vital difference too, is that the player who initiates the 4 N.T. bid must himself have a specific holding, that is, *either* three Aces *or* two Aces and the King of a suit bid by the partnership, whereas with the other conventions the initiator need have no special holding as long as he is morally certain that he will not be pushing the level of the bidding too high.

These positive requirements for the 4 N.T. bid can work two ways. The fact that a player can bid 4 N.T. gives what may be invaluable information to his partner but, on the other hand, a player may be most anxious to find out about his partner's Ace and King holdings and be unable to do so because he has not got the requirements for the 4 N.T. bid. There is, however, no doubt of the convention's efficacy when used correctly.

The responses, when partner has bid 4 N.T., are as follows:

(1) With two Aces *or* one Ace and the Kings of *all* suits bid by the partnership, bid 5 N.T.

(2) With one Ace only or a void, and that in a suit not already bid, bid 5 of that suit.

(3) With the Ace of a suit previously bid *or* the Kings of all suits previously bid, bid six of the best trump suit.

(4) With no Ace, sign-off by bidding five of the lowest ranking suit bid by the partnership.

In applying the Four-Five No Trump convention to the Acol system, it must be noted that when the opening bid has been the Acol conventional one of 2♣, the club suit does not rank as one bid by the partnership, and nor does the equally conventional 2◊ response.

An immediate bid of 4 N.T. is made in reply to an opening bid when responder is interested only in whether opener holds both the Ace and the King of the suit he has bid. If he does, the response is 5 N.T., as in No. 1 above, as in this case he holds the responding requirements of one Ace and the King of all suits bid.

♠ A
♡ A K J 8 5 4
◇ Q J 8 6
♣ A 6

If partner opens 1◇ and you find yourself holding such a hand as this, your immediate bid should be 4 N.T., which agrees diamonds as trumps and asks for the diamond Ace and King. If opener holds both, he bids 5 N.T. if he holds one of them only, he signs off in 5◇. If responder chooses to force in hearts before making this 4 N.T. bid, the issue will be clouded, as two suits will have been bid by the partnership.

4. THE BLACKWOOD CONVENTION

This well-tried favourite is the simplest of all to learn, to apply, and to interpret. Before using it there is only one essential, and that is that the trump suit must have been agreed, either directly or by inference.

A bid of 4 N.T. asks responder to show the number of Aces held, and this he does according to the following table:

With no Ace	..	5♣
„ one Ace	..	5◇
„ two Aces	..	5♡
„ three Aces	..	5♠
„ all four Aces		5♣

You will note that the response to show either no Ace at all or all four is the same, but this should not cause any possible risk of confusion because the partnership will not, I hope, be going "slamming" with no Aces at all between them! The 5♣ bid is used to show all four Aces so that a subsequent bid of 5 N.T. can be made asking for Kings, which responder must show on the same table but one step higher.

If an opponent intervenes over the 4 N.T. bid, and provided you don't want to double the intervention for penalties, the Blackwood responses are modified as follows:

With no Ace	..	Pass
With one Ace	..	Bid the suit ranking next above opponent's suit.
With two Aces	..	Bid the *next* higher ranking, and so on.

As with all intervening bids, this may run you into difficulties as, for instance, if you have to bid 6♣ over 5♠ to show one Ace. Here judgement must be your guide, with the rider that it is generally better to tell your partner the truth about your holding, and to answer any questions he may have asked.

A quantitative raise of an opening No Trump bid direct to 4 N.T. is always a slam try, but is not a conventional bid enquiring about Aces. It is, in any case, not a position where confusion will arise very frequently, as the mechanics available for investigation over an opening No Trumper are now increased by the addition of "Gerber".

There is another important feature of the Blackwood Convention which you should know, and that is how to deal with the situation when the 4 N.T. bid has asked for Aces and the response has, disappointingly, left you one short of slam requirements. It can also happen that, in this situation, you would like to play the hand in No Trumps, but, because it is a further conventional bid enquiring about Kings, cannot bid this. In this case the 4 N.T. bidder next bids *the lowest available suit not previously bid by the partnership*, which asks responder to return the contract to 5 N.T. This is not nearly as confusing as it sounds, and is really only a form of transfer bid. Look at this sequence:—

1♡—3◇   Responder to the original bid forced with
4◇—4 N.T.   3◇ which opener raised to 4◇. Ob-
5◇—5♠   viously in the hope of finding opener with
5 N.T.   at least two Aces, responder then bid
4 N.T., but was disappointed to hear
that the opening hand held only one. Wanting, for reasons
of his own (possibly with Match Points in view) to play the
hand in No Trumps, and unable to bid this himself as it
would be conventional, he bids 5♠—a suit not yet bid by
either partner—asking for the transfer back to 5 N.T., which
he will then pass.

You should remember one other thing, and that is
that Blackwood, as indeed all other conventions, is a
supplementary aid to good bidding and not a substitute for it. The making of a slam does not depend
solely on the position of Aces and Kings, so that
Blackwood should only be used when the information
it can elicit is really necessary, and after a decision has
been made as to the probable trick-taking capacity of
the combined hands.

THE ACOL DIRECT KING CONVENTION

The King Convention is an additional weapon
which modern Acol adds to the Blackwood convention,
and when using it, a bid of 4 N.T. by the partner of a
player who, by his bid has already specifically stated
his Ace holding, asks immediately about Kings. This
perhaps needs some clarification.

In Chapter 11 two sequences are explained,
2♣—2◇ and 2♣—2◇ where responder's final bids
2♠—4♠   2♠—4♡ both deny the possession of
any first round controls. In
the first, the double raise to 4♠ is conventional, showing
trump support and no Ace or void, and in the second,
the 4♡ bid shows a long solid trump suit missing the

Ace. The hand cannot contain an outside Ace or it would have been bid as a positive response in the first place. Then again, in Chapter 13, we have the double raise of an opening strong Two Bid, and the immediate bid of 3 N.T. opposite an opening Two Bid, showing 10—11 Aceless points. In addition there is the 4♣-4◇ Convention where responder will already have said that he holds either two or three Aces. Acol does not waste its bids, and there can be no object at all in asking partner what Aces he holds when he has already made a bid giving this information. In these circumstances, 4 N.T. asks at once for Kings, by-passing the request for Aces.

♠ K Q 9 8
♡ A K J 6 3
◇ A 7
♣ A 6

Suppose that the bidding has gone like this:—

2♣—2◇
2♡—4♡

4♡ is the conventional raise showing heart support in a hand with no first round controls but other scattered honour strength. The trump support will be at least as good as Q x x and probably better so that there will be an odds-on chance of losing no tricks in that suit, and if responder holds the two missing Kings as well, a 6♡ contract should be more than an odds-on bet. Missing one of the Kings it would be too dangerous, as the opening lead would very probably knock out one of the minor suit Aces while the opposition still hold the ♠A as an entry to get in to cash a trick in the suit concerned. Let us look at two possible response hands opposite our opening bid example, on both of which responder would raise opener's 2♡ to 4♡.

(a) ♠ 6
♡ Q 7 5 2
◇ K 10 8 6
♣ K 9 5 4

On this hand, of course, 6♡ is the correct contract and should be reached either with or without the King Convention. Without it, over 4 N.T. the response would be 5♣ to show no Aces, and over the subsequent 5 N.T. responder would show two Kings with 6♡, which opener passes.

253

Equally, using the convention, responder shows his two Kings by bidding 5♡ over 4 N.T., and opener raises to 6♡. Note, however, that if the response to 5 N.T. is 6◇, the partnership is forced into 6♡, as in this next example.

(b)   ♠ J 10 7   On this hand, when the ordinary
      ♡ Q 10 7 6   "Blackwood" 4 N.T. receives the
      ◇ K J 6   negative response of 5♣ to show no
      ♣ 10 3 2   Ace, the subsequent 5 N.T., if opener
                    risks bidding it, forces the contract
into the slam level whether two Kings are held by responder or not. Now, however, you can bid it thus:—

2♣   —2◇   You can stop in 5♡ if one of the Kings is
2♡   —4♡   missing or proceed to 6♡ if both are
4 N.T.—5◇   present and correct. The point, of course,
5 or 6♡   is that you are enabled to save a round of
                    bidding in the search for Kings without
having to risk being forced into a slam which is not on or missing one that is.

Similarly, of course, in the sequence 1♡—4◇, responder has shown three Aces, so 4 N.T. from opener asks immediately for Kings.

5. THE BOWERS VARIATION

This variation is a refinement of the Blackwood Convention, and it surprises me that it has not become more generally popular. I have tried it out myself and found it to be highly satisfactory, in that it has the effect of eliminating one of the unfortunate features of Blackwood, the difficulty of distinguishing just where responder's Aces and Kings are held. It can also be modified to include its own variation of the King Convention which we have just been discussing. I offer it to you, therefore, as a very reasonable alternative to either the Culbertson Four-Five No Trump or Blackwood itself, though you must remember to make very sure that your partner knows it too!

The Bowers variation is attributed to the American player, S. J. Bowers, and although mention of it has been made in print on more than one occasion, it appears to be very little known or used in this country. Give it a trial—I don't think you will be sorry.

In the normal Blackwood, responder to the 4 N.T. bid shows the *number* of Aces (and later, if asked, of Kings) which he holds, with no reference at all to which Aces or Kings they may be, information which may be of very great importance. Under the Bowers Variation this difficulty is largely eliminated, and the table of responses is as follows:

With no Ace	5♣
With one Ace *in a suit not bid by the partnership*	5◇
With one Ace *in a suit bid by either partner*	5♡
With two Aces	5♠
With three Aces	5 N.T.
With four Aces	6♣

The last two of these responses are most unlikely to be required, as the 4 N.T. bidder will exceedingly rarely be initiating the convention with either two or three Aces missing. If he should do so, it can only be because of his own heavy values in Kings and Queens so that he will be unlikely to need to bid 5 N.T. to ask for Kings when his partner has already used the bid to show three Aces. If it should happen, which is, of course, possible, then the question about Kings cannot be asked, but 5 N.T. over any response up to and including 5♠ asks for Kings in the normal way, and the same scale of responses is used.

As I have said, this convention can be adapted perfectly easily to cover the King Convention which is used in exactly the same way as explained already when responder has made a bid specifically showing his Ace holding, except that the table above should be used in responding.

The convention is as simple as Blackwood to operate, but perhaps just one explanatory example would be a help. Take this sequence:—

1♡—2♠   In response to this 4 N.T., 5◇ would
3♠—4 N.T.   indicate one Ace, either the club or
                       diamond as these have not yet been
bid. 5♡ would also show the possession of one Ace, this time either the heart or spade, as these are the two suits already bid by the partnership. 5♠ would show two Aces— any two Aces, of course—and so on. You may feel that this still leaves a wide margin for guessing which Aces they are, but in practice this is not really so as, in the great majority of cases the 4 N.T. bidder's own holding will make the position quite clear. If he, for example, gets the response of 5◇ showing one Ace in a suit not yet bid, and if he holds the ◇A himself, it is perfectly clear that his partner's Ace is the Club, and so on.

All the slam conventions have their difficulties and failures, the pitfall of "Blackwood in the minors" being too well known to need explanation here. For anyone who is not clear about it, though, you will readily understand that if your proposed trump suit is clubs, any enquiry for Aces which receives a positive response (i.e., 5◇ for one Ace) drives the contract into 6♣, for which reason it is highly dangerous to use Blackwood when seeking a club slam contract. This difficulty is not avoided with the Bowers variation, but after all, these things don't happen very often, and if and when they do you must go to even greater pains to find out about Aces and so on by way of cue bids before committing the partnership to an unmakeable slam.

THE MODIFIED GRAND SLAM FORCE

There is another modern modification which I should like to mention here, as it can be grafted onto any of these slam conventions without damage and with, in fact, considerable benefit. Under this modification a bid of 5 N.T., when not preceded by 4 N.T., asks partner to show *how many* of the three top honours are held in the agreed trump suit. Holding none, responder bids 6♣, holding one he bids six of the agreed trump suit, and holding two he bids a direct seven. Judged against the 5 N.T. bidder's own holding in the suit, this gives a pretty accurate picture. The advantage of this modification is that it allows a player who himself holds two of the three top honours to use the force.

West	*East*
♠ A K Q 8 4 2	♠ 7
♡ A Q	♡ J 9 8 5
◇ A Q 10 7	◇ K J 9 8 2
♣ 5	♣ A 9 8

Here is an example from a recent match. West opened 2♣ and was pleasantly surprised to get a positive response of 3◇ from East, showing an Ace and a King and a biddable diamond suit. Which Ace is already clear, but which King is vitally important and West, using this modification, was able to find out. An immediate bid of 5 N.T. agreed diamonds as trumps and East, holding one of the three top diamond honours, duly bid 6◇. West, with the other two, raised to 7◇.

CHAPTER 20

Acol Aids

THROUGHOUT this book it has been stressed that the best bidding as well as the most effective is the pure basic Acol, cutting out unnecessary elaborations and conventions, bidding your cards to the full, and not waiting for partner to bid them for you. Those of you, though, who have come all the way to this last chapter may have spotted what one might well call a fundamental fallacy in this.

To keep the Acol system pure and simple is not as simple as all that. It is all very well to tell you to omit unnecessary elaborations and conventions when a number of these have become both necessary and essential and are so much a part of the system that they need not even be mentioned as conventional. The fit-finding bids of clubs over No Trump openings—cue bids—trial bids—Blackwood or 4-5 N.T.—all these and others are conventions grafted onto the basic system without which it would be the poorer. They have, in fact, become an integral part of the system and others, no doubt, will do the same. Others, again, may be discarded or replaced.

As you will have realised, a number of the newest and most helpful of the modern techniques have already been incorporated in the text thus far. There are, however, a few others which have not fallen naturally into place, and it is important that they should not be overlooked. For the vast majority of hands, the Acol system will work fully and adequately without

them, but just as, from time to time, you need the
assistance of a particular conventional bid, so from
time to time you will find these additional aids of great
help in reaching the right resting-place without
guessing or "shooting".

If you are playing with a strange partner, check, as
you would do about any of the "reasonable alternatives" of slam conventions and so on, as to whether
he knows and understands their use. If he doesn't,
don't confuse him by trying to explain—the chances
are that you may go through a whole session without
even feeling the need for one of them. If he does know
and understand them, well and good—take full
advantage of it. If he doesn't, you won't be missing a
very great deal, and you will not be running the risk
of a major misunderstanding which may cost hundreds
of points. I am thinking now of two extremely competent players who had played through some 180 boards
at a Congress without one serious misunderstanding
and then, on the very last board of the very last session
"chucked" 1000 points at Aggregate Pairs because
of their different interpretation of the use of the
Unusual No Trump, a bid which had not cropped up
on any of the previous boards. This bid is one which
I propose to discuss in this Chapter, and we may as well
take it first.

THE UNUSUAL NO-TRUMP

As its name implies, this is a bid in No-Trumps in
any unusual situation or rather, when the bid cannot
be expected to be a genuine No Trump one. It may be
used at any level of the bidding, and its most usual
application is when the bidder of it is preparing to

"sacrifice", generally when not vulnerable against vulnerable opponents.

There are various schools of thought as to the most profitable method of using the bid, but you will not go far wrong if you regard it as a form of take-out double expressing shape rather than honour strength, though it may include the latter as well.

N. E. S. W.   Here, the 2 N.T. bid
1♢ — 1♠ 2 N.T. from West calls on East
          to bid the better of the
two remaining suits, in this case clubs or hearts, but if opponents have called only one major suit, as, for instance, 1♡—3♡, 3 N.T. would call on partner to show his better *minor* suit. If any two suits have been bid by opponents, then the No Trump bidder is asking for partner's choice between the other two.

N. E. S. W.   As already explained, the
1♠ — 2♡ — bid may be used at any
3♡ — 4♠ — level and here West, after
— 4N.T. — ? East's 4 N.T. bid, must
          show his preference as
between clubs and diamonds. Doubtless the reason for East not coming into the auction at a lower level was the vain hope that North-South would not bid to game. Now that they have reached 4♠ he sees no hope of defeating the contract, but does visualise a profitable "sacrifice" in one of the minors.

♠ 4   Such a hand as this would be typical
♡ J 6   if East were not vulnerable against
♢ K J 7 6 2 vulnerable opponents. It holds no
♣ Q J 9 7 6 defence at all but should develop
         reasonable playing tricks if partner
can produce some holding in clubs or diamonds.

In responding to an "unusual" No Trump bid,

partner must show whichever of the two suits he prefers, even if it is only the choice of a doubleton over a singleton. Whatever the holding, length must be preferred to honour strength.

Another important point to remember is that, as with a take-out double, an intervening bid lets responder "off the hook" and he should take the opportunity to pass unless he really has some length in one of the suits "asked". Thus the decision as to whether to double opponent's high contract or to seek the sacrifice by a further No Trump request can be left to partner. I am thinking here of the disaster I mentioned at the beginning of this chapter. The bidding had been:

N.	E.	S.	W.	
1♠	—	3♡	3N.T.	
4♠	5♣	6♠		

West, who had bid 3 N.T., not vulnerable against vulnerable opponents, had a singleton spade, six clubs to the Ace and six diamonds to the Ace. When East came in voluntarily with 5♣ and South still confidently bid to 6♠, West immediately visualised length in clubs with East and a void in the South hand which meant that his own hand was good for one trick— the ♢A—only. He therefore "sacrificed" in 7♣ which was doubled and four down when the 6♠ slam also would have gone down. East, instead of taking the opportunity to pass, had bid 5♣ on a 3-point hand with 4-3-3-3 distribution, the four-card suit being hearts.

Should the "unusual" No Trump bid be doubled a valuable choice of bids is now open to responder who, on the bidding thus far, cannot be expected to hold a very good hand. The double, however, enables him to tell his partner just where his strength, if any, lies. Thus:

(a) Holding strength only in the opponents' suits and nothing worth mentioning in the two "asked" suits, he passes the double, e.g., 1♠—No—2♡—2N.T.—A pass now shows x — ? only length to be in hearts or spades.

(b) With a marked preference for one or other of the two "asked" suits he bids that suit.

(c) With a reasonable holding in *both* the remaining suits, he redoubles, which tells his partner to make his own choice.

N.	E.	S.	W.
1♠	—	2♡	—
3♡	—	4♠	—
—	4N.T. x	?	

Holding:

♠ Q J 9 4
♡ J 10 3
◇ 7 6 3
♣ 8 6 5

Pass. The only strength in the hand, little though it is, is in opponents' hearts and spades. Without the double West would bid 5♣.

♠ 9 7 6
♡ 5 3
◇ J 10 9 6 5
♣ Q 7 5

Bid 5◇. The hand contains a very definite preference for the suit and should, with any luck, produce an excellent sacrifice even at the slam level.

♠ 8 7
♡ 7 3
◇ J 9 8 6 5
♣ Q 10 9 6

Redouble. In this case either clubs or diamonds will make an excellent choice as trumps and East may as well decide which he himself would prefer.

At the lower levels the bid may be used to make an immediate announcement of an enormous hand in the remaining two suits by jumping the level of the No Trump bid.

N.	E.	S.	W.
1♠	—	2♡	3N.T.

West's 3 N.T. bid would announce just about an Acol opening Two Bid in clubs and diamonds.

N.	E.	S.	W.
1◇	—	1♠	3N.T.

Here West's 3 N.T., again a jump bid, would show a strong two-suiter in clubs and hearts. Note that a bid of 1 N.T. would be natural and of 2 N.T., a mere two-suiter willing to compete.

N.	E.	S.	W.	Compare, however, this 2 N.T
1♡	2N.T.	—	—	bid by East, a normal "Unusual"
				N.T. asking for preference in
				the minors.

DIRECTIONAL ASKING BIDS

The use of a Directional Asking Bid is quite often the only means by which a partnership can find a No Trump contract in the face of an opponent's intervening bid. There are frequent instances of a strong hand anxious to play in No Trumps except for a weakness of, say, Q x only in the opposition's suit. All he needs to be able to find out is whether his partner has even half a stop in the suit, that is to say K x or J x x to support his own Q x.

♠ Q 8		*S.*	*W.*	*N.*	*E.*
♡ K J 6		1♢	—	1N.T.	2♠
♢ A K Q J 7 5		3♠			
♣ A 6					
South					

With a certain spade lead coming from East, South dare not bid 3 N.T. unless assured that North has some sort of a stop in the suit whereas the combined hands would be highly unlucky not to develop nine tricks between them if North holds even a partial guard in spades. South's 3♠ bid, therefore, is a Directional Asking Bid, requesting North to convert to 3 N.T. if he can offer the slender holding required to 'boost' South's own Q x in spades. Similarly,

S.	*W.*	*N.*	*E.*	the 2♠ from South is once
1♢	1♠	2♣	—	again a Directional Asking Bid
2♠				to which North should respond
				with 2 N.T. if he holds a partial
				guard in spades.

Confusion with cue bids is extremely unlikely to cause trouble because South can always remove the No Trump response. In the last sequence above, for example, if South had intended his 2♠ to show agreement of clubs as trumps coupled with first round control of spades, he could take out North's response into any appropriate number of clubs.

Whilst not forcing to game. Directional Asking Bids are, of course, unconditionally forcing for one round, and responder must bid in No Trumps or return to the most suitable trump contract, as his hand dictates.

If a player himself holds a certain guard in the opponent's suit, he can still make a Directional Asking Bid, this time in the hope of placing the No Trump contract with his partner as declarer. Take as an example such a deal as this:

West	East	E.	S.	W.	N.
♠ A 8 6 5 4	♠ Q J	1♣	—	1♠	2◇
♡ Q 7 4	♡ A J 9	?			
◇ Q 7	◇ A 8 6				
♣ 10 7 6	♣ K Q J 9 5				

In this case, if East bids the No Trumps, the diamond lead will come *through* any stopper West may hold, whereas if West is able to respond to a Directional Asking Bid by showing a partial stop in diamonds, the original lead will come up to him. If diamonds are led, this will give declarer two stops in the suit, or, alternatively, the defence will have to lose a 'tempo' towards clearing their diamonds by opening with another suit.

"SHARPLES" TWO CLUB OVERCALL

The menace of the weak No Trump opening bid is a very real one. Partner of the opening bidder may pass on as many as ten points so that the opposition will not know whether opener and his partner hold a combined count of 22 or more points or whether they themselves hold the balance of power, and are more than likely to be in doubt as to the best course to take. This, of course, is the main objective of the bid, as no one can deny that to open 1 N.T. on a meagre twelve points vulnerable can be asking for trouble in a big way. On balance, however, it is the opposition who get into trouble, either by letting the bid be passed out or by doubling it. As often as not 1 N.T. doubled creeps home, or the opposition pair get into an unmakeable contract over it and themselves go down or, alternatively, miss a comfortable part-score for their side. It is for this reason that I continually preach the virtues of the weak No Trump, and I am perfectly prepared to accept the few bad boards it may bring me.

In an endeavour to find a counter to this difficult-to-cope-with opening bid, the Sharples Two Club has been developed. It is in effect a weak take-out double of the opening No Trump bid, which leaves the double itself free to show a strong hand with a low limit of 16 points. Knowing that this count can be relied upon, the partner of the doubler is in a very much happier position when he has to judge whether or not to take the double out (on weakness) or whether he and his partner do, in fact, hold the balance of the points which gives them an odds-on chance of defeating the contract.

Holding a strong hand opposite to a double of 1 N.T., responder may elect to go on for a game or slam if his hand or the state of the score appear to make this more profitable.

Let us return to the Two Club overcall itself. If the double is to be made only on a strong hand of 16 or more points, this request for a take-out will be weaker, and the bid is particularly useful on hands containing

265

no better than a four-card suit which cannot be used in overcalling without misleading partner.

The Sharples Two Club may be used in either the direct overcalling or the protective position. This is a bid of 2♣, or 2◇ holding a singleton or void in clubs, on hands which are either not strong enough, or unsuitable, for a double of the opening 1 N.T. A rebid of 3♣ after an original over-call of 2◇ shows a minor two-suiter.

Partner should respond naturally (suits in ascending order if he has a choice). 2 N.T. shows 11-12 points, and 3 N.T. shows 13-14 points. These last two bids normally deny the holding of a biddable major.

The convention is negatived when used by a player who has already passed, i.e.,

S.	W.	N.	E.	In this sequence the 2◇ bid is
No	1 NT	No	No	natural, as too would a 2♣ bid
2◇				by South in this situation.*

The long and the short of it is that no sure way of dealing with a weak No Trump to the best advantage has yet been found, and it still remains largely a matter of luck—backed, of course, by some judgement—in most cases, whether you get the best result from passing overcalling, doubling, or bidding 2♣. This latter bid is, however, an added weapon which it is worth adding to your store.

FOURTH SUIT FORCING

The use of a bid in the fourth suit is another of which the meaning is open to different interpretations, though the Acol use of it is quite clear. The modern technique is to use it somewhat as an extension of the Directional Asking Bids for the purpose of investigating a possible

* Three American methods of countering opening No Trump bids are now available. They are "Ripstra", "Landy", and "Astro".

No Trump game contract. The one thing it is essential that you should understand is that the bid of the fourth suit does *not*, repeat **not,** show a good holding in the suit concerned, for which reason alone it must be treated as unconditionally forcing for one round.

It is a bid to be used when you are doubtful of what else to say—when you feel that between the two hands a game must be on—and particularly when you suspect that if partner can produce a partial guard in that mystic fourth suit, the game should be attempted in the cheaper No Trump contract rather than in a suit. Note at this point that if the bidder himself held a good stop in the suit, he could himself bid the No Trumps. Some examples may clarify the sort of situations where the bid may be found most useful.

♠ Q 5
♡ K 8 6
◇ K 9 2
♣ A K 9 6 4

Your partner deals and bids 1♡ to which you make the normal reply of 2♣, and partner rebids 2◇. This is a clear moment for the use of the fourth suit bid of 2♠, *asking* partner if he can provide a partial stop in spades to boost your own Q 5. In spite of your 15 points you dare not bid No Trumps yourself for fear of having a long spade suit run against you, yet surely your hand, opposite to an opening bid, should produce game. If partner confirms a spade stop by bidding 2 N.T., raise to 3 N.T. If he can only repeat one of his red suits you will have to raise to a game contract in a suit, requiring more tricks than 3 N.T. would do.

♠ Q 9
♡ A J 7
◇ A 9 8 6 5
♣ J 10 3

Here is another one. Partner opens 1♣ to which, in the natural course of events, you respond 1◇ and partner now rebids 1♡. What, you may well ask yourself, are you to bid next? With partner bidding clubs and hearts you dare not make the 2 N.T. bid your count demands with only a doubleton spade. Again, you resort to the 'fourth suit forcing' bid of 1♠, which gets you out of all trouble. If partner raises spades you revert to No Trumps. He will not raise you to game in spades, however good his holding in the suit, because he will recognise that you almost certainly have *not* got a biddable spade suit.

♠ A 6 5
♡ A 8 7
◇ Q J 9 8 2
♣ Q 5

Partner opens 1♠ to which you reply 2◇ and partner rebids 2♡. For the third time, without this fourth suit bid you are in difficulties. A jump preference in spades is not attractive on such an empty hand, yet a simple preference to 2♠ is an understatement of your values, so you make a 'fourth suit' bid of 3♣. Now if partner rebids his hearts you know he is 5-5, and you can give him a raise to 4♡, his first suit. If he rebids 3♠ you know he is 5-4 (or perhaps 6-4) and give him 4♠. If he bids 3 N.T. you can pass quite happily because you know that *he* knows he can't rely on you for more than a partial club stop, let alone a club suit.

One final word, and that is that the bidder of the fourth suit should confine himself to using it only when he has a minimum of Q x or J x x in it, that is to say, holding a partial guard himself which his partner's partial guard will support into a stop. Otherwise the partnership is quite likely to find itself in the ignominious position of reaching a highly scientific 3 N.T. contract with Q x of the fourth suit in one hand and J x in the other.

Epilogue

YOU should by now, if you have read this book and done the Revision Quizzes, be equipped to go out into the big wide world of Contract Bridge and say that you play Acol. At least you will have assimilated something, I hope, of the Acol technique, principles, and 'attitude of mind' which will, if you have any natural aptitude for the game, make you into an Acol player.

For the time being you will need to practice, to play against people who are better and more experienced than yourself, and to watch how they handle the various difficult situations which crop up. I'll give you two final examples, to end this book, of what I mean, both of which are based on the need to bid your own hand and not to wait for your partner to bid it for you. Both these hands come from what was really very much of a beginner's session, composed largely of Sixth Form Grammar School boys. They were all intelligent, interested, and keen, but inexperienced,

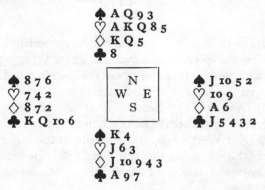

269

though most of them will become fine players in the future, but they were no match for one experienced Acol pair playing amongst them.

When North, the dealer, opened 1 ♡ South, in several instances, responded 1 N.T. It is true that this is a "text book" reply on a holding of 5-9 points, but these South bidders failed to remember that the bid, in addition to announcing the point count and ability to keep the bidding open, also announces the *inability* to bid anything more constructive. Here South held nine points, a heart fit, and a diamond suit of his own. Result? A final contract of 4♡ making six, instead of 6♡ bid and made. Anyway, what experienced Acol player would open only 1 ♡ on the North hand?

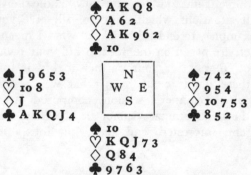

Here is the second example which is, perhaps, even more to the point. At Love All when West opened 1♣, not one pair other than the experienced one, managed to bid the 'cold' heart slam on the North-South hands. Why? Because most of them failed to recognise the fact that North's hand contained a force of 2♣ over West's 1♣, and opposite to the one North player who did make this call, South did not recognise the enormous power of his hand in response to the announced strength of the force. The experienced pair were in no doubt at all, and sailed merrily into 6♡ which, of course, cannot be defeated.

In Acol you **bid your own cards, and you don't wait for your partner to bid them for you**—he won't, he'll be too busy bidding his own. It is up to you, therefore, if you are North in a situation like the one above, to tell your partner of your enormous hand, and if you happen to be South instead, it is up to you to read the message and realise that your own hand has become enormous too. So practice, read the book again, and when you fail to bid a game or slam that more experienced bidders reach, make a mental note of where you went wrong so that you won't repeat the error.

Apart from some lucky distributional hands, you will inevitably find that missed contracts are the fault of under-bidding, of failure to bid your own cards to the full, or to revalue them in the light of what your partner has bid, of failure to force when you have the strength to do so—of failure, in fact, to adopt the Acol 'attitude of mind'. Once you have achieved this, you will wake up one day to find that you really are an Acol player! Don't let yourself remain one of the bidders that our Acol-ite is thinking of on the next page!

SOLILOQUY OF AN ACOL-ITE
by Rhoda Barrow

Respectfully dedicated to all those who, being blissfully
unaware of the basic principles of the Acol System,
which they profess to play, continue to frustrate their
partners with their knavish tricks. With deep apologies
also, to the Prince of Denmark.

To bid, or not to bid: that is the question:
Whether 'tis nobler in the mind to suffer
The calls and passes of outrageous partner,
Or to make bids against a sea of doubles
And, by revoking, lose them? To bid, to play:
No more; and by our calls to know we show
Our best suits from the thousand natural shapes
That hands are heir to—many's the combination
Devoutly to be wish'd. To bid, to play:
To play: perchance to win a good fat Rub.
For from that lead of King, what tricks may come,
When we have shuffled up this brand new pack,
Must give us pause: there's the finesse
That makes calamity of our long suit.
And who would bear the Yarboroughs and misfits,
Opponent's wrong and partner's contumely,
The pangs of trumpéd Ace, declarer's scorn,
Kibitzer's nasty sneers, and all the tricks
Palooka partner to the unworthy gives,
When he himself might the whole contract break
With his bare ten-spot? Who would part-scores call,
To grunt and sweat over the dreary cards,
But that the fear of cutting afterwards
The Acol-spoiling learner from whose mouth
No right bid ever comes, puzzles the will,
And makes us rather bear the one we have
Than risk the others that we know not of.
Thus Contract doth make cowards of us all,
And thus the simplest points of Acol bidding
Are sicklied o'er with the pale cast of thought,
And slam hands of great strength and moment
With this regard declarer plays awry,
To chuck both game and auction.

SUMMARY OF THE
ACOL SYSTEM

No: 1 OPENING SUIT BIDS OF ONE

REQUIREMENTS, VULNERABLE OR NOT VULNERABLE		
Point Value Minimum	*Distribution	Comments
LIGHT OPENING 9–10	6-card suit. Two 5-card major suits.	Tactical attacking bid when (a) A safe sign-off in 6-card suit is available, OR (b) Development is possible with two 5-card major suits.
12+	5-card trump suit. Two or three biddable 4-card suits.	Hand must offer a safe rebid. 5-card suit should be as good as K Q 10 x x.
12–14	Balanced and playing 'weak throughout' open 1 N.T. Playing 'variable' open 1 N.T. not vulnerable and one of a minor (3 card minimum) if vulnerable.	1 ♣ practically always a genuine suit bid if not vulnerable. If vulnerable a 3-card minor opening may be made to facilitate rebid which must be in No Trumps, unless holding 4-card support for partner.
Anything higher Maximum about 20	Any except well-balanced.	Strong hands are opened as one-bids if not qualifying for Two-Bid, 2 ♣ bid, or 2 N.T. Excess strength shown by jump rebid.
20 points and over	Any.	Almost always qualify for better than a one-bid. Exception is a 4-4-4-1 distribution which cannot be opened 2 N.T. or with a Two-Bid. Open suit below singleton except when singleton is clubs, when open 1 ♡.

*Distributional points are not included in these values.

No: 2 CHOICE OF BIDS

Division of suits	Order of Bidding in preparation for most convenient rebid
5 − 5 or 6 − 6	Suits of equal length, bid higher ranking suit first *except* when the suits are clubs and spades, then bid clubs first.
5 − 4	With adjacent suits at all times bid the longer suit first. On weak hands particularly, bid a higher-ranking 4-card suit only as support for partner.
6 − 5 7 − 6 7 − 5 6 − 4	Bid longer suit first unless the hand is weak and the suits are adjacent. Rebid in shorter suit, making second rebid in shorter suit if necessary, thus implying five cards for certain in shorter suit and, therefore, *five or more in first.* Bid and repeat six-card suit before bidding four-card suit, unless you can mention four-card *major* at the one-level as a rebid.
4 − 4	With both major suits: spades first. With both minor suits: diamonds first. With hearts and diamonds: hearts first. With spades and clubs: clubs first. With spades and diamonds: holding 3 hearts, spades first. holding 3 clubs, bid diamonds first. With hearts and clubs: clubs first.
4-4-4-1	Bid the suit below the singleton unless the singleton is in clubs, when bid 1 ♡.

No: 3 SUIT RESPONSES TO OPENING SUIT ONE BIDS

		TAKE-OUT TO ANOTHER SUIT	
Range	Point Value	Distribution	Comments
Simple Take-Out Bid in another suit at lowest level.	Minimum at the One-Level 5–6	4-card suit or longer, bid the suit.	Possibly weak response, forcing for one round. Indicates no greater values than would be required to bid 1 N.T.
	Minimum at the Two-Level 8	5-card suit or longer, bid the suit.	Still weak. Over 1♠, 1♡, or 1◇, 1 N.T. preferred to 2♣.
	Better than Minimum Up to 15	4-card suit or longer, bid the suit.	Full strength can be shown *after* opener's rebid.
Jump Take-Out One more only than needed for a simple take-out.	15+	4-card suit or longer, bid the suit. If expedient, force in a short minor.	Forcing to game response. Strongest response possible. Slam indication.
Double Jump Take Out More than needed for a forcing take-out.	6	7-card suit or longer, bid the suit.	Shows weakness except in the suit bid. Pre-emptive response to shut out opposition.

No: 4 SUIT LIMIT BIDS IN RESPONSE TO OPENING SUIT ONE BIDS

Raise	*Points	Distribution	Comments
Single raise in opener's suit	3–5	5-card or longer trump support with a void or singleton.	The weakest available response to an opening bid. Opener will not bid again except with a near opening Two Bid or to obstruct opponents.
	6–8	4-card trump support or at least three to a high honour if no other bid available.	
Double raise in opener's suit	In a Major 7–10	5-card or longer trump support with a void or singleton.	Not forcing but very encouraging. Partner will not bid again on a bare Light Opener but will go on to game or make a Cue Bid if he possibly can.
	11–12	4-card trump support.	
	In a Minor 11–12	At least 4-card trump support.	Again, not forcing, but may be taken by opener, if chances appear reasonable, as an invitation to bid 3 N.T.
Direct raise to game	In a Minor 8	6-card or longer trump support with voids or singletons.	Pre-emptive, to shut out the opposition.
	In a Major 0–5	Exceptional trump support, low point count, but with voids or singletons.	Pre-emptive, again used to block the opposition. Use either without or following an intervening bid.
Raise to 4♣	In a Major only	4-card or longer trump support and good "shape"	Conventional, showing strong hand with good trump support and TWO ACES.
Raise to 4◇	Ditto		Exactly the same except with THREE ACES.

*Distributional Points are not included in these counts.

No: 5 NO-TRUMP LIMIT BIDS IN RESPONSE

Response	Point Value	Distribution	Comments
ONE NO-TRUMP	5–9 over major suits	Balanced, with insufficient trump support for a direct raise.	Weak response. Where possible a suit response at the one-level should be preferred. This is logical as responder, with a weaker hand, would have made every effort to bid 1 ◇, 1 ♡, or 1 ♠ over 1 ♣, or 1 ♡ or 1 ♠ over 1 ◇, in order to keep the bidding at the lowest level possible.
	8–10 over 1 ♣	Ditto.	
	7–9 over 1 ◇	Ditto.	
TWO NO-TRUMPS	Over all suits 11–12	Balanced hand, of 4-3-3-3 or 4-4-3-2 pattern.	A strong Limit Bid. Not forcing.
THREE NO-TRUMPS	Over all suits 13–15 with good fillers	Balanced hand of 4-3-3-3 or 4-4-3-2 pattern.	A strong Limit Bid. Not a shut-out bid. Where a slam is indicated, however, a forcing suit bid should be preferred.

No: 6   NO-TRUMP BIDDING

Distribution: 4-3-3-3 or 4-4-3-2. Occasionally 5-3-3-2 if 5-card suit is a minor.

Opening Bid	Raises in No Trumps by Responder	Opener's Rebids In No Trumps
1 N.T. Weak (12–14 points)	2 N.T. on 11–12 points. 3 N.T. on 12+ or 13 points.	Pass on 12 points. Rebid 3 N.T. on 13+ points.
1 N.T. Strong (15–17 points)	2 N.T. on 8–9 points. 3 N.T. on 9+ points.	Pass on 15 points. Rebid 3 N.T. on 16+ points.
2 N.T. (20–22 points)	3 N.T. on 4–5 points.	
3 N.T.	A tactical bid made on an abnormal hand containing a long and strong minor suit and protection in at least two other suits, e.g.:— ♠ J 6 ♡ K 7 ◇ A K Q 10 8 6 2 ♣ K J	
4 N.T.	Conventional with responses as follows:— 1. With 2 Aces, 5 N.T. 2. With ◇A, ♡A or ♠A, bid five of that suit. 3. With ♣A, bid 6♣. 4. With no Aces, bid 5♣.	

See also Table on rebids after 2♣ opening bid.

No: 7 SUIT RESPONSES TO ONE NO-TRUMP OPENING BIDS

Response	Points Min.	Distribution	Comments
2◇, 2♡, or 2♠.	— 6	Any 6-card suit. Any 5-card suit.	Weak sign-off.
3♣, 3◇, 3♡ or 3♠.	8 10+	Good 6-card biddable suit. Good 5-card biddable suit.	Forcing to game, strong. Opener must raise to game in suit or rebid 3 N.T.
4♡, 4♠, 5♣ or 5◇.	6 or more	Very unbalanced. 7-card or longer suit.	Pre-emptive response on a hand containing little outside its suit, but having prospects of game in the suit bid.
2♣		Conventional.	See Tables 8 & 11.
4♣	High	Shape giving slam prospects. Conventional.	"Gerber" Conventional request for Ace-showing. Opener responds 4◇ with no Ace, 4♡ with one, 4♠ with two, 4N.T. with three and 5♣ with four. 5♣ from responder now asks for Kings on the same step principle.

SUIT RESPONSES TO TWO NO-TRUMP OPENING BIDS

Response	Points Min.	Distribution	Comments
3♡ or 3♠	Any	6-card suit. 5-card suit.	Inferential force. Game should follow.
3♣	Any	Fit-finding bid.	Conventional. See Table 11.
4♣	Any	Shape or points giving prospects of slam.	"Gerber" Conventional. As above.
3◇	0–3	6-card suit or longer.	"Transfer" bid to which opener must respond 3♡.

No: 8 TWO CLUBS OVER ONE NO-TRUMP

Response	Holding and bid	Comments
Over 1 N.T., weak or strong, respond 2♣ on:—	An unbalanced hand not suitable for No-Trumps *provided it is also suitable for a weak take-out or for a jump take-out and that a major suit contract seems preferable.*	The 2♣ bid is un-limited and may be made on anything from a rock-crusher to a Yarborough.
Over 2♣ opener rebids:—	Two of any four-card major suit held. If both majors are held show spades first. If no major is held, bid 2◇ *irrespective of diamond holding or of point count.*	Bid highest of touching suits first. Permits responder to rebid at the two-level.
Responder rebids: 1. If opener's major suit does not fit:	His own suit as a weak take-out at the two-level OR Reverts to 2 N.T. Raises to 3 N.T.	This presupposes a point count high enough for raise to 2 N.T. after losing hopes of suit fit. As above with point count high enough for direct raise.
2. If opener's major suit fits:	Pass if weak. Raise to 3 of suit if strong. Give direct raise to game in suit bid.	Responder may settle for a part score. Single raise to three is Limit Bid denying strength to raise to four.
If opener rebids 2◇:—	Rebid two of his own best suit. Pass 2◇. Force by raising 2◇ to 3◇.	Weak take-out to be passed by opener. Partner is known to have a maximum of six cards in the majors so is likely to have 3 or 4 diamonds. Opener must now show his *best* major suit at the three-level, pre-ferring length to strength.

No: 9   OPENER'S REBIDS

Holding	Rebid	Examples
Minimum hand or Acol Light Opener	Sign-off by rebidding long suit at lowest available level or showing second suit at lowest available level or making lowest possible No-Trump bid.	1♦–1♡ 2♦ or 1N.T.
		1♡–1♠ 2♡
		1♡–1♠ 2♦
Strong hand	Invitational but not forcing:— 2 N.T. over responder's change of suit. 16+ to 18 points. 2 N.T. over single raise from partner. 16+ to 18 points.	1♡–1♠ 2N.T.
		1♠–2♠ 2N.T.
	"Trial Bid" over single raise (may also be a second suit if in major).	1♡–2♡ 2♠
Better than minimum	Limit Bids—not forcing:— Jump rebid after change of suit.	1♡–1♠ 3♡
	Raise of responder's suit.	1♡–1♠ 2♠
	Double raise of responder's suit.	1♦–1♠ 3♠
Strong hand:—	Forcing to game:— Jump rebid in a new suit.	1♦–1♠ 3♡
Opener's rebids after responder's force	Sign-off:—	1♦–2♡ 2N.T.
	Neutral rebid showing suit length:	1♡–2♠ 3♡
	Showing alternative suit or support:	1♡–2♠ 3♦ or 3♠
	Conventional response showing solid trump suit:	1♠–3♡ 4♠

No: 10 RESPONDER'S REBIDS

Showing Minimum hand		*Showing Minimum hand*	
1♥ –1♠ 2 N.T.–3♠	Rebid of re- sponder's suit after 2 N.T.	1♦–1♥ 3♣–3 N.T.	Rebid of N.T.'s. at lowest level after opener's force.
1♠ –2♠ 3♥ –3♠	Rebid of opener's suit after Trial Bid.	1♠–1 N.T. 2♦–2♠	Rebid of opener's first suit showing preference only.
1♥ –1♠ 2♦ –2♠ 2 N.T.–3♠	Series of sign-off repeats of responder's suit.	1♥–1♠ 2♥–2♠	Rebid of respon- der's suit after rebid of opener's suit.

**The above sequences all illustrate minimum
or sign-off rebids by responder**

Inferential Forces.

1♥ –1♠ 2 N.T.–3♥	Return to opener's major suit after 2 N.T. rebid.	1♠–2♦ 2♥–3♣	Bid by responder in the fourth suit.
1♥ –2♣ 3♥ –4♣	Any bid following jump rebid of opener's suit.		

Unconditional Game Force.

1♥–2♣ 2♦–3♠	or	1♠–2♦ 2♠–4♣	A jump by responder in a new suit, even though opener has signed off.

Limit Bid but Not Forcing.

1♥–1♠ 2♣–3♠	or	3♥	A jump rebid in either opener's or responder's suit.

No: 11 ACOL AND THE CLUB SUIT

♣Opening Bid	Indications	Comments
1♣ not vul. 1♣ vul.	Practically always a normal suit opening bid. May be normal suit opener *or* 3-card minor if using variable No-Trump.	Not forcing. Responder bids one of a suit on 5 pts. and 1 N.T. on 8–10.
2♣ at any score	Minimum holding of 5 Q.T. unless predominant suit is clubs when the bid may be made on slightly shaded values.	All 2♣ opening bids forcing to game unless rebid in No-Trumps.
2♣ with 2 N.T. rebid.	23–24 points with a balanced hand.	Responder may pass on a blank hand.
2♣ with 3 N.T. rebid.	25 or more points with a balanced hand.	A game bid which responder can pass.
3♣ at any score	Weak pre-emptive bid *or* optional alternative, equivalent of strong Acol opening Two-Bid.	Responder may pass a strong 3♣ bid on a blank hand.
4♣	Weak pre-emptive bid with no defensive values or support for major suits.	Responder requires high values to raise a weak pre-emptive bid unless as a sacrifice.
♣*Responses* 2♣ over 1 N.T.	Conventional request for partner to show 4-card major suits, spades first if held.	With no 4-card major opener rebids 2◇.
3♣ over 2 N.T. or in sequence 2♣–2◇ 2NT–3♣	Conventional request for partner to show any 4-card suits held in ascending order.	If *only* 4-card suit is clubs opener rebids 3 N.T.
4♣ over 1 N.T. or 2 N.T.	"Gerber" request to opener to show the number of Aces held on the step principle.	A following bid of 5♣ asks opener to show Kings on the same principle.
4♣ over opponent's opening 3-bid.	"Lower available minor" convention asking for take-out over pre-emptive opener by opposition.	One of the reasonable alternatives.

No: 12 RESPONSES TO TWO CLUB OPENING BIDS

Response	Indications	Comments
2♦	Weakness response on a blank hand or any hand not having the requirements for a positive response.	Responder, having bid 2♦, *must* keep bidding open to game unless opener rebids in No-Trumps, when he may pass.
2♡, 2♠, 3♣, 3♦, or 2N.T.	Holding any one of the following: 1. An Ace and a King. 2. A fairly good biddable suit with 1½ H.T. 3. Any 9-point hand.	The 2 N.T. response shows the requirements under Nos: 1 or 2 but no biddable suit.

OPENER'S REBIDS AFTER TWO CLUB OPENING

If reply to 2♣ is:	Opener's Rebid	Responder's Rebid
2♦	2 N.T. on balanced hands of 23–24 points. 3 N.T. on balanced hands of 25 or more points.	(a) Pass on complete blank. (b) Raise on 3 points. (c) Bid any 6-card suit. Pass.
2♦	2♡, 2♠, 3♣ or 3♦.	(a) Raise on 3-card trump support. (b) Bid any 5-card suit. (c) Bid second negative of 2 N.T. if unable to raise or show suit. (d) Raise direct to game on good trump support, about 7 points and **no Ace or void.**

A Jump Rebid after a Two Club Opening:—

By Opener, after receiving a 2♦ response, asks partner to show any Ace he may hold by a cue bid of the Ace-suit. With no Ace he bids 3 N.T.

By Responder, he shows a solid suit *with* the Ace if this is his first response. If after bidding 2♦, responder then jumps the bidding, he shows a solid suit *without* the Ace, which may be invaluable information to the opener.

No: 13   ACOL OPENING TWO-BIDS

	OPENING BIDS OF 2♢, 2♡ AND 2♠.	
Type of Hand	Distribution	Comments
1. Combined high card and distributional values G U A R A N - TEEING NO LESS THAN 8 PLAYING TRICKS	Long and very strong SINGLE SUIT which, if opened with a one-bid, could not be rebid to show its values:— ♠ A K Q J 8 6 ♡ A 10 3 ♢ 5 ♣ A 8 7	Forcing for one round but not to game. Negative response is 2N.T. On this hand opener bids 2♠ and rebids 3♠ over 2N.T.
2. GAME-GOING STRENGTH needing little or no support from partner	A powerful two-suiter with which you require the absolute certainty of being able to show your second suit:— ♠ A Q J 7 3 2 ♡ K Q J 10 6 4 ♢ 3 ♣ —	This cannot be shown fully by an opening one-bid followed by a jump rebid. Open 2♠ and rebid 4♡. Partner can convert to 4♠ if preferred.
3. Distributional strength without five specific Quick Tricks.	A hand so big that, though it docs not qualify for a 2♣ open-ing, it still requires a second chance to show its strength. ♠ A K 10 5 4 ♡ 5 ♢ A J 10 9 ♣ A Q 7	This is the type of Two-Bid most often missed. On this hand, so nearly a 2♣ op-ener, open 2♠ and rebid 3♢.

The Acol Opening Two-Bid is unconditionally forcing for one round, but not forcing to game after the negative response of 2 N.T. unless a jump switch or reverse is made. The bidding of example No: 2 insists on a game contract by rebidding the second suit at game level. If the hand were slightly weaker the bidding could go 2♠–2N.T. 3♡– ? Which can be passed by responder.

If a positive response is given to an Opening Two-Bid, both partners have shown strength, after which it is inconceivable that the bidding should stop short of a game contract.

No: 14   RESPONSES TO ACOL OPENING TWO-BIDS

Response	Indications	Comments
2 N.T. Weakness	A completely blank hand or values not reaching one honour trick.	Responder can pass opener's rebid of three in the same suit, or any rebid other than a jump switch or release.
Single raise in bid suit	May be weak or strong: Weak includes trump support *with an Ace or void*. Strong includes trump support and one or more aces or voids.	The single raise is given to allow space for slam investigation. After raise Aces may be shown by cue bids.
Double raise (2♠–4♠ or 2◇–4◇)	Good trump support with about 10 points, but **no Aces or void**.	Not a shut-out response. Any rebid by opener is a slam enquiry. May be followed by use of Acol Direct King Convention.
Simple Take-Out: 2♡–2♠	At the Two-Level: A respectable biddable suit with a count of 8 or more points.	If the choice lies between a suit response or a direct raise, prefer direct raise with an honour in the suit opened.
2♡–3◇	At the three-level: A good biddable suit and at least 9 or more points.	
Jump Take-Out: 2♠–4♡ or 2◇–3♡	Shows the holding of a solid trump suit of one's own, with no losers—as good as six to the A K Q J or seven to the A K Q.	
3 N.T.	A well-balanced *Aceless* hand containing about 10–12 points.	Prefer a direct raise to game in opener's suit if the hand qualifies for it.

No: 15 PRE-EMPTIVE BIDS

	Object	Type of Hand	Comments
ACOL OPENING BID OF 3 OR MORE IN A SUIT	To obstruct opponents' bidding.	Containing one long suit only, equal to six playing tricks not vulnerable and seven if vulnerable.	Qualifying hands should be:— 1. Worthless in defence. 2. Useless in support of partner's hand. Unsuitable hands: 1. Any hand containing $1\frac{1}{2}$ honour tricks. 2. Any hand containing a 4-card major suit other than the suit bid.
RES-PONSES TO PRE-EMPTIVE BIDS	1. Raise to game on not less than 3–4 Honour Tricks. 2. Take out into another suit at game level only on a long and strong suit. Note: Any response at a lower level than game is a slam invitation showing control of the suit bid. 3. Take out into 3 N.T., which infers fit with opener's suit and controls in at least two other suits.		
OVER-CALLING OPPO-NENT'S PRE-EMPTIVE BID	1. Overcall in a suit holding length and strength in that suit only. 2. Double on a strong balanced hand that will in itself defeat the contract. Note: The double of a three-bid is primarily for penalties. Partner should not take out on weakness. 3. Overcall with lower available minor suit (3 ◇ over 3 ♣, 4 ♣ over all other 3-bids) or with 3 N.T., as preferred, when requiring partner to take out. Indications: A strong two-suiter or a strong hand containing support for any suit other than the suit bid. Either of these bids may be used conventionally as the equivalent of a Take-Out double and partner must respond accordingly.		

No: 16 INTERVENING BIDS

Objects: 1. To take the offensive and to counter-attack.
2. To disturb the course of the bidding and to disrupt opponent's lines of communication.
3. To contest a part score.
4. To direct partner's lead.

Type of Overcall:	Requirements
Simple Overcall in a suit, i.e., a bid at the lowest level necessary.	Playing strength rather than honour tricks. The total of possible playing tricks should be:— (a) Within TWO tricks of the bid if vulnerable. (b) Within THREE tricks of the bid if not vulnerable.
Jump Overcall in a suit, i.e., a bid of one and only one more than required for a simple overcall.	Playing strength equal to eight playing tricks, including a strong trump suit or two good suits. Not forcing, but highly invitational and partner should find a response if he reasonably can.
Pre-emptive over-call in a suit, i.e., a bid at any higher level than a jump overcall.	Shows weakness except in the suit bid, which should provide at least eight playing tricks. The bid is made with the object of obstructing opponents, and is in no way forcing.
Overcalls in No-Trumps.	A balanced hand of about 16 points, the equivalent of an opening bid of One No-Trump vulnerable, and including a good stopper in opponent's suit.

No: 17   FORCING OVERCALLS

Overcall	Requirements
Immediate Overcall in Opponent's suit: N. E. S. W.) (1♠ 2♠)	A strong hand unsuitable for a take-out double.
Forcing for one round.	Avoids the danger of a penalty pass from partner.
1♣ 2♣ — 2♡ — 3♣	Partner responds on first round as to a take-out double. Thereafter uses judgement.
Second bid in opponent's suit is forcing to game.	UNCONDITIONALLY FORCING TO GAME. Responder bids as for a Take-Out double.
TWO NO-TRUMPS OVER OPPONENT'S OPENING ONE-NO-TRUMP BID.	A hand calling for a take-out double which cannot be made, as a double of an opening 1 N.T. is always a business double.
An Acol Conventional bid.	A strong but unbalanced hand of freak distribution. FORCING TO GAME. Responder bids as for a take-out double.

No: 18   TAKE-OUT DOUBLES

Conditions	Requirements
A double of an opening bid of one or two of a suit, provided:— 1. It is made at the first opportunity, AND 2. The doubler's partner has not bid, doubled, or made a penalty pass. Note: A double of an opening bid of three or of 1 N.T. is a business double.	A fair hand with a minimum of 12 points containing:— 1. Support for every unbid suit. OR 2. A good long suit with support in another suit, preferably an unbid major suit. Note: A double of a major suit always infers strong interest in the other major suit.
PENALTY PASS	A Penalty Pass of a Take-Out Double may occasionally be made when doubler's partner has strength in opponent's suit (equal to three trump tricks) and anticipates a substantial gain by defeating the doubled contract.
DOUBLES OF NO-TRUMPS	A double of an opening bid of One or more No-Trumps is a Penalty Double.
DOUBLING PRE-EMPTIVE OPENING BIDS	A double of an opening suit bid of three is primarily intended as a Penalty Double, but in exceptional cases partner may use his discretion to take out if he thinks it may be advantageous to do so on *strength*, not weakness.

No: 19 RESPONSES TO TAKE-OUT DOUBLES

	Where there has been no intervening bid
Holding 0–3 points	(a) Take out into longest suit. (b) With two 4-card suits, bid the one that can be shown at the lowest level. (c) If the only 4-card suit is the suit doubled, bid the next higher ranking 3-card suit. (d) If the take-out must be made at the two-level, bid 2♣ in preference to bidding a weak 4-card suit.
Holding 4–8 points	(a) Generally take out into the longest suit, but prefer a 4-card major to a 5-card minor suit.
Holding 8–10 points	(a) On a balanced hand of 8–10 points, take out into 1 N.T. with or without a stop in opponent's suit. *Doubler should have opponent's suit stopped to bid on in No-Trumps.* (b) Jump the bidding by one step in the longest suit. (c) Take out into 2 N.T. on a balanced hand with two stops in opponent's suit.
Holding 11 or more points	Make a forcing-to-game take-out by bidding opponent's suit, i.e., the suit doubled. Example: N. E. S. W. 1♠ x — 2♠
	Following an intervening bid (or redouble)
	(a) Pass on a completely worthless hand. There is now no obligation to bid. (b) Show a four-card major, even on a worthless hand, if this can be done at the one-level. (c) Bid any 5-card suit. (d) With 8 points or more and a good biddable suit, make a jump bid in that suit.

No: 20 SLAM CONVENTIONS

Blackwood Convention	Comment
Without any particular holding, but when there is slam expectancy, a bid of 4 N.T. by either partner asks for Aces. The forced responses are:—	Before making a conventional 4 N.T. bid, the previous bidding should have disclosed slam prospects and the final trump suit should have been agreed, either verbally or by inference.

Holding	Response
No Ace	5 ♣
1 Ace	5 ♦
2 Aces	5 ♥
3 Aces	5 ♠
4 Aces	5 ♣

A quantitative raise to 4N.T. is a slam try, but not a conventional demand to show Aces.

If the 4 N.T. bidder rebids 5 N.T. Kings must be shown on a corresponding scale:—

Holding	Response
No King	6 ♣
1 King	6 ♦
2 Kings	6 ♥
3 Kings	6 ♠
4 Kings	6 N.T.

A bid of 5 N.T. should only be made when the partners hold the four Aces between them, and when a response at the 6-level will not embarrass the 5 N.T. bidder.

If an opponent intervenes after a 4 N.T. bid, the Blackwood responses are:—

Holding	Response
No Ace	Pass
1 Ace	Bid the suit ranking next above opponent's suit.
2 Aces	Bid the *next* suit and so on.

Note: The response to show all four Aces or none is identical, but there is no risk of confusion. You will only very rarely be slamming with no Ace at all and will then be heavy with King-Queen tricks.

When the best contract would be in No-Trumps and when the 4 N.T. bidder has found two Aces missing, his bid of 5 in an *unbid* suit asks his partner to bid 5 N.T., which becomes the final contract.

DIRECT KING CONVENTION

When a player has made a response which specifically denies the holding of any Ace (such as 2 ♥–4 ♥), or has already shown the number of Aces he holds (1 ♥–4 ♣ or 1 ♥–4 ♦), a bid of 4 N.T. asks immediately for Kings.

No: 21   SLAM CONVENTIONS

Culbertson 4-5 N.T. Convention	Comment
When previous bidding suggests slam possibilities, a bid of 4N.T. by either partner guarantees the bidder has:— 3 Aces OR 2 Aces+King of any bid suit. Partner must not pass. Forced responses are:—	4 N.T. is not conventional when it is used as a *direct* slam try, i.e., when it is a quantitative raise of an opening No-Trump bid or a raise of partner's jump rebid in No-Trumps.

Holding	Response	
(1) 2 Aces or 1 Ace+King of all suits previously bid.	5 N.T.	In applying the 4-5 N.T. convention to the Acol system, the reference to suits previously bid does *not* include clubs or diamonds when the opening was the conventional Two-Club Bid and 2◇ negative response.
(2) 1 Ace or void in any unbid suit.	5 of the suit.	
(3) Ace of a suit bid or Kings of all suits bid.	6 in the best trump suit.	
(4) No Aces and no void.	5 of the lowest suit bid (sign-off).	

When a player who has previously made a conventional 4 N.T. bid rebids 5N.T., it shows that he holds ALL FOUR ACES.

ACOL FOUR NO-TRUMP OPENING BID

A conventional bid reserved for those hands where the opener is interested only in Aces.
Responses: With 2 Aces, respond 5 N.T.
              With ♠A, ♡A or ◇A, respond 5 of the suit.
              With ♣A respond 6♣.
              With no Aces respond 5♣.

MODIFIED GRAND SLAM FORCE

A direct bid of 5 N.T., if not preceded by 4 N.T., asks responder *how many* of the three top honours in the agreed trump suit are held. Holding none, responder bids 6♣, holding one he bids six of the trump suit, and holding two he bids seven.